D1453702

The
Socialist
Mayor

The Socialist Mayor

Bernard Sanders in Burlington, Vermont

Steven Soifer

Bergin & Garvey
New York • Westport, Connecticut • London

Library of Congress Cataloging-in-Publication Data

Soifer, Steven.
   The socialist mayor : Bernard Sanders in Burlington, Vermont /
Steven Soifer.
    p.   cm.
   Includes bibliographical references and index.
   ISBN 0-89789-219-4 (alk. paper)
   1. Burlington (Vt.)—Politics and government. 2. Socialism—
Vermont—Burlington—History—20th century. 3. Sanders, Bernard.
I. Title.
F59.B9S57   1991
320.9743'17—dc20   90-48954

British Library Cataloguing in Publication Data is available.

Library of Congress Catalog Card Number: 90-48954
ISBN: 0-89789-219-4

First published in 1991

Bergin & Garvey, One Madison Avenue, New York, NY 10010
An imprint of Greenwood Publishing Group, Inc.

Printed in the United States of America

The paper used in this book complies with the
Permanent Paper Standard issued by the National
Information Standards Organization (Z39.48-1984).

10 9 8 7 6 5 4 3 2 1

To progressives everywhere
working to bring about
a just and equitable world.

Contents

Preface

Over the past several decades, as the U.S. political climate has increasingly swung to the right, my socialist convictions have grown stronger. My interest in socialism goes back to a junior high school social studies class in which we read Michael Harrington's *The Other America.* The fact that hunger existed in this country, despite its great wealth, made a profound impression on me. I remember concluding that an economic and political system that actually met the basic needs of all its people was preferable to the current U.S. economic and political order.

Like many others of my generation, I was exposed to a Marxist analysis of the United States while in college. In examining what was wrong in this country, I tried to figure out for myself how best to transform our society. The vision of a just and equitable social order—one in which everyone would maximize his or her full potential—always guided me. I wanted to see a society in which the economic, political, and social rewards were fairly distributed among all. In the new social order, no one would be exploited in any way and oppression would be nonexistent. Those who were able to work would do so to their full capacity in a meaningful job, while those who were unable to work, for whatever reason, would be taken care of by society. And people would have not only the rights mentioned above but also various responsibilities to society. Marx's dictum, "From each according to his [and her] ability, to each according to his [and her] need," would be the way of life.

After graduation, I decided to put my political beliefs and convictions into practice. I went to work as a community organizer for the Association of Community Organizations for Reform Now (ACORN) in 1976. This organization worked to help improve the lives of low- and moderate-income people at local, state, and national levels. While working for ACORN in Fort Worth, Texas, I was exposed to local electoral politics. There, ACORN endorsed and worked for local candidates who supported the organization's position on key issues. As a consequence, we played a role in shaping the complexion of local politics by altering the composition of the Fort Worth City Council.

I became further involved in local politics in Vermont as the statewide director of the Vermont Alliance—a citizens' action group of poor and working-class people. Two Vermont Alliance members ran for and were elected to the Burlington Board of Aldermen in 1981. During the mayoral race that same year, Vermont Alliance neighborhood groups, in conjunction with other neighborhood groups in the city, sponsored a mayoral debate. This forum helped give Bernard Sanders additional grass-roots legitimacy in the low- and moderate-income wards of Burlington, which helped carry him to victory.

The election of Vermont Alliance members to the Board of Aldermen and Sanders's mayoral victory in 1981 (which completely surprised just about everyone at the time) epitomizes the use of electoral politics to effect social change and a just society. Now that Sanders has stepped aside as mayor (having been reelected three times: in 1983, 1985, and 1987) and the Progressive Coalition (a loose-knit electoral alliance of liberal Democrats and nonaligned progressives in Burlington) still controls the mayoralty and six of thirteen aldermanic seats, the time is right to study this contemporary and important electoral phenomenon.

This book is an attempt to evaluate the role local electoral politics can play in incorporating democratic-socialist principles into U.S. society. It is an extensive case study of one contemporary experiment in municipal socialist politics—the administration of Mayor Bernard Sanders in Burlington, Vermont.

The study relies on over eighty interviews with people both inside and outside of the Sanders administration. Within the administration, those interviewed include the mayor, his various campaign managers, the assistant city attorney, the city clerk, the city treasurer, the director of the Community and Economic Development Office, and the heads of various city departments. Outside the administration's orbit, those interviewed include members of Burlington's Progressive Coalition, both on the Board of Aldermen and in the community at large, leaders and members of the local Democratic and Republican Parties, members of the business community, and reporters for the daily and weekly newspapers.

Much written material published before and during Sanders's years in office also is utilized. An exhaustive search of newspaper articles from the archives of *The Burlington Free Press*, the city's only daily newspaper, was conducted, supplemented by articles from three other newspapers: the Burlington-based weekly *Vermont Vanguard Press*, the Barre-Montpelier *Times-Argus*, and the *Rutland-Herald*. Other examined written information includes the Burlington city charter, Burlington's annual reports, various reports issued by the city's Community and Economic Development Office, and Sanders's campaign literature.

Chapter 1 lays out a historical and theoretical framework for discussing the Sanders administration. The conditions surrounding the election of a socialist to the mayoralty and the success of the Progressive Coalition in Burlington are explored in Chapter 2. Burlington's governmental structure and the handling of the city's finances under the Sanders administration is examined in Chapter 3. Development and growth issues, especially concerning the waterfront and the Southern Connector, are introduced in Chapter 4. Then, the workings of democracy under a municipal socialist administration are investigated in Chapter 5, focusing on electoral involvement, neighborhood groups, and tenants' issues. Chapter 6 looks at questions of ownership under a municipal socialist administration using several case examples, such as the Burlington Community Land Trust and the attempt to municipalize the city's privately owned cable company. Chapter 7 examines Sanders's role in relation to tax issues and the redistribution of wealth, focusing on issues like property taxes, the gross receipts tax, and the excavation fee. Chapter 8 concentrates on some quality-of-life issues and how groups like the Mayor's Council of the Arts, the Mayor's Youth Office, and the Burlington Women's Council have affected them. Sanders's foreign policy, an unusual preoccupation for a mayor, is looked at in Chapter 9, with special emphasis on Nicaragua. Chapter 10, the conclusion, discusses how Sanders has been able to uniquely influence local and state politics in Vermont and examines the question of whether he really is a socialist. The epilogue tells the story of how in November 1990, Sanders became the first socialist to be elected to the U.S. Congress in decades.

This study is a critically sympathetic look at the Sanders administration. The book chronicles the beginning of Congressman Bernie Sanders's successful political career. I hope that this work will shed some light on the important question of the relationship of electoral politics to social change in the United States.

Acknowledgments

During the long gestation period for this project, many people contributed their talents, support, and expertise to make this book possible. Jim Bergin, publisher of Bergin and Garvey, always had faith in this manuscript. I greatly appreciate the help of Susan Mesner-Hage, my manuscript editor, whose insightful questions and tactful suggestions helped to shape this book. I also am grateful to Sophy Craze, my acquisitions editor, who guided me through the labyrinth of publishing and brought this work into print. Finally, I wish to thank Nina Neimark, my project editor, Rebecca Perry, my copy editor, Christina Haley, my indexer, and Margaret Benton, my proofreader, for their indispensable work in helping to complete the book.

I also wish to thank my friend Bryan Pfeiffer for helping to put together a sample chapter of this book. His technical assistance and critical thinking got this project off to a good start.

David Gil of the Heller School, Brandeis University, deserves special mention. His work as a teacher, writer, and activist has served as an inspiration and a model for my own. David's excellent thinking and sage advice have heavily influenced me.

My life partner, Naomi Almeleh, has seen me through the book. I appreciate her valuable computer assistance, feedback on the manuscript, and emotional support. I also am grateful to my parents, Lawrence and Evelyn Soifer, for their support throughout this process.

Barbara Von Braun, formerly the *Burlington Free Press*'s archives librarian, also deserves credit. I appreciate her assistance in helping me locate many articles on the Sanders administration. I also want to thank Sue Trainor, the mayor's assistant during the time of my study, who answered my many questions and found ways to fit me into the former mayor's busy schedule.

Finally, I want to acknowledge all the Vermonters who generously allowed me to interview them. While those who offered their opinions and observations about the Sanders administration for this book may or may not agree with my conclusions, I deeply appreciate the cooperation and contributions of each person with whom I spoke.

I would especially like to thank the former Burlington mayor, Bernard Sanders, for lending his support to this endeavor. While still in office, he made his files available and gave me many hours of his time. I also want to thank Bernie for his fierce belief in democratic socialism. Without his hard work as mayor of Burlington, there would have been no story.

The
Socialist
Mayor

Historical Background and Theoretical Framework on Socialist Municipalities

SOCIALIST PARTY OF AMERICA: A BRIEF RETROSPECTIVE

Bernard Sanders reveres Eugene Debs, one of the founders of the Socialist Party of America. In his influential study of the Socialist Party of America, James Weinstein[1] argues that the party, begun in 1901, reached its zenith in 1912 and began its decline after that. According to the author, "the old Socialist Party . . . [had] a commitment to the fulfillment of the promises of American democracy and a belief that this dream is frustrated in a society dominated by corporate capitalism and subordinate to its imperatives."[2]

In 1901, the Socialist Party had about 10,000 members and by 1912, it had over 100,000 members. The party successfully placed about 1,200 of its members in office around the country, with elected officials "in 340 municipalities from coast to coast, among them 79 mayors in 24 states." However, by 1917, only seventeen Socialist mayors were left in office.[3]

There were four tendencies within the Socialist Party of America: right wing, moderate, left wing, and syndicalist. Victor Berger, who essentially built the local Socialist Party branch in Milwaukee, represented the right wing. He wanted the Socialist Party to be "relevant to the existing problems of American workers." He also championed "social reform," which led others in the party to charge that he identified "socialism with progressivism." Berger was, in a sense, an incrementalist, believing that socialism would eventually be attained through the winning of small victories.[4]

Morris Hillquit, who led the New York base of the party, represented the center of the Socialist Party. He often attempted to mediate the disputes between other factions within the party. For Hillquit, it was important to open up the party to people from classes other than workers.[5]

The left wing of the party was epitomized by the thoughts and deeds of Eugene Debs. For the leader of the Socialist Party, elections were not an end in themselves, but rather a means for educating the masses about the virtues of socialism. If the "consciousness" of the working class was heightened due to an election, then it was a success. Debs, however, was skeptical of how much Socialists were capable of achieving once elected to local office.[6]

Finally, William Haywood represented the syndicalist faction of the party. The only value in engaging in the electoral process and winning office, according to Haywood, was to "use the powers of the police to protect strikers." For him, workers should gain control of the state through means other than elections—for example, a general strike.[7]

At times, Socialists elected to local office got so much criticism from their fellow party members for not bringing about municipal socialism that they left the party. Not only did elected Socialists have to face internal party attacks, but they often had to contend with "fusion" candidates in their reelection bids, frequently losing to these "Republicrat" candidates. While some in the party saw these electoral races against fusion candidates as a virtue because they "put the issue of capitalism versus socialism before the voters," in reality they made it very difficult for Socialists to hold on to their well-earned victories.[8]

Even when elected, Socialists could not really implement socialism on the local level. Says Weinstein:

> The Socialists ... were severely limited in what they could do when in control of a municipality. They could not bring socialism to one city while the rest of the country remained capitalist. Furthermore, even if charter restrictions permitted (which they rarely did), Socialists could not put through reforms which would seriously impinge upon business interests, lest industry be driven from their city.[9]

In Weinstein's estimation, only limited social changes could be wrought by elected Socialists on the municipal level, and even these changes were not limited to socialist administrations. He states:

> In practice, a Socialist administration could press for public ownership of utilities and transportation facilities; increase social, recreational and cultural services; and adopt a friendly at-

titude toward unions, especially in times of strikes. But some or all of these things could be done, and at times were done, by non-Socialist reformers.[10]

Concerning business communities' attitudes toward municipal socialist administrations, Weinstein writes: "On a municipal level, Socialist administrations often met with the approval, implicit if not explicit, of the larger and more sophisticated business interests."[11]

Weinstein's analysis seems borne out by several historical case studies of municipal socialist administrations in the early to mid-twentieth century. In his anthology *Socialism and the Cities,* Bruce Stave[12] presents a number of interesting examples of the limits and possibilities of reforms on the local level, including Milwaukee, Wisconsin; Bridgeport, Connecticut; and Schenectady, New York. In addition to these historical case studies, three contemporary California municipal socialist administrations, namely Berkeley, Santa Cruz, and Santa Monica, also have relevance in comparison to the Sanders administration in Burlington, Vermont.

Looking briefly at some of the historical case studies, several interesting trends emerge. In describing the socialist experiment in Milwaukee, Sally Miller[13] points to four key Milwaukee Social Democratic Party (later affiliated with the Socialist Party of America) 1898 platform issues—"class struggle," "municipal ownership of utilities," "an equitable tax burden," and "social and cultural measures"—which also are issues that take a front seat during the Sanders years. Victor Berger, elected mayor in 1910 only to lose to a unity candidate two years later, worked for "home rule, governmental honesty, and modernization," also Sanders's themes. The attempt of Milwaukee's Social Democratic Party to incorporate other classes into its electoral base also applies to the situation in Burlington, as evidenced by Sanders's efforts to keep a lid on property taxes, which has appeal to more conservative voters.

Actual Milwaukee Socialist reforms are remarkably similar to those achieved in Burlington: the efficient management of local government, targeting big business to pay its fair share of taxes, providing free concerts, and economically and politically reinvigorating the city. Moreover, Milwaukee Socialists confronted similar structural problems to the Sanders administration in the implementation of their agenda. City charter limitations and the obstructionist tactics of the Wisconsin legislature also were present during the era of the Milwaukee Socialists. Even the accusations hurled at the Milwaukee Social Democratic Party for being reformist in nature and therefore just like the Progressive municipal administrations of the time sound like charges made by some of Sanders's critics that he is nothing more than a liberal Democrat.

The latter years of the Milwaukee Social Democratic Party, under the leadership of Daniel Hoan from 1916 to 1940 and Frank Zeidler from 1948 to 1960, provide similar analogies to the Sanders administration. The major difference between Hoan and his Progressive era counterparts was his opposition to the commission form of government and his advocacy for the municipal ownership of various utilities. Other accomplishments of the Hoan administration, such as centralized purchasing, were continuations of earlier municipal socialist initiatives, and could equally be applied to Burlington in the 1980s. Regarding Zeidler's administration, he too ended up following typical municipal socialist reforms, such as municipalization, fiscal reforms, taxing big business more, and various recreational activities—all familiar themes in the Sanders administration.[14]

Jasper McLevy's socialist rule in Bridgeport from 1933 to 1957 presents similar comparisons. According to Bruce Stave,[15] good, honest, and efficient government was the hallmark of McLevy's administration, and it is true of Burlington, too. Municipalization, good labor relations, good fiscal management, home rule, and public involvement in decision making were also themes of McLevy's administration—as they are of Sanders's administration. McLevy faced many of the restrictions—such as city charter restraints and at least initial opposition from the Connecticut legislature—that Burlington confronted many years later. Finally, even though McLevy (and Emil Seidel, Milwaukee's first Socialist mayor) had the support of the majority of members on their respective city councils, while Hoan and Zeidler did not enjoy such a majority, there were few differences between these administrations' accomplishments. (This would indicate that even if the Progressive Coalition in Burlington had won control of the Board of Aldermen, discussed in Chapter 2, it probably would have made only a relatively small difference regarding the accomplishments of the Sanders administration.)

McLevy was attacked for practicing "sewer socialism" by the National Executive Committee of the Socialist Party, primarily because he put getting elected and reelected to office ahead of the education of the public concerning the virtues of socialism. The committee said that municipal Socialists had one of two choices: either work to educate people about the benefits of a socialist society or try to gain political power. It warned that the latter strategy could compromise socialist principles by trying to convince people of the virtues of socialism through public example. This would not work, said the committee, because "an administration and officials elected by non-Socialists do not represent Socialism."[16]

The committee was quite clear that there were many obstacles to the implementation of socialism on the local level, and what the priorities should be:

> And after all, municipal Socialism is not what we want. Without the state and national government, we can never really have Socialism. . . .
>
> Municipal office and the pursuit of it, are primarily useful to us in attaining a strong organization with which to build the workers commonwealth. It is not, and must never be, an end in itself. . . .
>
> The Socialist who campaigns for local office should be a Socialist first and a candidate second; he should never for one moment forget that Socialism will not be attained through city hall.[17]

If the Socialist Party of America's National Executive Committee had still been around in the 1980s, it might have hurled similar criticisms at Sanders.

The last historical case to mention is the Reverend George Lunn of Schenectady. Facing even more constraints than his Socialist comrades in other cities, Lunn's major accomplishments, says Kenneth Hendrickson,[18] also were in the areas of efficiency, financial management, upgrading city services, and various creative municipalization experiments. Says Hendrickson:

> The Socialists . . . upgraded the efficiency of city government by overhauling the filing system in the offices at City Hall, increasing the salaries of city employees, instituting a new purchasing and record keeping system, caring for the streets efficiently, . . . increasing the number of parks, improving the sewer system, improving garbage collection, and improving the water system with new piping.[19]

These accomplishments are strikingly similar to the Burlington experience.

Lunn's support cut across the political spectrum, as does Sanders's. Like his contemporary in Burlington, Lunn knew the limits of his power in office. During his inauguration, the Schenectady mayor told his supporters:

> We know . . . that we cannot abolish the capitalist system in Schenectady, but we can and will demonstrate to all the spirit of Socialism and the application of Socialist principles in so far as possible with the handicap of laws framed to establish and sustain capitalism.[20]

The authors of these case studies on early to mid-twentieth-century U.S. municipal Socialists, on the whole, present a rather dim view of these electoral experiments. Sally Miller, for example, feels the major accomplishment of Milwaukee's legacy was placing labor issues on city hall's agenda. However, she sees little real difference between the Milwaukee Socialists and their Progressive counterparts of the time. For Miller, the Socialists were really nothing more than effective reformers. Similarly, Bruce Stave believes that McLevy's rule in Bridgeport brought few, if any, major reforms. Over the years, McLevy, for all intents and purposes, abandoned his socialist roots and catered more and more to the strata of Bridgeport's population that went from being working class to middle class. Regarding Schenectady, there is scathing criticism of that socialist experiment by a former Socialist himself, Walter Lippman. For him, Lunn's Schenectady wasn't a socialist haven at all but rather a reformist administration, since it desired to hold down taxes rather than raising them to fund various needed social service programs.[21]

Stave's overall conclusions about these municipal socialist experiments are disheartening too (reinforcing, in many ways, the position of the National Executive Committee). He accurately points to a number of local, state, and capitalistic constraints on these administrations. These constraints lent a reformist character to these administrations, especially in the areas of finance, efficiency, municipalization, and government regulation. Thus, they seemed to fare no differently than progressively oriented administrations of that era. The end result was the inability to achieve the socialist dream, that is, "nationalization of the means of production and distribution, democratic planning and production for use rather than profit."[22]

The California municipal socialist experiments in Berkeley, Santa Monica, and Santa Cruz during the 1980s also look very similar to the Burlington socialist experiment in many ways. For example, in Berkeley,[23] under the leadership of Gus Newport and Berkeley Citizen Action from 1979 to 1986, tenants' concerns—especially around rent control—were a main issue. Also, development issues (the preservation of open land), taxation (making business pay more of its fair share), and foreign policy issues (Reagan's war in Central America) were important priorities—as in Burlington. Santa Monica[24] was no different: Renters' issues catapulted Santa Monicans for Renters'

Rights (SMRR) into the mayor's office and gave it control of the city council in 1981. Development issues, good fiscal management, citizens' involvement in local government, union issues, worker self-management, and housing co-ops were all important issues during SMRR's tenure, as they are in Burlington.

Finally, in Santa Cruz[25] local socialist feminist officeholders struggled with similar themes, such as renters' concerns, development issues, and environmental problems. Also, citizen involvement, the concerns of low- and moderate-income people, confronting big business, municipalization issues, and domestic and foreign policy concerns were raised, just like in Burlington. Accommodation with the business community happened here—as it did in Berkeley, Santa Monica, and Burlington, too.

In summary, there are remarkable similarities between the occurrences in Burlington of the 1980s and the experience of other municipal socialist experiments in the early and late twentieth century. In the case examples of Milwaukee, Bridgeport, Schenectady, Berkeley, Santa Monica, and Santa Cruz, the parallels are much more striking than the divergences. What stands out most clearly are the constraints on municipal socialists everywhere, including cities with home rule. And, due to the restrictions of city charters in many instances, the interference of state government, the challenges of the legal system, and most importantly, capitalist economic and ideological hegemony, socialists elected to local office, even when they had a local legislative majority, seem to operate within a narrow, fairly well-defined range of options, most often in the category of "reformist reforms," to be described shortly.

Another interesting parallel is the similarity in the types of reforms undertaken by municipal socialists. A more open government, the more efficient management of finances, cost-saving measures, municipal ownership where and when possible, holding the line on property tax increases (though often for very different reasons), limited attempts to redistribute wealth, and a slant toward the poor and working classes (especially the latter) were and are the hallmarks of many municipal socialist administrations, although more contemporary socialist administrations openly address foreign policy issues, too.

WHAT ARE THE LIMITATIONS ON AND POSSIBILITIES OF MUNICIPAL SOCIALISM?

Why is socialism on the municipal level, at least in a capitalist country like the United States, a virtual impossibility? Capitalism is perpetuated through two crucial mechanisms. The first is "ideological hegemony." This means that the ideas of the capitalist class permeate society and exert subtle control over other classes through various institutions and symbols. In the absence of a counter ideology, the ruling class's version of reality prevails.[26]

The second critical factor is the "logic of capitalist accumulation," that is, the desire of capitalists to accumulate greater and greater wealth for the purpose of business expansion and personal gain. In a real sense, this is the engine of capitalism. Because capitalism is the dominant mode of economic production, all state functions must work to support this system. Elected and appointed officials, then, have a very narrow choice when it comes to the implementation of state policy, assuming they want to stay in office or retain their appointed job. If these people do not follow capitalist logic regarding the accumulation of profit, they will either be defeated in the electoral arena or removed from their bureaucratic positions. If an elected official decides to seriously challenge the capitalist economic system or its manifestations, the ruling class can provoke an economic crisis, thus ensuring a capitalist victory in the long run. In the final analysis, it really does not seem to matter what the political persuasion of various elected or appointed officials is, since in terms of state policies, the end result will be roughly the same.[27]

The implementation of state policies, then, appears structurally limited by the ruling class and the overall dynamics of the capitalist system. This means that certain state policies can never be achieved under capitalism, such as the nationalization of major industries. State policies are carefully "selected" by politicians, bureaucrats, and various interest groups. Of all the possible choices available to them, some are preferred to others by the capitalist class. At certain times, though, the ideal option of the ruling class cannot be implemented. In such cases, state policies with contradictory elements may be chosen because they are essential to the preservation or enhancement of the capitalist system. Finally, in a few rare cases, state policies that are clearly inimical to the reproduction of the capitalist economy are put into place, as long as they do not pose a serious threat to the established order.[28]

Two different categories of reform are available to leftists working through the state. One is the category of "reformist reforms," that is, those types of reforms that do nothing to challenge the ruling class's "ideological hegemony" or to alter the "logic of capitalist accumulation."[29] On the national level, an example of such a reform would be the battle concerning the contraction or expansion of various benefits available to social service programs. On the local level, an example would be providing more or less Community Development Block Grant program money to low- and moderate-income neighborhoods.

The second category is "nonreformist reforms," that is, those reforms that question the dominant capitalist ideology and/or change the nature of capitalist relations. These reforms, such as socialized medicine in the form of a national health system or, on the local level, the promotion of worker-owned and -controlled businesses or community land trusts, can be revolutionary in nature. There are several criteria for these kinds of reform. They are: 1) a power shift away from the ruling class and toward the disenfranchised in society, which may involve challenging the logic of capitalist accumulation and bringing about the decentralization of decision-making powers; 2) the presentation of a new, democratic-socialist vision of society, which challenges the prevailing ideological hegemony of the ruling class; and 3) the altering of people's consciousness so that they begin to perceive that a new social order is necessary in order to address the problems of capitalism.[30]

SANDERS'S BRAND OF SOCIALISM

Socialism is the heart and soul of Sanders's life. He describes himself as a "democratic socialist, with an emphasis on the economic rights of working people." In addition, "he favors free, universal national health care, more worker participation in government and industry, and public ownership of large utilities" (but not small businesses).[31]

During an interview, the mayor expanded on his definition of democratic socialism:

[It's] a vision of society where poverty is absolutely unnecessary, where international relations are not based on greed . . . but on cooperation, [and] . . . where human beings can own the means of production and work together rather than having to work as semi-slaves to other people who can hire and fire.[32]

Asked whether it was possible to have socialism, as he defined it, on the municipal level in the United States, Sanders replied: "Of course not." He added that for the most part, "significant radical change" on the local level was not possible either. What was possible, from his perspective, was "a lot of good things," such as worker ownership. "The role we play within the city can be safely defined as very progressive, but there's nothing particularly socialistic about it," said Sanders. "It's basically having to deal with very, very difficult [and] impossible situations and doing the best that we can."[33]

The mayor was in agreement with the National Executive Committee of the Socialist Party of America's view of the possibility of municipal socialism: "Anyone who thinks you bring about socialism or radical change to one city—ignoring what goes on at the state or national level—is absolutely incorrect. . . . There is no way in God's Earth that local government alone can radically improve the conditions in one city."[34]

Sanders described what a professed socialist like himself could do when elected to office:

> What being a socialist means is ... that you hold out a vision which ... is very different.... I think what socialists do and should do in local politics is precisely talk about the inability of local government to deal with problems because of what goes on at the national and state level.[35]

As a socialist, Sanders concluded, it is important to "hold out a vision of what the world might look like if you had a sane economic order." By doing so, it is possible to "show people how radical change can and must occur."[36]

In the case of Burlington, Vermont, the reforms undertaken by the Sanders administration are placed in the context of the local social, political, and cultural milieu as well as the issues at hand. Along the way, we will see history repeat itself in the rise of "fusion" candidates, the systematic constraints on a socialist mayor in a capitalist economy, the kinds of issues addressed, the charges leveled by critics, and the limits of possible reforms on the local level.

However, this is not the whole story. The battles and accomplishments of the Sanders administration were not the only criteria by which to judge the "socialist" experiment in Burlington. For, by the sheer force of his charismatic personality, Sanders would have effected change regardless of his political stripes. In some ways, his socialism was incidental to the change he wrought. While the color he brought to local politics in Burlington was of a different shade than most other politicians, we must try to understand how much of what he achieved was due to Sanders the man versus Sanders the socialist.

Sanders is not your conventional politician, and most in Burlington recognize this. He has never been afraid to take unpopular stands. Few politicians today could openly run as a socialist and win political office. But Sanders did. Because Sanders honestly believes in what he says, he comes across as a sincere politician, something that is rare today. He also is a caliber of politician that few others in Vermont can match. In many interviews with Burlingtonians from across the political spectrum, this is one characteristic that stood out above all others.

Sanders inspires those who traditionally have been disenfranchised from electoral politics to get involved in the local political process. Sanders, unlike most politicians today, can get those who usually don't have a reason to get involved in the political process to the polls. People living in Burlington's low- and moderate-income wards today are voting in equal percentages in local elections to voters from the city's more affluent wards. Such results are due to Sanders's grass-roots campaign style, his ability to address issues of concern to low- and moderate-income people, and his fiery speeches. In short, Sanders inspires people—both to vote for him and, once elected, to work hard for him.

But it's not just low- and moderate-income voters who have cast a ballot for Sanders. The mayor picks up a sizable proportion of upper-middle-class votes too, in part because of his charisma and his ability to articulate what he stands for and in part due to his administration's ability to manage city finances better than previous local administrations, both Democratic and Republican. Sanders's appeal cuts across class and party affiliation lines.

Burlington's quality of life has improved since Sanders took office. It is true that the improvements cannot be wholly credited to Sanders—for example, the economy probably would have been better under any administration, due more to national trends than anything done locally; and certain changes, like the completion of the Church Street Marketplace, were already under way before he was elected mayor. Nonetheless, his administration has overseen important changes that have made Burlington more attractive and livelier to live in. The vibrancy of the downtown area, the cultural offerings now available, and the improvements in the lives of ordinary people can be partially, at least, attributed to Sanders. *U.S. News and World Report* recently recognized Sanders as "one of the nation's 20 top mayors," acknowledging his role in "preserving affordable housing, keeping property tax increases to a minimum and—in a state where cities enjoy little autonomy—sparking a statewide push for home rule." In 1988, the U.S. Conference of Mayors named Burlington (and one other city) as the most livable city in the country with a population under 100,000.[37]

If nothing else, Sanders has shown that socialists can govern at least as well, if not better, than Democrats and Republicans, at least on the local level. Socialists *are* a viable alternative to Democrats and Republicans, and this is of tremendous symbolic importance, for it shows that socialism can do as well, if not better, in meeting people's needs than capitalism.

This is a study of Sanders's eight years in office and the possibilities and limitations of democratic socialism in municipal government. By studying his administration's record on various issues—local finances, development, participatory democracy, redistribution of wealth, municipal ownership, quality of life, and foreign policy concerns—issues that historically have been on the socialist agenda, we will compare Sanders's record to his own vision of a democratic-socialist society and a "sane economic order," and see how Sanders—the man and the socialist—has fared.

Burlington, Bernard Sanders, and the Progressive Coalition

In this chapter, a brief description and history of Burlington, Vermont, will be given. This will set the stage for discussing the phenomenon of Bernard Sanders and the Progressive Coalition. Who is Bernard Sanders? How was it possible for a socialist to win the mayoralty in Vermont's largest city, and for the Progressive Coalition that sprung up around him to gain control of six of the thirteen seats on the Burlington Board of Aldermen? What is the future of Burlington's experiment in progressive politics?

SETTING THE STAGE: A PICTURE OF BURLINGTON, VERMONT

The city of Burlington is nestled between the Green Mountains and Lake Champlain in the northwestern part of the state of Vermont. Burlington itself has a population of slightly over 38,000, while the greater Burlington area—which includes many of the smaller population centers in the Chittenden County area—has 123,000 people. Thus, in a state with a population of only 535,000 (the 48th smallest state in the country), the greater Burlington area has over one-fifth of the total.[1]

Historical records show that Lake Champlain itself was first discovered by the Frenchman Samuel de Champlain in 1609. During the next 150 years, French settlers and a Native American tribe (the Abenakis) "shared" the area. In 1763, the British won control of the area from the French, leading English immigrants to come to the Lake Champlain region. One of the best known of these settlers—Ira

Allen—is considered the "founding father of Burlington." He and "his Onion River Land Company owned nearly 200,000 acres in the Champlain Valley and as much as 80% of the Burlington area."[2]

In the 1800s, Burlington was known as the lumber capital of the area. Vermont's wooded hills provided excellent sites for logging, while the fledgling city had the ability to turn the timber into useful products. However, in the mid-1800s, with the coming of the railway and the depletion of Vermont woods, lumber began to be imported from Canada and finished in Burlington. By the 1870s, "Burlington was the third largest lumber port in the nation, behind Chicago and Albany." In addition, cotton mills and woolen mills rounded out Burlington's industrial base.[3]

By the early 1900s, Burlington was divided into three social classes: the working class, the middle class, and small business owners. Between "80–95% of the laborers were of French-Canadian stock," while the middle class was comprised of "Italians, Irish, Yankees, Greeks, Jewish [sic] and Germans."[4]

According to historical accounts, the greatest conflict at the beginning of the twentieth century occurred between different ethnic and religious groups, not between the different classes. During the last seventy years or so, however, class conflict has come to predominate over ethnic or religious differences. Burlington, following the cycle of many other U.S. cities, has seen its downtown neighborhoods become the home of primarily the poor and working classes, while the newer, outlying suburbs provide homes to the middle and upper-middle classes.[5]

Burlington's industrial base has changed over the years, too. Like much of the nation, Burlington has undergone rapid changes in the last fifty years. General Electric located an industrial plant in the city, and the University of Vermont and the adjoining Medical Center Hospital of Vermont have provided work for many Burlingtonians over the years. The recent attraction of International Business Machines and Digital Equipment Corporation to the greater Burlington area has created many well-paying jobs for area residents, too.[6]

There also has been a tremendous growth in service sector jobs and in "manufacturing and retail and wholesale trade" jobs in the Burlington area. All of this substantially changed the city's demographic composition and helped set the stage for the major political upheaval that began in 1981.[7]

Burlington's power structure is another factor that helps explain the political events examined in this book. A small city like Burlington does not have a *concentrated* power elite. Instead, various small "elites" exist, some of which wield more power than others. In Burlington, these groups include the banks, insurance companies, real estate brokers, large firms (such as General Electric), the Chamber of Commerce, the Democratic and Republican Parties, the daily newspaper (*The Burlington Free Press*), and various wealthy individuals. Although Burlington has its millionaires, and even multimillionaires, there are few, if any, large-scale capitalists that reside in the city.[8] For the most part, Burlington's elite is comprised of relatively small-scale capitalists.

Before Sanders was elected, the Democratic Party was the ruling party and certain businesspeople had a lot of clout at city hall, especially those who were members of the Ethan Allen Club—an exclusively men's club in Burlington. As a result, certain economic and development decisions were made over the years that were not necessarily in the best interests of most Burlingtonians, since they favored business interests over the general welfare of the city's low- and moderate-income residents. After Sanders was elected, most of the businessmen who had leveraged political clout in the past were no longer influential at city hall. However, they still were able to exert indirect influence over events in Burlington.

BRIEF BACKGROUND ON BERNARD SANDERS

Bernard Sanders (everyone calls him Bernie) was born in the Flatbush section of Brooklyn, New York, in 1942. His father had emigrated from Poland to the United States and became a paint salesman; his mother was a housewife and raised Sanders and an older brother in a small apartment. "Money was a constant anxiety," Sanders said, but "we never were poor in the sense of not having food on the table. . . . [We lived] a solid lower-middle-class existence."[9]

An early influence on Sanders's consciousness was his Judaism. Sanders noted: "Being Jewish has greatly influenced my intellectual and emotional development. I was very conscious as a kid that my father's whole family was killed by Hitler. The understanding of what went on in Germany made me sensitive to the fact of activities [that is, the Holocaust] like that."[10]

Sanders recalled his early childhood years as being a "happy period." Much of his time was taken up "playing ball." One of the "major disappointments in life was that I didn't make the junior varsity [team]," he said. Overcoming this, Sanders became a very good cross-country runner and co-captain of the track team in high school. "I always had good endurance," he said. At one point during his track career, Sanders came in third place in the New York City one-mile race. During this time, he found himself floating back and forth between the "jocks" and the "intellectuals," never feeling completely comfortable with either group.[11]

While his parents did not influence his evolution as a socialist (both parents were Democrats), his brother was active in progressive politics when Sanders was growing up. "From earliest memories, I was a rebel and a non-conformist," said Sanders. He elaborated: "Something that was with me ever since I was little was an instinct to not do what other people did because they did it."[12] As we shall see, this "instinct" has served Sanders well in the political arena.

Sanders lost his first political race for president of his high-school class. One of his campaign platforms had been for "the school to adopt a Korean child." (This was in the period following the Korean War.) Although rejecting his campaign, the school and its students took up Sanders's suggestion.[13]

Sanders wanted a track scholarship to an Ivy League school, but his grades weren't quite good enough. He went instead to Brooklyn College for one year and then decided to finish his education at the University of Chicago. This experience was to have a "profound impact" on his development. The Hyde Park community in which the school is located provided fertile ground for Sanders's political development. For the first time he met blacks, and he became active in the civil rights movement. A member of the Student Peace Union and the Congress on Racial Equality, he described himself at this time as a "classic liberal," concerned with issues like civil rights, economic justice, and nuclear war. He also protested against the Vietnam War. Said Sanders: "I really did not understand that these problems . . . had a common root," that is, the capitalist economic system.[14]

When he first entered college, socialism was not something that attracted Sanders. "Socialism meant to me exactly what it meant to every other kid—which is that's communism and something you don't go near." In a funny incident he relates, Sanders describes discovering the Eugene V. Debs club at Brooklyn College and, not knowing what it was, he asked someone. When he found out it was a socialist club, Sanders was "absolutely shocked" to find out there were socialists in his school.[15]

At the University of Chicago, Sanders wasn't clear on "what I wanted to do or what I wanted to be." He thought about being a psychiatrist or a psychologist because he was interested in what made people tick, wanted to know what made people crazy, and was fascinated by mass psychology. However, he failed biology twice, at which point the dean told him to take a break from school. Said Sanders: "I got my education after I had temporarily flunked out of school [because] I had the opportunity to read." And read he did. He read psychology, history, sociology, and socialism—works by Marx, Lenin, and Trotsky. This was a very fertile period for him and one that left a lasting impression on his intellectual consciousness. During this time period, Sanders's "emotional rebelliousness and sense of fairness became mated with an intellectual analysis of why things occur." He graduated from the university with a degree in political science.[16]

After graduating in 1964, Sanders worked in a Head Start program with children. He also attended graduate school in psychology for a brief period, but decided it was not for him. Sanders's political activities at this time included belonging to Students for a Democratic Society. In the years following his graduation, he eked out an existence doing many different jobs, spending his summers in Vermont, where he and his first wife owned land. In 1968, Sanders made a fortuitous decision: He moved permanently to the Green Mountain State.[17]

In the summer of 1971, Sanders made his first foray into Vermont politics. A good friend invited him to a meeting of the Liberty Union Party. This new, alternative party had been formed in 1969 and had a radical platform that included everything from taking over the state's electric utility companies to the nationalization of the country's banks. Sanders was so impressed with the Liberty Union Party that he went to its convention later that year, and when the floor was open to nominations, he put forward his own name as the party's candidate for the U.S. Senate. He got the nomination, an event that launched his political career.[18]

In the special U.S. Senate election of January 1972, Sanders got a grand total of 2.2 percent of the statewide vote. In November of 1972, Sanders became the Liberty Union candidate for governor, but received only 1.2 percent of the statewide vote (though he did get a greater number of votes than in the earlier special election).[19]

Far from being discouraged, Sanders actually became the chairperson of the Liberty Union Party in 1973. Sanders worked tirelessly to help build the party. In the 1974 elections, the work that Sanders and others had put into the party began to pay off. That fall, the Liberty Union Party gained major party standing by garnering a little under 7 percent of the statewide vote. Furthermore, Sanders almost doubled his own vote total from two years before in his second bid for a U.S. Senate seat.[20]

The Liberty Union Party's strength in Vermont peaked during the next few years. In 1975, the Liberty Union candidate for mayor of Burlington, Vermont, won 28 percent of the vote. When Sanders made his second bid for the governorship of the state in 1976, he received over 11,000 votes statewide and about 12 percent of the total votes cast in Burlington.[21]

By this time, the relationship between Sanders and the Liberty Union Party had become somewhat strained. He had given up the party chairperson position almost two years before his 1976 race, saying that he desired some "breathing space" from all its pressures. Less than a year after his 1976 race he left the Liberty Union Party forever, claiming that the faltering party could no longer "remain active on a year round basis in the struggles of working people against the banks and corporations which own and control Vermont and the nation."[22]

After leaving the Liberty Union Party, Sanders continued his work as the director of a nonprofit historical society, making filmstrips and videos about people such as Eugene Debs. For the most part, Sanders was not active in Vermont politics from the time he left the Liberty Union Party until he made his historic bid for the mayoralty of Burlington, Vermont, in 1981.[23]

THE MAYORAL RACE OF 1981

It was late in the summer of 1980 that Sanders seriously thought about running for mayor. "I think it was . . . my idea that he run for mayor," said a close friend of and political advisor to Sanders. "The match between . . . Bernie and the city was a good one. [At first], Bernie was somewhat hesitant, but he warmed to the idea," said the advisor.

Sanders "felt that because Liberty Union candidates had received up to 30 percent of the vote in some Burlington wards, that in a proper campaign and the correct race, it was possible for a radical to win," said one progressive alderman. Election records showed that in his last gubernatorial race, Sanders had garnered 16 percent of the vote in Burlington's working-class wards. So, in September of 1980, a meeting was called between Sanders and some of his friends at a low-income housing project to discuss his running for mayor. The meeting focused on five-term, ten-year incumbent Democratic mayor Gordon Paquette's vulnerability, and there was a feeling that Sanders would make the best candidate because of his commitment, the fact that he was an excellent speaker, and because he "reaches people where they are at," said a Sanders advisor.

Sanders formally announced his independent bid for mayor in fall 1980. At the beginning of the campaign, one of Sanders's advisors was "not convinced that Bernie would win, but that Paquette could be beaten." The advisor and Sanders calculated that it would take 4,000 votes to defeat Paquette, and that given the size of Burlington, it was possible to run a grass-roots, door-to-door campaign and conceivably pull off an upset victory. Sanders was advised to focus on the specific concerns of Burlingtonians. The initial strategy was to lay out a socially conservative but fairly radical economic platform, with an emphasis on "fiscal responsibility." The traditional "liberal ethos" was discarded, replaced by a "new vision," according to this advisor.

Sanders chose several pertinent issues to frame his 1981 campaign. His campaign theme was "It's Time for a Change, a *Real* Change." The main issues he ran on were (1) *waterfront development*—he opposed Burlington developer Tony Pomerleau's plans for a twin tower, eighteen-story condominium complex on the waterfront, with each condo priced at $200,000 (one of Sanders's campaign slogans was "Burlington's not for sale"); (2) *housing*—he supported new housing for low- and moderate-income people and a form of rent control; (3) *property taxes*—he was opposed to property tax hikes and he supported alternative forms of taxation; (4) *Southern Connector*—he opposed a proposed four-lane road through the residential South End of Burlington; and (5) *police and crime*—he supported the city's police officers and an effort to prevent crime, especially in Burlington's low- and moderate-income ward neighborhoods.[24]

Sanders's campaign platform, while not very radical in nature, was well-crafted to the political situation and addressed many Burlingtonians' real concerns and fears. Furthermore, Sanders opposed most of Paquette's less popular stands with voters.

In the last month of the campaign, there were three mayoral forums sponsored by various groups, at which Sanders's skills as a debater were evident, according to one of his campaign aides. A further encouraging sign was that Sanders's campaign really seemed to pull itself together in the last few weeks. "A week before the election, we had a sense that we would either win big or lose big, and neither result would surprise us," said a Sanders campaign worker. The last-minute advice of a well-seasoned political operative helped, too. With the aid of about 100 volunteers and only $3,000, the Sanders campaign tackled coordination of "election day strategies . . . [such as] get out the vote, publicity and advertising," said the political operative.

The momentum of the Sanders campaign had been building for weeks, and as election day approached, there was a sense of excitement and anticipation. Sanders's charisma had set the city buzzing, especially in the poor and working-class neighborhoods. Yet, Burlington's political pundits, as late as a few days before the election, predicted that incumbent Paquette would receive 56 percent of the vote, while challenger Sanders would get only 24 percent of the vote. On election day, though, Sanders stunned the city's "political establishment," squeaking past Paquette by a 4,035 to 4,023 vote margin—a mere twelve-vote difference. Ten days later, after a tense recount, Sanders was declared the official winner, but by an even slimmer ten-vote margin. The "underdog in the campaign" had won an amazing victory.[25]

How do we explain the extraordinary upset of Bernard Sanders over Democratic mayor Gordon Paquette? In talking with many Burlingtonians about it, a number of key reasons emerged. Sanders's upset victory was due, in part, to the nature of the Burlington Democratic Party. The party, for the most part, had been in control of local politics in Burlington for more than thirty years. In 1981, the Democratic Party not only controlled the mayor's seat, but ten of the thirteen seats on the Board of Aldermen as well (with the Republicans holding the other three seats). Gordon Paquette had functioned as a "fusion candidate" for the Democrats and Republicans in several of the past mayoral elections. Sanders's ability to win in 1981 "shatter[ed] the myth of a Burlington Democratic organization that [could] guarantee votes necessary to win elections."[26]

A further reason was Paquette's complacency in the mayoral campaign; he believed that Sanders did not pose a serious threat to his reelection. This was perhaps most evident in Paquette's push for a 65-cent property tax increase during the campaign, which Sanders opposed. The challenger's ability to appear as a fiscal conservative through his opposition to a large tax increase broadened his popular appeal, especially among the city's conservative voters, said one Burlington progressive.

The lack of a Republican candidate and the presence of three independent candidates, including Sanders, also was critical to Paquette's defeat. One of those independent candidates, restauranteur Dick Bove, ran against the incumbent after losing in the Democratic Party city caucus. If Bove had not gotten the 1,000 votes he did, Paquette almost surely would have won the election.[27]

The history of progressive community and political work in the city during the previous decade and changing demographics also were contributing factors. Many different groups, such as tenants' organizations and neighborhood groups, helped create a conducive climate for a progressive to run for electoral office and win, said another Burlington progressive. That decade also saw major changes in the demographic character of Burlington. One report indicated that "in a five-year period between 1975 and 1980, 14,694 residents, or 41% of the City's population, was new to the City." Also, while the fifteen to thirty-four-year-old age group comprised 31 percent of the population in 1960, in 1980 it skyrocketed to 51.4 percent of the population. Neither the Democratic nor the Republican Parties picked up on these trends, leaving Sanders the political beneficiary of these changes.[28]

The endorsement of the Burlington Patrolman's Association a week before the election was still another crucial factor. Paquette had alienated this group over the years, and the socialist challenger actively courted their support. One Sanders administration official commented that the endorsement "probably took him [Sanders] from . . . being a strong candidate, but certainly not a majority candidate, to a situation where he was now a real legitimate contender." And one newspaper reporter confided that it "gave Bernie an endorsement from a very credible source that in and of itself negated all the possible . . . red-baiting that would have gone Bernie's way. . . . I mean, how can you be a communist if the police are for [you]?"

The news media also played an important role. One of Sanders's campaign workers said: "Bernie was brilliant at dealing with the media the first time, and the media was very friendly. They obviously didn't like Paquette, and found Sanders to be interesting. They were as supportive as could be." Thus, by giving Sanders a lot of coverage, the news media helped turn him into a major contender in the election. Said one progressive: "I can't believe he [Sanders] would have won as mayor if he had not been on the news almost every night—and sympathetically so."

The outcome was influenced, too, by the attraction of about 1,000 new voters to the 1981 mayoral race. Additionally, there was a strong protest vote against Paquette, coupled with a higher than normal turnout for a local election. What did not influence the election, or even become an issue, was Sanders's political philosophy. "The media knew [he was a socialist], but the public didn't know. To the public, he was an independent," commented one progressive. One campaign worker said Sanders's identification as a socialist was "never brought up by the media or Paquette, even though the campaign was ready for it." Immediately after the election, however, a story appeared in *The Burlington Free Press* on Sanders's socialist beliefs and philosophy, making it widely known for the first time.

Almost no one, with the exception of Sanders himself and a few of his campaign staff, really expected him to win. Said one peace activist: "I think most people, especially on the left, were amazed that he won." Sanders's victory at the polls prompted many to speculate on his good fortune, with some concluding that his election was a fluke, and others suggesting that his success was the result of a well-calculated, brilliant electoral strategy. One newspaper reporter who was interviewed said that Sanders's election was a matter of "25 different levers . . . switch[ing] at the right time in synch."

In a paper analyzing Sanders's first two mayoral campaigns (1981 and 1983), Tom Rice, assistant professor of political science at the University of Vermont, made some interesting observations concerning Sanders's 1981 campaign. Rice's findings showed that Sanders did better among working-class and liberal voters than he did among middle-class and conservative ones, yet he still managed to pick up between 33 and 50 percent of the conservative vote. Sanders, as might be expected, also ran well among the Democrats, the young, and those who had been in Burlington only a short while. The study concluded that in the 1981 election, two "traditional socialist themes"—class background and ideology—were a factor, as both working-class people and people with a liberal ideology strongly supported Sanders.[29]

Clearly, no one variable was responsible for Sanders's remarkable victory in 1981. A series of events occurred which, when combined, created the stunning upset.

POLITICAL GAINS FROM THE 1982 ALDERMANIC RACES

After winning the mayoralty, Sanders attempted to send positive signals to the Board of Aldermen, telling them he would be working with them for at least the next two years: "I extend the olive branch. I do not want to go to war with anybody. I do not want to fight every step of the way, and [I] hope we'll work in cooperation."[30]

This was not to happen. Unfortunately, but perhaps not unexpectedly, "war" did break out between the newly elected mayor and the Board of Aldermen. The first big battle occurred when the Board of Aldermen, still controlled by the Democrats (the breakdown on the Board of Aldermen after the 1981 elections was eight Democrats, three Republicans, and two allies of Sanders), refused to grant Sanders any of his appointments to various city positions. The Democrats, out to show that Sanders's 1981 victory was nothing more than a fluke, interfered with almost all of Sanders's initiatives that first year. For example, besides blocking his appointments, the Board of Aldermen fired Sanders's newly appointed secretary, Linda Niedweske (though she was rehired later).[31]

The major issue in the 1982 Board of Aldermanic elections, then, was one of fairness, with voters judging whether or not the board was treating the new mayor in an appropriate way. On election day, the progressive slate did very well. Three progressives won—Rik Musty, Citizens' Party candidate in Ward 1; Zoe Breiner, Citizens' Party candidate in Ward 2; and Gary DeCarolis, an independent from Ward 3. Two more progressive candidates were able to force runoff elections which they eventually lost. (It should be noted that the presence of the Citizens' Party in Burlington was short-lived and that those who ran and won under that label eventually became members of the local Progressive Coalition, which didn't formalize itself until 1984.)[32]

Sanders and his supporters thus controlled five of the thirteen aldermanic seats.

Because this election was seen as a referendum on the Sanders administration, a great deal of interest was stirred up among the electorate. There was a record turnout for aldermanic elections in 1982; over 10,000 voters showed up at the polls. The net result of the March aldermanic elections was that "all Democratic incumbents who tried during the past year to block Sanders's appointees and proposals were either defeated or forced into runoffs."[33]

To fully understand the victory and close defeats of progressive forces on election day, it is necessary to look at the ward compositions in the city of Burlington. Each one of Burlington's six wards is quite distinct. Ward 1 (commonly referred to as the Hill Section) is predominantly middle to upper-middle class, dominated by most of the city's colleges (and by extension, their students and faculty) and the Medical Center of Vermont. The Old North End, which encompasses Wards 2 and 3, is the poorest section of Burlington, with about one-third of its inhabitants living in poverty. However, these two wards together have over one-quarter of the city's registered voters, and before the Sanders "revolution," had voted Democratic for more than a decade. Ward 4, or the New North End, is solidly middle class, primarily a single-family home area, "where one-quarter of the city's residents and registered voters live," and which usually is represented by a bloc of Republican aldermen. The South End's Ward 5 is described by Sanders as a "suburban-type ward," but it also is probably Burlington's most diverse ward, having its share of both low-income and very well-to-do residents. Moreover, it is a very ethnic, Democratic ward, with about 14 percent of the city's registered voters. Finally, Ward 6 is described by one observer as "a monied, liberal-Republican, Gucci, preppied kind of ward." The city's wealthiest ward, it has about 12 percent of the city's registered voters. There is also a significant student presence in this ward.[34]

Though Sanders failed to get a majority on the Board of Aldermen, he and his backers did achieve the ability to sustain a mayoral veto on the board. One administration insider said that whereas in 1981 the opposition on the Board of Aldermen could essentially work around the mayor, the election of three progressive candidates in 1982 "basically changed the political reality to one where the Board of Aldermen now had to deal with the mayor." The 1982 elections proved to be a watershed in Burlington politics in a larger sense. Said another administration insider: "It really solidified [the progressives'] power base and gave us the opportunity to . . . put forward some of our initiatives and put us in a better bargaining position."

THE 1983 ELECTIONS: SOLIDIFYING POWER

The 1983 mayoral election proved to be a major turning point for the Sanders administration. The opposition to Sanders, most notably the city's economic and political establishment, "thought Bernie was a fluke, and there was . . . an all out effort to defeat him," said an administration insider. As early as summer 1982, there were efforts to map out a strategy to defeat Sanders. "Leading Democrats, Republicans, and members of the city's business establishment are quietly planning Sanders's overthrow," reported the daily newspaper. Democratic and Republican party leaders were talking about running a fusion candidate against Sanders. The mayor responded: "I think it exposes the system for what it is. As quick as a flash, when the establishment is threatened, all these great traditions of the two-party system fade away into the dust."[35] The Democrats and Republicans, however, couldn't agree on a unity candidate.

On election day, Sanders achieved a resounding victory, garnering 52 percent of the vote against both a Republican and a Democratic challenger. He won all but one ward (4) and got almost 70 percent of the vote in Wards 2 and 3. With a "record turnout" of over 13,000 voters (more than 40 percent of the electorate), this was indeed a stunning victory for the socialist mayor. In addition, the progressives held on to their five seats on the Board of Aldermen. They completely dominated Wards 2 and 3, but made no further inroads into Ward 1 and could not break into Ward 5. Wards 4 and 6, meanwhile, remained an enclave for the city's Republicans. The composition of the Board of Aldermen, then, was unchanged after the 1983 aldermanic elections: five seats for the progressives, five seats for the Republicans, and three for the Democrats.[36]

Sanders's challengers in the 1983 elections included James Gilson, a conservative Republican businessman, and Judith Stephany, the liberal Democratic statehouse minority leader. Gilson was obviously not in sympathy with many of Sanders's ideas, clearly opposing his "socialist approach." However, Gilson lacked personal charisma, he was not a good campaigner, and he ran on a "pro-business" platform while attacking the incumbent as "anti-business."[37]

Stephany, who jumped into the race very late in the game, was unable to get her campaign off the ground until several weeks before the election. Stephany wanted to run a "positive campaign," and said that she agreed with many of Sanders's ideas but disagreed with his confrontational approach. Her line was that "those who made the revolution are not always the best to lead after the coup." However, Stephany was "caught in a political sandwich, with Sanders taking votes from her on the left and Gilson taking votes from the right of

Burlington's fractious Democratic party," and essentially she ran "a campaign long on style and short of substance."[38]

From the day that Sanders announced his intention to run again, it was clear his opponents were going to have trouble defeating him. Said the daily newspaper:

> Sanders may be in better political shape than at any time since he was elected. Sanders announced for the second year in a row . . . [no] property tax increase. With the city apparently in a good financial position, the mayor will be able to stress the Republican theme of good financial management as a campaign issue . . . [while] . . . the School Board Chairman [Gilson] . . . [is] stung by an audit that showed the School Department had a deficit last year.[39]

A few weeks before the election, the newspaper gave this glowing account of Sanders's accomplishments:

> By most conventional political measures, Sanders has forged a good record. He has brought new people into the political process, awakened interest in city politics, handled city finances well, and managed to reform areas of city government, for which even his opponents give him grudging praise.[40]

In interviews with people about the 1983 election, the most frequent response to the question "Why did Sanders win reelection against both Democratic and Republican challengers?" can be summed up in one progressive businessman's response: "He did a good job." There also was a strong consensus that Sanders won reelection because he ran against relatively weak opponents. On election day, Stephany and Gilson got only 31 percent and 17 percent of the vote, respectively. But the 1983 election differed from the previous mayoral election in several important ways. Sanders received more than 50 percent of the vote in a three-way election that saw a record-setting turnout. Clearly, many Democrats, some Republicans, and quite a few independents voted for Sanders.[41]

The 1983 mayoral campaign was "much more complicated, much more expensive, and much more sophisticated" than in 1981, said one Sanders campaign worker. It was the costliest in Burlington's history, with the candidates' combined expenditures exceeding $85,000. Gilson was the top spender at close to $35,000, Sanders second with over $28,000, and Stephany a close third at over $24,000.

One neighborhood group leader stated that Sanders "had a better political team than anyone else could put together: more energy, more lists, more phone calls, more door-to-door people." Voter registration drives helped add a lot of new people to the Burlington voting lists. Sanders's reelection campaign also motivated many people to get involved in it, according to a Sanders campaign worker. A Burlington environmental and peace activist commented: "The impressive thing about . . . Bernie's reelection campaign was . . . [that] . . . 200 to 300 people were involved in one way or another." A Vermont progressive political activist explained that "progressives, at all costs, want[ed] him kept in office" because Sanders's beliefs and his commitment to addressing the big issues made him an important spokesperson for the left.

An administration insider assessed the impact of the election in these terms: "Bernie's political power was finally recognized." He added that "it told the old political establishment that in fact the new political establishment . . . [was] legitimate—that they [Sanders's supporters] really did have a power base—that it wasn't a fluke."

The praise was not unanimous, however. A progressive critic expressed disappointment in Sanders's reelection campaign:

> The subsequent elections have been less ideological. . . . His [campaign] slogan in '83 was "Leadership that's keeping Burlington strong." It's not a radical posture to take. And the content of it [the campaign]—street improvements, keeping taxes down, efficiency in government, saving money . . . at best they're kind of a democratic, reform-oriented platform. He [Sanders], in fact, does what almost all politicians do, which is he runs left between elections and then back right, right before the election—not so much in the spoken word—but in what the machine produces. And the machine gets the word out real well.

University of Vermont political scientist Tom Rice's analysis of the 1983 mayoral race showed that Sanders did much better among the young and those who had lived in the city a short time, a finding that corresponded to his analysis of the 1981 election. Furthermore, Sanders polled very well among Democrats and independents. However, the "liberalness" of one's ideology or one's class background played a much less significant role in the 1983 election than it did in 1981. Instead, party affiliation and age were the most significant factors in determining voting patterns in the election. This seems to suggest, concluded Rice, "that in the United States, a Socialist can gather substantial support among the traditional Socialist constituencies—

the working class and liberals . . . and also that a Socialist's appeal need not only be limited to traditional Socialist constituencies."[42]

The 1983 Burlington elections were a watershed for the Sanders administration and the progressives, an event that consolidated their power. Despite widespread skepticism from many in the city's Democratic and Republican Parties and in the business community, Sanders and the progressives had left their stamp on Burlington, which would remain as part of the political milieu for the foreseeable future.

1984 ALDERMANIC ELECTIONS: CLOSE, BUT NOT QUITE

Progressives in the city of Burlington, now calling themselves the Progressive Coalition, almost gained control of the Board of Aldermen in 1984. One academician predicted: "'84 is the peak for Sanders. This is really the . . . year it comes together for Sanders, or so it looks." The daily newspaper, four weeks before the March elections, said: "The [Progressive] Coalition has the early lead, at least in organizing. . . . [It] has raised about $2,500 . . . [and] also has access to a computer, and has a network of several hundred volunteers."[43]

The 1984 elections, however, had a different feel to them than the two previous mayoral races. "There is no theme to this election. This is not a referendum on Bernie Sanders," commented an academician. More surprisingly, those aldermanic candidates running under the Democratic and Republican party labels went to great lengths to praise Sanders. For example, one Republican candidate who eventually won a seat on the board and became one of Sanders's more outspoken critics, said before the election: "I think Bernie has done a number of good things. He's had some good advisors, he's made some good moves."[44]

Election day in March 1984 was a tense one. When it was over, the Progressive Coalition had picked up one more aldermanic seat—for a total of six—but still was one short of board control. Composition of the new board was six progressives, five Republicans, and two Democrats. The Progressive Coalition, although lacking a majority, had at least gained a plurality on the Board of Aldermen. Perhaps the most striking thing about the election was that it marked the low point for the Democratic Party in Burlington. The Democrats had run seven candidates for the Board of Aldermen, and they all were defeated.[45]

The Progressive Coalition held on to three of its seats (Wards 1, 2, and 3), picked up a seat (Ward 5), and for the first time ever, won two seats on the School Board, thereby proving it was a power to be reckoned with. Reelection campaigns of the progressives were even more significant, explained one progressive alderman, because the Democrats and Republicans joined forces to defeat the Progressive Coalition candidates. Consequently, in the races in Wards 1, 2, 3, and 5, instead of facing Republican and Democratic opponents (which would have given the Progressive Coalition candidates a significant advantage since only 40 percent is needed to win), Sanders's allies faced only one Democratic opponent, said this progressive alderman.

The gain of an additional seat on the board increased the Progressive Coalition's power in one important way: When the Board of Aldermen met as the city council, the mayor became a voting member. The progressives and the Democratic/Republican opposition now each had seven votes on the council, creating a stalemate that became a very powerful bargaining chip for the progressives. Said one administration insider: "The real political significance of the 1984 election was the inroads it allowed the Progressive Coalition to make regarding commission appointments" [an appointive power of the city council].

The Progressive Coalition had another chance to win a majority on the Board of Aldermen in spring 1984 when Linda Burns, an incumbent Democratic alderwoman from Ward 5 and the sister of Democratic alderman James Burns, decided to resign from the board. The two contestants in the race were Paul Lafayette, a Democrat who was born and raised in Burlington with roots in the community and a Francophone last name, and Samuel "Frank" Sampson, a Progressive Coalition candidate who was a member of the Planning Commission and a sociology professor at the University of Vermont. The overriding issue in the race became whether or not Sanders would get a majority on the board. The race proved to be no contest: On election day, Lafayette rolled over Sampson by a 2–1 margin.[46]

The special aldermanic election in May 1984 gave the Progressive Coalition one of their best shots at winning a majority on the board, but they were unable to take advantage of the opportunity. Instead, the Democrats finally stopped their electoral skid, winning the election by a comfortable margin. The election of Paul Lafayette to the Board of Aldermen would come back to plague the Sanders administration later.

THE 1985 MAYORAL AND ALDERMANIC ELECTIONS: MAINTAINING THE STATUS QUO

By the 1985 election, Sanders had pretty well consolidated his political power in the city of Burlington, a fact that did not escape the

Democrats and Republicans. In summer 1984, members of both parties began talking seriously again about running a unity candidate. Reported the daily newspaper: "City Republicans and Democrats have held meetings on the topic [of a unity candidate], and most agree: Mayor Bernard Sanders, the socialist independent once considered a fluke, is so firmly ensconced that it will take a candidate with the backing of both traditional parties to pry him loose."[47]

On the surface, the discussion between the two parties seemed to accomplish little. However, in fall 1984, the editors of *The Burlington Free Press* made the unusual move of suggesting that Maggie Green, a Republican city planning commissioner, run as a fusion candidate. One of the editors, Dan Costello, said that "the need to defeat Sanders was compelling enough to warrant the unusual timing."[48]

Sanders had been considering staying out of the race for a third term as mayor, primarily because of the long hours and huge commitment required for the office. However, the daily newspaper's suggestion of a fusion candidate irked him. He saw the move as a verification that there was a "one-party system" in town, the "Republicrats, before the progressive movement was born in Burlington."[49]

Shortly after the daily newspaper suggested Green as the fusion candidate of their choice, she gracefully declined to run. Said one political observer: "After Green refused to run, a Republican alderwoman, Diane Gallagher, said she would run for mayor, acknowledging she would be an underdog." Shortly thereafter, Sanders decided that he would run again. A few weeks later, Brian Burns, a former Democratic Lieutenant Governor and gubernatorial candidate, also announced his candidacy for mayor of Burlington.[50]

The 1985 mayoral race took an interesting twist when Diane Gallagher was forced to withdraw from the race as a Republican and run as an independent. After Burns announced his candidacy, "Gallagher [was] . . . pressured by members of the Burlington business community to withdraw from the Burlington mayoral race to improve the chances for Democrat Brian Burns to defeat independent Mayor Bernard Sanders." Prominent Democrats and Republicans, especially in the business community, were behind this move. Burns even contemplated attending the Republican caucus to wrest that nomination from Gallagher, but decided against it. However, since there was a distinct possibility that the caucus would not have nominated anyone because of divisions within the Republican Party over which candidate to support, Gallagher chose the route of an independent candidacy rather than risk possible rejection by her own party. Said the daily newspaper: "Gallagher attributed some of the opposition to her independent voting record and to the fact that she is a woman."[51]

Soon after Sanders announced his bid for a third term, *The Burlington Free Press* published a poll which indicated that "two-thirds of Burlingtonians polled approved of the job Sanders is doing as mayor. Further . . . two-thirds of those polled believed the economic climate of the city has improved in the last few years, a phenomen[on] which could hamstring the Mayor's opponents' efforts to label him as bad for business." The polling data led the daily newspaper to comment a few weeks later that "the Burlington mayoral campaign will focus on the record of Mayor Bernard Sanders, according to his opponents, and that suits the Mayor fine."[52]

Yet Sanders was handicapped going into the 1985 contest by his late announcement, and his campaign was slow to get into gear. According to one administration insider, Sanders finally decided to enter the race despite his reservations because he felt some obligation to the progressive electoral movement he helped start and he really did not want to see Brian Burns become mayor of Burlington.

Sanders ran a campaign based on his strong mayoral record over the previous four years. It paid off: On election day, Sanders won an expected victory, garnering 55.3 percent of the vote to Burns's 31.5 percent and Gallagher's 11.9 percent. The combined effect of a heavy snowstorm the night before and the results of a poll conducted several weeks prior to the election (showing Sanders with a strong lead) resulted in a light turnout, with only 10,400 showing up to vote (about 3,000 less than in the 1983 mayoral race).[53]

Sanders won a third term, in part, because his opponents ran poor campaigns. Gallagher was plagued by the internal problems of her own party and was unable to galvanize opposition to the Sanders administration. Brian Burns was the Democrats' great liberal hope for defeating Sanders. As it turned out, however, his campaign fizzled too. Burns mounted an aggressive campaign, personally attacking the mayor on his appointments, his inability to accomplish anything, and the kinds of initiatives he had put forth. But about halfway through the campaign he reversed gears. At a press conference, the Democratic candidate announced that people would no longer see "Mr. Tough Guy." Instead he was going to focus on his positive vision for the city. Switching strategies midstream did not help his campaign; if anything, it probably hurt it.[54]

Sanders viewed the 1985 campaign as "a judgment of what we've accomplished—on the direction we're taking the city—and the people seem to feel [good about it]." He portrayed Brian Burns as representing the "Old Democrats," and characterized the basic campaign issue as: "Does that [progressive] fight continue, or does the old guard and the big money behind them come back to control City Hall"?[55]

Sanders received the continued support of the labor movement (seven trade unions, including the local American Federation of State, County, and Municipal Employees [AFSCME] union, supported his candidacy), as well as support from a group of University of Vermont professors. However, it wasn't just these endorsements that solidified Sanders's support. Two well-known Democrats not only endorsed him but worked for him as well.[56]

The 1985 mayoral race was considerably less expensive than the previous race, costing a total of only about $60,000. Still, Sanders and Burns spent about $25,000 each, while Gallagher spent around $10,000.[57] One campaign worker speculated that once it became clear Burns wasn't going to beat Sanders, less money came into the Burns campaign, and consequently the Sanders campaign could spend less too.

There was a grass-roots spirit to the Sanders campaign which, according to one campaign worker and peace activist, made the election feel like "a team of people who all made it look like fun . . . [and] it all seemed an expression of the community movement." Another peace activist said: "The fact that they [the Sanders administration] addressed issues that were felt by grass-roots activists [to be important] really contributed to the Sanders administration being able to maintain their level of support" [among this group].

In his analysis of why people voted for Sanders in 1985, Tom Rice noted that Burlington voters, who were only slightly more left of center than the nation, saw their mayor as being very liberal, if not radical. Although Sanders's socialist identity was something of which Burlington voters were aware (if not by the mayor's own pronunciations, then by the media's constant mentioning of it), they *didn't* vote for Sanders because he is a socialist. In fact, over 80 percent of Burlington voters identified with either the Democratic or the Republican Parties, 14 percent considered themselves independent, and only 4 percent were affiliated with a third party or didn't reply to the question. Concluded Rice: "In sum, it appears that Burlington is not in the midst of a Socialist revolution. The citizenry does not lean far to the left and doesn't identify with the Socialist party. Instead, Sanders's success seems due primarily to his personality, and, to a lesser degree, to his stands on the issues."[58]

The Board of Aldermen elections that same year were crucial to the Progressive Coalition's attempt to gain control of the board. One seat in each of the city's wards—for a total of six —were up, and each major political faction in Burlington had two seats up for grabs. Since the progressives' seats in Wards 2 and 3 were relatively safe, they had a good shot at picking up a seventh seat in either Ward 1, where the Democratic incumbent was not running again, or in Ward 6, where a

Democrat was running who was sympathetic to the Progressive Coalition.[59]

Even though Sanders, once his own reelection was virtually assured, campaigned hard for key Progressive Coalition candidates, the seventh seat eluded them. The results were a blow to the Progressive Coalition. The progressives had a clear shot to control both the mayor's office and the board, but again weren't able to pull it off.[60]

1986 ALDERMANIC ELECTIONS: TOO CLOSE FOR COMFORT

The Progressive Coalition, which had come so close to controlling the Board of Aldermen in 1985, faced a difficult challenge in 1986: With four of its six seats up for challenge, could it retain at least five seats in order to sustain the mayor's veto power? As it turned out, the coalition held on, but just barely.

The coalition's task was made all the more difficult because three of the four incumbents chose not to run for reelection. Acknowledging this critical juncture, the mayor said: "This is going to be a hard time, a time of testing for the progressive movement.... It's harder to maintain the excitement when the fights are long-term fights. It cannot, is not, and never will be a one-person show. It cannot depend on one personality." The daily newspaper also commented: "For the first time since 1981, the progressives have the most to lose."[61]

On election day, the results were ambiguous. The Progressive Coalition held on to aldermanic seats in its two strongest wards—2 and 3. They lost badly in Ward 5 and were forced into a runoff election in Ward 1 against a conservative Republican. The runoff election between Progressive Coalition member Erhard Mahnke and Republican Walter Simendinger really stretched the Progressive Coalition's ability to get out the vote. The mayor's veto power was at stake, and the daily newspaper reported that the "outcome may hinge on the depth of opposition to or support for Mayor Bernard Sanders." When the runoff election was held several weeks after the general election, Mahnke won by thirty-one votes. Simendinger had run a campaign in which he "sharply criticized Sanders's socialism." The election again showed that attacking Sanders's socialism was a mistake. The Progressive Coalition had proved it was capable, through hard work and sheer persistence, of winning when it really counted.[62]

The board elections gave the Progressive Coalition and the Republicans five seats each, the Democrats three. Despite a difficult situation, the progressives were able to minimize their loss and, by retaining mayoral veto power, continue to have an active say in the shape of city politics.

1987 ELECTIONS: WE'RE HERE TO STAY

After Sanders's unsuccessful 1986 gubernatorial bid,[63] the daily newspaper speculated that he would run for mayor again, especially to keep himself in the limelight to launch yet another bid for governor. As if to confirm expectations, Sanders, in an interview with Burlington's weekly newspaper, claimed that his run for governor had "revitalized" him.[64]

At the beginning of December, Sanders threw his hat into the ring. He timed the announcement to come shortly before the Progressive Coalition's citywide meeting to endorse a mayoral candidate. After receiving the Progressive Coalition's endorsement, Sanders announced that regardless of the outcome, this would be his last race for mayor.[65]

Early on the Republicans, for one reason or another, were having trouble finding a mayoral candidate for the 1987 race. The daily newspaper editorialized that it would behoove the Republican Party to find a candidate in order to give the voters a maximum range of possibilities. Despite the newspaper's encouragement, the Republicans were unable to field a candidate.[66]

What the Republican Party lacked, the Democratic Party promised to make up. The daily newspaper predicted that the Democratic Party's caucus in the middle of January was going to be large, and it was correct. A record-breaking 1,000 people attended the caucus, at which time Paul Lafayette handily defeated Caryl Stewart for the Democratic mayoral nomination. For a change, the Democrats looked good. Their party seemed revitalized, and this time, there was only one major opponent facing Sanders. Even the mayor admitted that it was probably going to be a close race.[67]

As the race unfolded, there were a number of surprises. For example, Sanders proposed a 4-cent tax increase to hire more police officers and administrative personnel and to buy more police cruisers—his first proposed tax increase since 1983. (In that year, Sanders requested a 16-cent splinter tax for the streets.) On another front, Sanders received a rude shock when the city's municipal employees' union, a strong supporter of the mayor in the past two elections, endorsed Lafayette. Finally, the union at the General Electric plant, the International Union of Electrical Workers, also decided to support Lafayette—the first time this union had ever backed a candidate for mayor. All of a sudden, Sanders appeared in trouble. According to one Republican alderman, Lafayette already had about "35 to 40 percent [of the vote] from the 'Anybody but Sanders' crowd," and was now eating into traditional Sanders supporters.[68]

Many observers thought the race could go either way. One reporter noted that Lafayette had "widespread support among both Democrats and Republicans," and that Lafayette's campaign tactics differed from those used in previous races in that he stressed positive rather than negative themes.[69]

Sanders's campaign strategy was clear; he was running on his impressive record. In a campaign piece put out during the election, Sanders stressed his accomplishments over the years, highlighting improvements to the city while holding the line on property taxes and finding alternative sources of revenue, the creation of more jobs, and various people-oriented initiatives of his administration.[70]

The biggest surprise of the election, however, came when *The Burlington Free Press*, whose editors were long-time critics of the Sanders administration, endorsed the incumbent. The editorial praised Sanders for his leadership and criticized Lafayette for his hesitant approach to issues and his lack of vision for the city. In conclusion, the editorial said: "While the *Free Press* will continue to oppose some of Sanders's policies, we believe he is the better qualified of the two candidates for mayor and suggest voters re-elect him to a fourth term." Few people, especially the mayor, were prepared for this endorsement.[71]

Election day once again proved the political pundits wrong. Sanders easily won his fourth term, coasting to a 55.6 percent to 44.4 percent victory over Lafayette (which equaled, percentage-wise, his previous best showing). The mayor won five of six wards, including Lafayette's (and Sanders's) home ward (5). Sanders overwhelmed Lafayette in Wards 2 and 3, and also in Ward 1, winning by nearly 2–1 margins in them.[72]

The Progressive Coalition also did surprisingly well on election day. They regained their sixth seat and with it the chance to gain a majority on the Board of Aldermen. The only disappointment for the coalition was the defeat of their candidate in Ward 5 in the runoff election held several weeks after the general election.[73]

This last mayoral race dispelled the myth that if only the opposition could find a strong unity candidate to challenge Bernard Sanders, it could kick him out of office. Such a strategy could conceivably have worked in 1983, but by 1987 Sanders had consolidated his power base, making it virtually impossible to dislodge him from the mayor's office.

The 1987 electoral race had the potential to be a lot closer than any of the previous ones. However, Sanders proved to be the consummate politician, picking up on Lafayette's weaknesses and chipping away at them, while running on his own very solid record. The strong showing of the Progressive Coalition as well was an indication of its superb organizational skills and its recent efforts to create a real organization apart from Sanders. As it became more institutionalized, the Progressive Coalition carved itself a deeper niche in Burlington politics.

1988 ALDERMANIC ELECTIONS: MAINTAINING THE STATUS QUO

To a large degree, the 1988 aldermanic elections were anticlimactic. Other than the Democrats winning a third seat on the board at the expense of the Republicans, things remained the same. While the Progressive Coalition had a tough fight retaining one of its two seats in Ward 3 (the newcomer progressive candidate won by only seven votes), incumbent Progressive Coalition aldermen won easily in Wards 1 and 2. Although Sanders declared that "we were extremely nervous, and we worked as hard as we could," early election results made it clear that the Progressive Coalition, at the very least, would retain its ability to sustain a mayoral veto. After the 1988 aldermanic elections were over, the board composition was six progressives, five Republicans, and three Democrats.[74]

1989: THE CHANGING OF THE GUARD

The year 1989 was important for Burlington's progressive movement. After his narrow defeat in the 1988 congressional race,[75] Sanders made it clear that he would not run for mayor again in 1989. With the loss of its standard-bearer, the Progressive Coalition had to come together as never before.

In December 1988, the Progressive Coalition held a citywide meeting to elect a successor to Sanders. Initially, it appeared that there would be three contenders for the position. Before the meeting, however, city treasurer Jonathan Leopold, Jr., decided not to run, and alderman Terrill Bouricius pronounced at the meeting (attended by over 100 people) that he would not challenge Community and Economic Development Office (CEDO) director Peter Clavelle for the nomination.[76]

Meanwhile, the Democrats were busy selecting their own candidate to run against Clavelle. Nancy Chioffi, president of the Board of Aldermen and a businesswoman, narrowly won a caucus victory, setting up a race between herself and Clavelle. Since the two had similar positions on a number of issues, it seemed the mayoral race would be close.[77]

The mayoral race was further complicated by the entry of a Greens candidate. Sandra Baird, an attorney and former Progressive Coalition supporter, decided to join the contest because she felt neither of the other candidates would seriously address environmental concerns. There was speculation that Baird's run could jeopardize Clavelle's chance to succeed Mayor Sanders, especially since again there was no Republican mayoral candidate in the race.[78]

While Clavelle's style was much lower-key than Sanders's, his positions on the issues were virtually identical. Given the popularity of Sanders, Chioffi faced the difficult task of proving that she was different enough from his heir apparent, Peter Clavelle, for voters to choose her, while at the same time not threatening to change too much.[79]

Several weeks before the election, *The Burlington Free Press* published a poll showing Peter Clavelle holding a nine-point lead in the race, but 21 percent of the voters still were undecided. Six percent said they were backing Greens candidate Baird. The same day, the daily newspaper gave the Clavelle campaign an added boost by endorsing him for mayor.[80]

Election day was sweet for the Progressive Coalition. Progressive Coalition mayoral candidate Peter Clavelle received almost 54 percent of the vote, while Democrat Nancy Chioffi got 42 percent. Greens candidate Baird tallied slightly more than 3 percent of the vote. Clavelle had proven that the Progressive Coalition had staying power, even without Sanders at the helm. Moreover, the Progressive Coalition held on to its six aldermanic seats.[81]

THE IMPACT AND FUTURE OF BURLINGTON'S PROGRESSIVE EXPERIMENT

Bernard Sanders and the Progressive Coalition have clearly transformed the nature of local politics in Burlington, Vermont. In essence, Sanders and the coalition have created a viable third electoral force in the city that has successfully challenged the traditional two-party structure—at least for now.

However, it would be a mistake to assume that because of these events, Burlington has been turned into a socialist city and that the electoral changes in the city are permanent. Sanders was not elected and reelected mayor of Burlington because he is a socialist. Rather, as

Tom Rice has clearly shown, Sanders enjoyed support because of his charisma and his stand on certain issues.

Elections in the United States are very much a politics of personalities rather than a politics of ideologies—especially on the local level. It is no small irony that Sanders's electoral career has paralleled in time that of Ronald Reagan's—with obvious ideological differences. The fact that some Burlingtonians have voted for *both* Sanders and Reagan indicates that many voters seek strong political leaders with firm stances regardless of their ideology.

Sanders is a talented politician—one who stands above the crowd in Burlington and who can compete effectively for statewide office in Vermont. While there is no doubt that he is a socialist, he no longer seems to flaunt it as he did during his Liberty Union days. Consequently, while the average Burlingtonian probably is aware of his socialist proclivities, that does not seem to negatively affect the voter on election day. Moreover, attempts by Democratic and Republican opposition candidates to raise the red specter have, for the most part, backfired.

The Progressive Coalition has moved in recent years from being a loose-knit, informal network of progressives to being a more permanent organization. Prior to 1986, the coalition had been relatively disorganized, due in part to Sanders's opposition—both overt and covert—to the creation of a formal political organization. Then, in summer 1986, about fifty members of the coalition met to formally adopt a structure, a platform, and bylaws for the organization.[82] One result of the formal institutionalization of the Progressive Coalition was its strong showing in the 1987 and 1988 aldermanic elections.

But Burlington's Progressive Coalition still has some difficulties ahead. According to a poll conducted by Tom Rice's Campaign Marketing Associates firm after the 1987 elections, Burlingtonians identified their political allegiance this way: 36 percent Democrats, 23 percent Republicans, 18 percent independents, 12 percent undecided or otherwise affiliated, and only 11 percent Progressive Coalition. Rice felt that the results indicated shallow support for the coalition and that the reason it continued to do well was directly related to its standard-bearer, Bernard Sanders. Interviews with a number of people reinforced the view that Sanders was the glue that held the Progressive Coalition together. The implication was that without Sanders, the coalition would fall apart.[83]

The Progressive Coalition in Burlington was remarkably successful from 1981 to 1989, even though it never won the seventh aldermanic seat. But these victories do not guarantee its long-term survival. When Sanders made it clear that he would not run for mayor again in 1989, the coalition was faced with a major challenge. Once

Sanders left municipal office, the charismatic personality around which the coalition was built vanished. But Peter Clavelle proved that Sanders's charisma isn't the only force holding the Progressive Coalition together. Clavelle's ability to win the 1989 mayoral election and the Progressive Coalition's retention of six seats on the Board of Aldermen indicates that voters' allegiance to the coalition runs deeper than just to Sanders.

Still, third-party movements historically have fared poorly in the UnitedStates.[84] While the Progressive Coalition has been loosely connected to the Vermont Rainbow Coalition[85] under the banner of the Progressive Vermont Alliance as of May 1990, the coalition's isolation may eventually take it down the path of extinction even faster than past third-party efforts in the United States. Although there is discussion about creating a new progressive third-party in Vermont (a move Sanders probably would support), this step might only be a temporary palliative, especially since there are few, if any, similar occurrences in the United States today.

One ironic long-term consequence of the Sanders "revolution" in Burlington may be the eventual revitalization of Burlington's two-party system. Before Sanders was elected, the Democratic Party convincingly ruled Burlington, in effect making it a one-party town. Because of the city's demographic changes and the inflexibility of the city's Democratic Party at the time to accommodate these newcomers, many turned elsewhere, to Bernard Sanders and the Progressive Coalition. In the future, there will likely be a realignment of the Burlington electorate—with liberal Democrats now in the Progressive Coalition rejoining the city's Democratic Party, forcing it to become more liberal in the process. Depending on how liberal the party becomes, the remnants of the "old-guard" conservative Democrats may join the ranks of the newly revitalized city Republican Party. This would then complete the realignment of the Burlington electorate.

Local Government and City Finances in Burlington

The events that transpired under the Sanders administration need to be examined in light of the city government's structure—including the executive role of the mayor, the legislative function of the Board of Aldermen, and the role of the city commissions—and its day-to-day operation. The structure and function of municipal government can determine, to a large extent, the power wielded by its highest offices, and Sanders has been forced to adjust his expectations to comply with these inherent limitations. Still, in the areas of appointments and city finances, the mayor has accomplished a lot.

STRUCTURE OF BURLINGTON'S CITY GOVERNMENT

Burlington often is referred to as having a "commission form of government." This is misleading. Said one Burlington activist: "We don't have a commission form of government; what we have is a mayor and council form of government." This distinction is important. What people meant when they said "commission form of government," commented this activist, was the early-twentieth-century movement which saw "administrative and legislative power centralized in one body." This never was (and is not) the form of government in Burlington.

The disagreement over Burlington's form of government is compounded by the perception that it is a "weak mayor form" of government. However, terms such as strong or weak mayor forms of government were "misnomers," according to a former socialist mayor, because many mayors play a strong role in city government despite their formal powers "by virtue of their ability to nominate [and] hand out positions as rewards."

Commissions have been with Burlington since its incorporation as a city in 1865, said a knowledgeable Burlington activist. Initially, there were only three commissions (probably streets, fire, and police), but over the years more and more commissions were added. "The structure [of Burlington's city government] has essentially remained the same since the incorporation of the city," concluded the activist.

THE ROLE OF THE MAYOR

Burlington's city charter grants a number of formal powers to the mayor. First, the mayor has the power of making some appointments. The city charter states:

> The mayor shall appoint on the first Monday of June, and annually thereafter . . . one assessor, a building inspector . . . a city clerk and one or more assistant city clerks, a city treasurer and one or more assistant city treasurers, a city attorney and one or more assistant city attorneys, a city constable . . . city engineer . . . civil defense director, all with the approval of a majority of the Board of Aldermen.[1]

The mayor also can appoint the director of the newly created Community and Economic Development Office. (See Chapter 4 for a detailed examination of this office.)

The charter grants the mayor of Burlington considerable control over the budget, which originates with the mayor. By effectively wielding the power of the purse, a good deal of political power can be exerted, including indirect control over city departments. In addition, the city attorney ruled in 1981 that the mayor and aldermen together— rather than the city's Planning Commission—decide how federal grants are spent.[2]

The mayor's other significant power is the veto. As in the federal system, the mayor can veto any proposed board legislation and a two-thirds majority vote is required by the aldermen to override the veto. Thus, with five supporters, a mayoral veto can be upheld.

By virtue of his or her position, the mayor is a member of the city council, the fourteen-person body comprised of the mayor and the thirteen aldermen. The city council's most important function is appointing city commissioners. Since the mayor can vote on the city council (the mayor has no vote on the Board of Aldermen), six supporters effectively allows the mayor to stalemate meetings and there-fore force compromises on commission appointments.

THE FUNCTION OF BURLINGTON'S BOARD OF ALDERMEN

Burlington's Board of Aldermen is comprised of thirteen mem-bers—two members from each ward serving staggered terms, except in Ward 4, which has three aldermen serving it. After each election, the board elects a president from amongst its members. The board president chairs aldermanic meetings, votes to break board ties (or abstains from voting to bring about a board tie, thus effectively killing a measure), and determines the composition of various aldermanic committees. Thus, the board president wields a lot of power.[3]

According to the daily newspaper, "the Board of Aldermen is where the power lies in Burlington government." Actually, the board's power is officially quite limited. The mayor's appointments to various offices require approval of a majority of aldermen, as does removing an item from the mayor's budget. A two-thirds majority of the board is necessary to add to or reallocate items in the mayor's budget or to override a mayoral veto. [4]

Although the city clerk is responsible for putting together the board's agenda, the aldermen have the power, by a majority vote, to change the order or to take an item off the agenda. By a two-thirds vote, the board can place an item on the agenda. More importantly, the Board of Aldermen has the power to consolidate or add city commissions and, as members of the city council, to appoint city commissioners.

THE ROLE OF CITY COMMISSIONS

Most of Burlington's city departments—including electric, fire, parks and recreation, planning, police, public health and safety, public works, and water resources—are governed by commissions. In addi-tion, there are commissions for the airport, the housing authority, the library, Church Street marketplace, and the waterfront. Most of the city commission appointments are made by the city council; however, a few are appointed by the Board of Aldermen and a couple by the mayor alone.[5]

The commissions' budgets rest in the hands of the mayor and the Board of Aldermen. However, commissions have a good deal of inde-pendence from the executive and legislative branches of government in running the day-to-day affairs of the various departments. They are responsible for appointing and getting rid of department heads, with "the mayor and the Board of Aldermen hav[ing] no role whatsoever in the process." Department heads are answerable to their respective commission, not the mayor or aldermen, and their loyalty (not to mention their job security) usually rests with their commission. Most commissioners were appointed to five-year terms until March 1983, when Burlington voters overwhelmingly approved a ballot item changing many commission terms from five years to three years.[6]

Burlington's form of government is unusual due to the role of its commissions and their legislated powers. Some of the obstacles Sanders initially faced were due to the city's governmental structure. Over time, though, the mayor and his allies learned to work around these barriers. Regardless of whether Burlington's form of government can properly be called a "weak mayor form," Sanders clearly has wielded significant political power. His formal powers coupled with his ability to sustain a veto on some important issues have meant considerable control of budgetary matters. And through commission appointments, he and his supporters have been able to gain control of or have significant influence on many of the city's commissions.

SANDERS AND LOCAL GOVERNMENT

Appointments

Immediately after Sanders was elected mayor, he began to experience difficulties with the Board of Aldermen. At the very first meeting of the board, city aldermen fired Sanders's secretary, Linda Niedweske. The aldermen did so "because she [Niedweske] did not fit the job's previous requirements and because the Mayor had not asked to lift a city hiring freeze," according to the daily newspaper. However, after sending Sanders this message of who was in charge, the board agreed to a compromise that permitted her to be rehired.[7] According to one administration insider, the aldermen "waived the freeze and redesigned the position to be that of an administrative assistant," as opposed to executive secretary.

Shortly after this first skirmish, a bigger battle began to brew. Sanders, deciding to ignore a suggestion from the Board of Aldermen that he simply "reappoint" various city officials, recommended the appointment of five of his allies to the crucial positions of city treasurer, city clerk, assistant city clerk, civil defense director, and assistant city attorney.[8]

At the board meeting to consider Sanders's candidates, the aldermen, on an 11–2 vote, flatly denied Sanders his appointments. Democrats and Republicans teamed up to hand the mayor his first major defeat, claiming that "the mayor was making a radical change by sweeping out incumbents and politicizing administration jobs." Joyce Desautels, then president of the board, accused Sanders of attempting to "expand . . . the base of the Socialist Party in Burlington." In the first round of a power struggle between the mayor and the Board of Aldermen over who decided key city appointments, the aldermen came out ahead.[9]

Sanders refused to succumb to pressure. The mayor brought a lawsuit against the board, claiming that his appointees were never given a fair hearing by the aldermen, and several hundred people rallied at city hall to protest the board's action.[10] According to one administration official, not getting the appointments was initially a "major defeat," because it prevented the Sanders administration from moving ahead with its agenda. In the long run, though, it turned out to be a "blessing in disguise." The board's action created public sympathy for Sanders, dampened public expectations about what Sanders could do without help on the board, and gave the administration much-needed time to pull things together, according to this administration insider.

During the fracas, the city's civil defense director decided to leave his position. This was a strategic blow to Sanders's opposition on the board. They tried to get him to reconsider his decision, but the city attorney put a stop to their plans when he ruled that the board did not have the power to revoke an appointed official's resignation.[11]

The resignation provided Sanders with the opening he needed. The mayor went back to the board and asked it to reconsider his initial appointment for the position of civil defense director—David Clavelle. Sanders also requested that his appointment for Public Health and Safety administrator, Steve Goodkind, be reconsidered too, since the present administrator was retiring. Shortly after Sanders made his requests, the aldermen granted them, partly due to public pressure. The board voted unanimously to appoint Goodkind, and only two aldermen voted against the appointment of Clavelle. Although not key posts, the mayor was gratified to at least get his first two appointments—and therefore supporters—within the administration.[12]

Meanwhile, Sanders's suit against the aldermen was dismissed in superior court, and he decided to appeal the decision to the Vermont Supreme Court. The daily newspaper said: "He [Sanders] hopes the high court will require aldermen to give the [remaining] rejected appointees a 'fair' hearing." The board, however, threw Sanders a monkey wrench when it voted not to pay the mayor's legal bills in the case. The board reversed itself several weeks later and paid the bill.[13]

The mayor's problems were not confined to the board. In summer 1981, Sanders had to discipline the city clerk, Frank Wagner, because he stole a letter addressed to the mayor. Wagner was suspended and not paid for three weeks. During the fall, Sanders again took action against Wagner when the city clerk—without telling the mayor—took three weeks off.[14]

Mayoral appointments were stalemated until the March 1982 aldermanic elections, when the Progressive Coalition captured three more seats. Sanders, with five supporters now on the board, geared up for another battle on his appointments. Immediately taking the offensive, he issued a statement asking the board to quickly and positively act on his nominees for key city posts and said that the aldermen's decision "will set the tone" for future aldermanic meetings. At the board meeting to consider his appointees, the aldermen proved to be remarkably cooperative, approving three of his nominees (Jim Rader—city clerk, Jeanne Keller—assistant city clerk, and John Franco—assistant city attorney), with only a few aldermen casting negative votes against Rader and Keller. "The victories of Republican and Sanders supporters at the March [1983] city elections gave Sanders the support to get the appointees," reported the daily newspaper.[15] With the progressives in control of five seats on the Board of Aldermen after the election, Republicans, and even some Democrats, saw the writing on the wall and began to cooperate with Sanders, said one administration insider.

A few months later, Sanders's triumph was almost complete when the Board of Aldermen confirmed the mayor's nominations for city treasurer (Jonathan Leopold, Jr.) and city personnel director (Peter Clavelle). However, the board held up the confirmation of Sanders's nominee for assistant city treasurer (Barr Swennerfelt) for several weeks. She finally was confirmed by the board, which "gave the Mayor the final appointment he wanted in City Hall administrative posts."[16]

Sanders had scored a major victory in getting his appointments to key city positions. This was confirmed a year later when both progressives and Republicans teamed up to easily reconfirm all the previous year's appointments. "The appointments had none of the recriminations and shouting matches that marked Sanders's first two years in office," said the daily newspaper.[17]

The way Burlington's city charter reads, the question of mayoral power over appointments is an ambiguous one. The mayor is allowed to appoint people on a yearly basis, but the board must approve those appointments. Current appointments tend to stay in their positions even when administrations change. Sanders bucked the status quo by taking the aldermen to court over the appointments issue. One can only speculate on the outcome if the board had refused to confirm the mayor's appointments. But given the political nature of the issue, it would seem Sanders was not on firm legal ground, which the judge confirmed when he refused to issue a ruling on the matter.

The March 1982 aldermanic elections broke the political stalemate over the appointment issue. With Sanders's political strength in evidence and the effect of the board's noncooperative attitude toward the mayor clearly reflected in the election results, the board was forced to concede to the mayor's wishes—or possibly face even greater political repercussions. The shift in the board's attitude after the election was remarkable: Within three months, Sanders was able to get six important positions filled in city hall.

There is general agreement that the caliber of most of Sanders's appointments has been high. Doreen Kraft, former director of the Mayor's Council on the Arts, said: "He [Sanders] decided to bring some of the smartest, brightest and committed people to surround him and he wasn't scared of how much talent people had." She also added that "this is something which I think is one of his most admirable qualities."[18]

One Republican alderman and a past president of the Board of Aldermen (who himself had occasionally gotten into some heated arguments with Sanders), felt positive about the mayor's appointments. One newspaper reporter agreed, saying that Sanders's appointments "had won the respect" of the Burlington community and thereby "countered Bernie's negative image."

City Finances

Soon after Sanders took office, he began to tackle the question of city finances. One of the first things that the administration did was to put the city insurance policies out to bid. For about a generation, the policies had been in the hands of a cartel of nine insurance companies which divided them up as they saw fit. By bidding them out, the city hoped to save about $200,000 a year. Another cost-saving measure implemented early in his administration was an increase in the "city building permit fees for large developers" and "police and fire alarm user fees."[19]

At the end of 1982, a $1.9 million surplus was discovered by the city treasurer's office. From 1965 to 1982, the city's surplus revenues had increased from a little over $100,000 to almost $2 million—a surprise to everyone, including former mayor Gordon Paquette. (Some Republicans on the Board of Aldermen who had cursorily examined the city's financial records suspected something was amiss with the annual budgets presented to the board.)[20] The uncovering of the surplus by the treasurer's office was a coup for the administration, which had been looking for a way to fund various capital improvement projects in the city. Shortly after the discovery of the surplus, the office did "an audit of the city's pension retirement fund" and discovered that 97 percent of all retirees were receiving incorrect benefit amounts. Jonathan Leopold, Jr., the city treasurer, commented that this was the "biggest joke anyone ever heard of." Cleaning up this mess, along with the discovery of the surplus, "built up an enormous amount of credibility" for the office, said Leopold.

The treasurer's office took other steps to save the city money. Leopold stated that his office could save $100,000 a year through "centralized purchasing by department heads, better investment policies, and changes in the telephone system." Shortly after becoming treasurer, Leopold discovered that the Paquette administration had stashed away $500,000 of the city's surplus funds "in a zero interest checking account." Furthermore, another $500,000 was tucked away "in a 5.25 percent interest passbook account." Only then, said Leopold, was the remaining city money invested in certificate of deposit accounts. This all changed when Leopold began "bid[ding] out the city's financial business to the bank that g[ave] the highest rates." Leopold said that under past banking practices, the city in 1981 "lost about $70,000 by not investing short-term money" and that he hoped to earn "an additional $50,000 a year in interest under new banking practices in a different bank." In response to a reporter's question about these new banking practices, Sanders joked: "You don't appreciate how much free enterprise we bring to the city. . . . Now, every moment the city's money will be at work."[21]

The city also made money through "arbitrage," according to Leopold. "When the city borrows money, we borrow it on a tax- exempt basis, which means we get a lower rate. We turn around and invest the money at commercial rates, so we get a higher rate of return than our cost of borrowing," he said.[22] One administration insider commented that arbitrage was a way the city "can make money by borrowing money."

Another improvement brought about by the city treasurer's office was to computerize city finances.[23] When Leopold took over the office, the accounting procedure he discovered was "almost identical to what you would have encountered if you had walked into Scrooge's business and asked Bob Cratchit what he was doing . . . [because it was a] mid-nineteenth-century accounting system." The computer system installed in city hall brought Burlington into the twentieth century as far as modern accounting practices were concerned, said Leopold.

Additionally, Leopold helped redefine the role of city treasurer from the "manager of cash flow and writer of checks" under the Paquette administration to "the chief financial officer . . . of the city" under the Sanders administration. Said Leopold: "My role is to ensure that the government does what the Mayor and the city council[sic] wants and to accomplish that through the financial authority and the administrative power that that financial authority can give you."

Implementing the city treasurer's new role was not easy. Although the city charter gave the mayor the legal authority to control the budget, the Board of Aldermen quite easily circumvented Sanders in this matter. Before Leopold took office, members of the Sanders administration thought that the board took too much control of budgetary matters from the mayor, but were not quite sure how to challenge it. Consequently, Sanders was unable to "determine priorities for use of resources or to insure that priorities funded under the budget were accomplished," said Leopold.

Leopold felt that his becoming city treasurer was "probably the most significant event in enabling the mayor to accomplish his agenda . . . in terms of what he wanted city government to do." Previous to his hiring, Sanders had "minimal control over the budget . . . and the financial affairs of various departments of the city." Moreover, the mayor lacked the "financial management tools" to accomplish his goals. Now, stated Leopold, all the changes his office had brought about had "enabl[ed] the mayor to properly exercise his legal responsibilities."

According to Leopold, the "key power" of elected officials was their ability to "control the money." To assure Sanders of effective control, the city treasurer did several things. First, Leopold pushed the question of the mayor's legal authority over the budget, which resulted in a legal opinion issued by the city attorney's office in December 1981. The ruling held that the use of all monies, whether for departmental use or federal grants, must first be authorized by the mayor's office and then approved by the Board of Aldermen.

Second, Leopold created for Burlington a "program-based budgeting [process which] allows for the generation and management of the [necessary] detail to enable the elected officials to determine, from a policy standpoint, the allocation of resources that [the] city has." In this way, said Leopold, it was possible to "determine exactly what is going to be available and exactly what we want to spend it on." The end result, stated Leopold, was that Sanders now had "the ability to absolutely control every single penny that was being spent."

Third, the city treasurer's office set up "accurate accounting systems," giving elected officials the necessary information to make budget decisions and to maximize the use of the city's money. Leopold discussed the importance of "accurate accounting systems." He said the way city budgets were put together before he arrived was a "joke" because the mayor and the Board of Aldermen "virtually had no impact in terms of defining the policies and priorities of departments." It was now possible, through the use of the mayor's budget, to determine "the allocation of resources to accomplish objectives." The end result, according to Leopold, was the ability of the electorate to hold their public officials "accountable" for the implementation of various programs, thus ensuring "a real democracy."

The efficiency improvements implemented by the city treasurer's office under the Sanders administration have saved the city of Burlington many hundreds of thousands of dollars, some of which was expended to set up a capital improvements program, commented Leopold. Beginning in late 1982, the city created a $2.5 million fund that financed several projects, such as a street repaving program, repairing the Lakeside underpass, start-up funds for the Community Land Trust program, fixing up Memorial auditorium, and initiating a small business revolving loan fund.

The capital improvements program was new for Burlington, and appeared to be a good use of the surplus funds. By late 1985, the surplus money had disappeared. The city also was facing a $1 million deficit for the 1986 fiscal year beginning in July due to federal cutbacks in revenue sharing funds. At the end of 1985, however, an audit of the city finances showed it to be financially sound—with a $700,000 surplus. By the end of fiscal 1986, the city's surplus was over $1 million again. The general fund balances for fiscal years 1987 to 1989 were $616,000, $302,000, and $1.6 million, respectively.[24]

The reform of Burlington's finances was viewed by many as a big accomplishment of the Sanders administration. But those interviewed had somewhat different interpretations of what the Sanders administration's fiscal reforms and financial savings meant to the city of Burlington. Sanders himself stated that "he doubts either a Republican or Democratic mayor could have reformed as many areas of city finances" as he had. Jonathan Leopold, Jr., the man most responsible for fiscal savings and budget changes, thought his office's fiscal reforms were a sign of "progressive government," both because it now made the government bureaucracy accountable to the people who put it in office and because the Sanders administration, with increased control over the budgetary process, could more easily put through its progressive policy objectives. One administration insider felt that the reform program instituted by her department was "progressive" because it was "up-to-date, modern, and efficient . . . [but] actually it's [also] very Republican as far as being fiscally sound." Another administration insider said the administration's philosophy regarding financial matters was to mitigate the impact of the unfair property tax (which, from the progressives' viewpoint, disproportionately hurts low- and moderate-income people) by wisely spending people's money and by running an efficient government. Furthermore, said this insider, there was no reason why one political party (traditionally, the Republicans) should lay exclusive claim to the issue of fiscal responsibility.[25]

Most Progressive Coalition supporters felt positive about the fiscal reforms and the fiscally responsible image the administration portrayed. One said that the emphasis on "government efficiency" was important to the administration's credibility. Another commented that by being good on fiscal issues, the Progressive Coalition was able to "establish ourselves and prove we were good administrators and [could] run the city."

One administration official mentioned that there was enormous pressure on the new administration to prove itself, since the opposition was waiting to attack its every mistake. By doing such a good job with the city finances, the Sanders administration took a potential issue away from the opposition and showed itself to be competent beyond everyone's expectations, including its own. However, this meant certain compromises by the administration. By being fiscally sound, the city's ability to provide significant wage increases or comprehensive health care coverage to its employees was constrained. Being in a situation where you would either have to "ask taxpayers to cover salary increases [of city workers] or ask city workers to hold the line" [on salary increases] put the administration in a "no win" position, said this official.

Some administration officials, Progressive Coalition members, and progressives in the Burlington community, however, questioned whether or not the administration's fiscal policies were truly progressive. One Progressive Coalition member stated: "A lot of things done fiscally in the city are simply accepted practices in most other municipalities or in the business world, like bidding out your insurance. That's not a socialist idea, that's just good fiscal management. A lot of what we've done ... [is] good Republican management ideas." Another Progressive Coalition member and activist commented that "a lot of it [the administration's fiscal policies] is just good capitalism at work." Still another stated that Sanders was "probably more of a fiscal conservative than Paquette was."[26]

Even the daily newspaper saw fit to comment on the seeming paradox of a socialist mayor using capitalist financial tools: "When it comes to saving money in city government ... the Sanders administration is using free market principles that Adam Smith or any corporation chieftain would applaud." Sanders did nothing to dispel this critique when he said: "One of the major priorities of the first period since I've been mayor is to take the city from what was a very inefficient government and make it into a modern corporation."[27]

One of Sanders's progressive critics strongly felt that Sanders's comment about running the city like a corporation was indicative of the sellout of his socialist principles. Said this critic about Sanders:

He respects capitalists; . . . their efficiency is something that he's trying to emulate. The big fact is he's running the city like a corporation. The city's not an ethical community to him, it's a corporation . . . and the question is who's going to get the best shake: the middle management employees, the blue collar employees, or the upper class employees. And when push comes to shove, he sometimes gets confused between all three. If this is socialism, I don't know what capitalism is.

Democrats and Republicans alike were critical of the administration's fiscal policies, but for very different reasons than progressives. One Democratic alderman claimed that "the city financially is much worse off today than it has been since the days of the Democratic administration. First of all, we had the large surplus . . . [and] right now . . . there's hardly sufficient monies to pay the monthly bills." (The alderman was referring to the supposed financial crisis the city was facing in fiscal 1986 with the cutbacks in revenue sharing funds.)

A former Republican state administration official felt that Sanders was creating "programs and services through one-time, non-recurring revenue sources." By not implementing small, steady property tax increases to fund these projects, Sanders was "spending at a rate that far exceeds his revenues . . . [and has thereby] taken a significant fund balance and eroded [it]." A former Republican alderman first claimed that the Sanders administration was "trying to out-Republican the Republicans" and then changed his tune several years later, claiming that "we've [the Republicans] been telling them [the Sanders administration] for the last three years that they're going to run out of money . . . [and] Sanders didn't know enough to plan ahead."[28] Another Republican alderman had this to say:

I don't think he's [Sanders] been prudent in the way city finances have been accomplished, mainly in the continuation of the Paquette process of using revenue sharing for operating expenses as opposed to using revenue sharing for capital expenses. Everyone has known for years and years that that money [revenue sharing] was going to disappear, and yet rather than ask for moderate property tax increases from year to year, he

[Sanders] continued that process of using that revenue sharing money to pay for firemen's salaries.

Not surprisingly, local businesspeople in the Burlington community were generally impressed by the Sanders administration's fiscal practices. Said one prominent business owner: "They're [the Sanders administration] really managing a lot better, they're bidding a lot more stuff, they're just running it [the city] in a very business-like, well-planned, well-organized way." He also added that he felt the administration was not perceived as a "big-spender." Another prominent business owner commented that Sanders "straightened out things in city hall—[for example] the treasurer's office—he's made considerable savings on consolidation of purchasing [and] insurance programs."

Many of the Sanders administration's fiscal accomplishments— such as discovering a $1.9 million surplus, consolidating the purchasing power of the city, implementing new accounting methods, reinvesting city money in high-interest yield accounts, and using new budgetary planning and management techniques—have, over the years, saved and earned Burlington many hundreds of thousands of dollars and given the mayor new powers of control over the city budget. Most of the new fiscal policies can be considered good government reforms, but whether they can be considered progressive, or for that matter, socialistic, is another matter. By helping to save the taxpayers' money, these types of reforms serve a useful function. But any good Republican municipal administration would pride itself on such accomplishments. After all, being careful with taxpayers' money and efficient, well-managed local government are traditional Republican themes. But competent, responsible government also has been a trademark of municipal socialist governments since the beginning of the twentieth century (see Chapter 1). The application of capitalist, free-market principles to the running of local government (such as putting insurance contracts out to bid and running Burlington like a "modern corporation"), however, should not be seen as a hallmark of socialism. While accomplishments like these certainly lent credibility to the Sanders administration, they also led to wry comments about Sanders trying to "out-Republican the Republicans."

The Republicans, who had their favorite themes snatched away, were forced to turn elsewhere to criticize the Sanders administration. Thus, they attacked the administration's taxing and spending policies. The Democrats also criticized Sanders, but less so than the Republicans. Criticism of Sanders's handling of the city finances also came from the left, which objected to the way Sanders used capitalist principles to run the city. To them, it was a real indication of his departure from socialist ideas. Ironically, it was the local business community that heaped praise on Sanders for his fiscal management of the city.

How should a socialist mayor prioritize funding needs of local government? How are the often-conflicting needs of government employees' salaries, capital improvements to the city, and the city's taxpayers to be balanced? And how should surplus city funds be spent?

Clearly, the Sanders administration could not spend all it desired without considering the practical and political consequences of such actions. Insiders within Sanders's government described well the dilemmas facing a socialist administration in local office. However, by saving a little bit of the city taxpayers' money here and there and by discovering large surpluses in the city's general fund, the Sanders administration could put that revenue to good use. City services grew, for the most part, without having to raise taxes—an important accomplishment. And while it is true, as some critics have pointed out, that the administration funded various projects out of nonrecurring revenue sources, most of those projects would not require sustained funding over the years.

In some ways, Sanders has helped forge a "new" model for today's progressive and leftist politicians, though earlier socialist administrations had already paved the way (see Chapter 1). Fiscally conservative in some respects, Sanders presents an economically liberal (and even radical in some respects) program and a very progressive social agenda. Although the application of capitalist principles to run local government may seem contradictory to socialist ideals, there appear to be few alternatives given the nature of the capitalist economy.

The criterion, then, by which to judge a socialist municipal administration becomes how earned income or saved dollars are utilized; that is, are they used to benefit low- and moderate-income people, thereby addressing existing class inequities in the city? For the most part, the Sanders administration does seem to have fufilled this criterion.

City Commission Appointments

City commission appointments were another major area of struggle, usually pitting the Sanders administration and his Progressive Coalition against the Democratic and Republican Parties and the various department heads. The initial struggle over appointments began even before Sanders officially took office. After the March 1981 election, the mayor-elect asked the Board of Aldermen to wait until he took office before appointing three commissioners; the aldermen refused.[29]

The following year, when it was time for yearly appointments to be made by the city council, Sanders and the Progressive Coalition (which now claimed five aldermanic seats] were unsuccessful in getting any of their appointments on the city commissions. The daily newspaper said:

Burlington Republicans and Democrats joined forces . . . to deny supporters of Mayor Bernard Sanders seats on more than 20 city Boards and commissions. . . . Sanders was most upset when the coalition of Republicans and Democrats voted to oust chairman Antonio Pomerleau, one of the few city commissioners with whom Sanders has worked well.[30]

In fall 1982, a report in the daily newspaper stated: "Of the 104 commissioners in the city, just one . . . lives in Ward 3, . . . Burlington's poorest area." Only three commissioners were from Ward 2, the Old North End. The fact that low- and moderate-income people—Bernie Sanders's constituency—were not represented on the various city commissions had become a public issue.[31]

The 1983 spring elections saw a change in the length of time appointees served on city commissions. By a healthy 69 percent, Burlington residents approved a charter change reducing the terms of city commissioners from five years to three years. This was a victory for Sanders, who had not been able to make any significant inroads regarding commission appointments.[32]

After the spring election, the tide began to turn. That summer, thirty-one positions on various city commissions were up for appointment. There were 158 people interested in these city appointments, up substantially from previous years. In 1983, the Republicans on the board, seeing that it was to their advantage to work with the now-established progressive power block on the board, changed tactics and decided to deal with them rather than the waning Democrats. According to the daily newspaper, "the Mayor's backers and the GOP combined to name the most important commission positions, leaving Democrats out in the cold in some instances." Furthermore, the city council reinstated Antonio Pomerleau to the Police Commission, which pleased Sanders.[33]

The summer 1984 commission appointment process marked the beginning of real gains for the Progressive Coalition. By picking up a sixth seat on the Board of Aldermen (giving the Sanders administration and his supporters seven seats on the city council), the Progressive Coalition could assert its power by stalemating the appointment process. A battle raged over a vacant seat on the Airport Commission, with balloting going seventy-one times. In the end, the Progressive

Coalition gave up the Airport seat and five other commission appointments in exchange for seats on the important Electric Commission and the Planning Commission. In December, the Progressive Coalition had another opportunity to fill several vacancies. According to the daily newspaper, "Burlington's Progressive Coalition, enjoying a City Council majority due to the absence of a Republican alderman, won its second seat on the city Electric Commission without having to resort to the usual horse-trading."[34]

The progressives continued to use their power in the 1985 commission appointment process. That year, in a deal worked out with Republicans, the Progressive Coalition won a majority on the Electric Commission. In exchange, the Republicans got a seat on the Planning Commission, making its composition three progressives, three Republicans, and one independent. A compromise candidate was agreed upon for the Police Commission.[35]

By summer 1985, Sanders and the Progressive Coalition had begun to wield considerable influence on some of the city's commissions. An analysis in the daily newspaper said:

> Four years after Mayor Bernard Sanders won election, his influence is beginning to permeate the commissions that oversee the operations of city departments. . . . After years of pecking away, the coalition will now control two commissions [Electric and Street Commissions] and be within reach of three . . . [Planning, Parks and Recreation, and Police Commissions]. . . . Because [of] the nature of the commission system, the Progressive influence on the commissions is likely to linger long after Sanders is gone.[36]

The Progressive Coalition's loss of an aldermanic seat in the spring 1986 elections negatively impacted their commission appointments that summer. At the appointment session, the Republicans and Democrats took advantage of the progressives' weakened position and denied Sanders and his allies two reappointments. However, Jim Schumacher, one of the progressives' appointees to the newly created Public Works Commission, retained his seat after eight rounds of voting. Sanders commented that "the loss of an aldermanic seat last March hurt the Progressives' negotiating power."[37]

Over the next few years, the Progressive Coalition was able to maintain their significant influence on the commissions, though their control over the various commissions fluctuated. For example, while the Progressive Coalition lost control of the Electric Commission in 1987, they gained control over the new and important Public Works Commission. In 1988, the coalition also won a majority of seats on the Fire and Library Commissions.[38]

The Progressive Coalition's control of six seats on the Board of Aldermen had marked the real turning point, according to one administration insider, and this event allowed them to win twenty to thirty commission seats. In order to do so, however, compromises were necessary. Commented one progressive alderman: "Unless we talk, no one gets appointed." Said another: "It's really the Republicans we talk to. The Democrats haven't been willing to make any deals or work with us in any way."

Several Republican aldermen corroborated the fact that they and members of the Progressive Coalition were able to work together on commission appointments. To assure that aldermen wouldn't take weeks to make commission appointments, said one, "you say: 'OK, who's the least obnoxious to you and who's the least obnoxious to us and [let's] see if we can reach a middle ground.'" Another Republican alderman commented: "I've had reasonably good success in dealing with them [the Progressive Coalition] . . . on . . . commission appointments. . . . They've exhibited . . . a sense of compromise."

One Progressive Coalition commission member spoke about the positive impact of getting progressives onto the various commissions: "If you look at the commissioners now, there aren't just Republican businessmen [on them]. . . . On [the Electric] Commission, three of the five people [used to be from] . . . the five largest companies in the city using electricity . . . and you better believe that had an effect on . . . policies."

Another Progressive Coalition commissioner said: "Without active commissions, departments [are] not held accountable, so many [are] run poorly, and people complained. . . . But no one was responsible . . . [because] the commissioners . . . [are] not elected." The big accomplishment progressives have made, said this commissioner, was that "we're taking an active role in running the departments."

With control of certain commissions, the Progressive Coalition has increased its power in this area of government, but not as much as might be expected. For example, even though the Progressive Coalition was technically in control of the Electric Commission, it was unable to oust the department head. At best, then, it seems that the coalition's presence on the various commissions has allowed it to influence certain policies, but rarely, if ever, to make dramatic changes in the way various departments operate.

City Commission Form of Government

When Sanders first won election in 1981, many people, including some of the city's department chiefs, thought it was a fluke. According to one Progressive Coalition alderman, it was the department heads' intention to "sabotage him [and] ignore him . . . [in hopes that] he'll soon be gone." This, of course, did not occur.

Early into Sanders's second year, a letter from a number of department heads listing their grievances with the mayor was leaked to the press. In the letter, concern was expressed over "the Mayor's lack of regard for the input of commissions and of appointed staff." An aldermanic meeting was set up so that several of the issues raised by department heads could be discussed. The issues included meetings between Sanders and department employees without supervisors being present, inadequate input from department heads regarding the formulation of department budgets, and the mayor setting up alternative structures of city government that infringed on departmental turf. At the board meeting, a lot of angry words were fired back and forth, but nothing of substance occurred.[39]

One of the department heads involved in that skirmish felt that the leaking of the letter to the press was "extremely unfortunate" and that it was probably done by "a department head with a political axe to grind." He then went on to explain what he saw to be the key issues between department heads and the mayor-elect:

> As department heads, we were kind of in the middle of [a] crunch with a very strong mayor and with a commission form of government. Most of the commissioners were appointed by the previous administration with very little turnover. . . . I think what we were trying to say was: "Look, we have a system of government in place. If you want to change that system of government, fine, change it. But try to appreciate the fact that if you disregard it, and try to act [as if this were] . . . a strong mayor form of government, and as if indeed you did appoint department heads, then we're nowhere. We're trying to react to what you tell us, and yet we have commissioners that hold our appointments in their power, and we must take our direction from commissioners."

Regarding the resolution of the issues, this department head commented that the Board of Aldermen addressed the issues to some degree but ultimately did nothing substantive about them. Consequently, an air of animosity and confusion between the mayor and the department heads continued for almost a year.

According to the same department head, the conflict had pretty much been resolved by 1985:

> I think there's really been an accommodation, if nothing more —certainly that—between the mayor, department heads, and myself. Both Bernie and I realize our personalities clash. I think

the mayor has mellowed . . . from his former days of real radical pursuit of social concerns, and appreciates that there is only that much that he [can really] accomplish. And I think those department heads that have survived . . . have learned to accommodate his demands for immediate action by simply saying: "Look, it's a small thing, for God's sake, let's do it and get it done." And if we have to adjust our own thinking of where money, manpower . . . [and other things go], we adjust.

While department heads were learning to live with the mayor, Sanders and his allies were slowing learning to coexist with the commission form of government. At the outset of his administration, Sanders was opposed to the commission form of government. He criticized the commissions for being unresponsive and unaccountable to the will of the people, and he clearly "favor[ed] direct control of city departments by the mayor and the Board of Aldermen." Sanders was quoted as saying: "The commissions are the bulwark of conservative government, especially when they're dominated by conservative people." This is not surprising, since as mayor, Sanders had little control over the commissions and their department heads. The insular nature of the commissions bothered Sanders, since it was difficult, if not impossible, to effect change.[40]

Progressive Coalition members expressed similar sentiments early on. One alderman commented: "Ultimately, I think we should get rid of the commissions." An administration insider stated that the city commissions had become "little fiefdoms."[41]

One Progressive Coalition commissioner said about the commissions:

They can't really accomplish much; they're an amazingly ineffective body. In theory, what a commission is supposed to do is hire and fire department heads and set long-range policy. In practice, what almost all commissions do, until progressives started getting on them, is not doing anything, except automatically rehiring the person they're supposed to be in charge of, who, if . . . [the department head has] been around the city long enough, is usually quite effective in manipulating them [the commissioners].

The commissioner then explained why the commission system had not worked well:

The problem with commissions [is that] they've tried to run departments [and] it's not possible. . . . You are an unpaid, political appointee and even if you spend (which I have done) 20 to 30 hours some weeks, trying to understand what's going on, you're not there. You don't make the day-to-day decisions. You shouldn't be making decisions like that; it's not your job. That's what makes commissions not work.

A number of department heads in Burlington, however, saw things differently. One supported the "commission form of government," saying that it had "worked well" and had created a "decentralization of power." Another also expressed a preference for the commission style of government. He said: "I prefer being accountable to a board rather than an individual."

Still another department head commented:

I think the idea of a number of strong commissions—a few commissions but strong commissions—protects the so-called public administrator from the . . . very political atmosphere in any city. You [the public administrator] want to work for a commission that is hopefully made up of a number of parties . . . or [where there is] a city or town manager.

In the middle of 1983, Sanders decided to set up "a task force to study the role of commissions, a form of government that has been done away with in most other Vermont and New England cities." Eventually, the task force turned into a nine-person Citizens' Panel under the blessing of the Board of Aldermen—comprised of a good cross section of Burlington's community.[42]

At hearings held on the commission form of government, many different opinions emerged. The president of one of the local colleges criticized the commission form of government for decentralizing power too much and for being undemocratic. At the same hearing, one administration official commented: "Who runs the city? No one. We have a weak mayor, who is held responsible but who has little author-ity, a Board of Aldermen who are burdened with administrative tasks, and department heads responsible to no central authority." Thus, both argued for a "strong mayor" system. On the other hand, a Republican alderman responded that "the city enjoys efficient, responsible and effective government. The strong-mayor system would be further from participatory democracy."[43]

The debate on the commission form of government was summed up in the daily newspaper this way:

To most Republicans and Democrats, the citizen commissions that oversee city departments are an integral part of Burlington's government. Once they are appointed by aldermen, the commissions should be left pretty much alone and allowed autonomy in setting department policies. . . . To supporters of independent Mayor Bernard Sanders, the commissions are an antiquated and inefficient way of administrating departments. The commission system insulates most department policies [from] scrutiny by Sanders and aldermen, where Sanders believes most important decisions should lie.[44]

During Sanders's second term, though, the mayor and his Progressive Coalition allies on the Board of Aldermen began to have a change of heart. One reason was the charter change passed by Burlington voters, which cut commissioners' terms by two years. Also, once Sanders and his allies got the sixth seat on the board, they could effectively stymie all commission appointments. Thus, they forced the opposition to compromise, and Progressive Coalition members or their supporters began to get appointed to the city commissions.

Over the years, the Progressive Coalition gained control of about one-quarter to one-third of the commissions' seats and won control of a number of commissions, even a few of the more important ones. As a consequence, Sanders and the coalition no longer vociferously called for a change in Burlington's form of government. Commented one Progressive Coalition alderman: "I think we've learned to live with the commission form of government."

When the Citizens' Panel finally issued its report in fall 1985, it called for some major changes but did not recommend the dismantling of the commission form of government. The report recommended increasing the mayor's power by allowing him or her to "hire and fire department heads," and it built in a provision for "aldermanic oversight" of the mayor's newly acquired powers. The report also recommended that "voters [should] elect the members of the eight most important city commissions."[45]

As of 1988, no changes in the commission form of government seemed imminent. One activist who sat on the Citizens' Panel that came up with recommended changes for the structure of Burlington's city government commented that while Sanders [had] "always been real adamantly opposed to the commission system," after he saw the report, he appeared to have moderated his viewpoint on this issue. One reason, said the activist, was probably due to the recommendations concerning increased mayoral control over the department heads and particularly the election of key commissioners. Given the Sanders administration's recent success with appointments to commissions, its zeal to change the commission form of government seems to have dissipated.

CONCLUSION

Clearly, the structure of local government places certain constraints on a socialist mayor. Regardless of whether Burlington actually has a "weak mayor" form of government, there are built-in limitations on what Bernard Sanders was able to do in Burlington, such as the dispersion of power that exists between the executive office and the legislative body in the city and the system of city commissions.

Despite these difficulties, Sanders was remarkably successful in pushing his agenda at city hall. By forcefully fighting to get his appointments, Sanders successfully surrounded himself with a group of very competent people who in turn helped to augment Sanders's mayoral powers in a variety of ways. And although the existence of city commissions initially hampered the Sanders administration, once the Progressive Coalition garnered six seats on the Board of Aldermen, it was able to effectively wield power in the appointment process.

It appears that it is not so much the form of government as it is the power wielded within whatever form of government that is crucial to a reform-minded administration. In actual practice, then, the structure of local government has little real impact on what a Socialist administration can or can not do. Sanders and his administration demonstrated "good government" practices, which can cut across party lines. The key difference, as we have seen, is who benefits from these practices. In Burlington, a strong argument can be made that poor and working people have been the prime beneficiaries.

Development and Growth Issues and the Sanders Administration

Development issues were a dominant theme in Burlington during the Sanders years. From the proposed development of Burlington's waterfront to the building of the Southern Connector, Sanders played a major role in determining the nature of Burlington's future. But did Mayor Sanders, an avowed socialist, forge a socialist development policy—and what would such a policy look like?

We will first explore general economic and development issues confronting the Sanders administration from the perspective of those most intimately involved with them. From there, we will examine the creation of the city's Community and Economic Development Office (CEDO), and then delve into an in-depth examination of two important development issues in Burlington—the waterfront and the Southern Connector.

DEVELOPMENT AND GROWTH ISSUES

Sanders has sustained attacks from both his left and his right on various development issues. From the left has come vociferous criticism leveled at Sanders for supposedly abandoning his socialist principles, while many in the business community and those in the Democratic and Republican Parties have attacked him as anti-business. Sanders's position on development is straightforward: "We are pro-development, but that development has got to serve the needs of the people of Burlington."[1] He has further defined his approach by saying:

There are many, many communities where someone walks in and development by definition is good. That is not my belief. If it's good, why is it good? Is it attractive? Does it produce decent jobs? Does it fit into the master plan of the city? We don't believe that development [is] an end in itself. . . .

Development has to serve a social purpose. Also, increasingly, we've been raising the issue, as they are in Boston, about leveraging. That is, if you want to develop in the city of Burlington, what do you have to offer the people of Burlington? What are you going to do for them? It's a negotiating principle. I think underlying it all is that development is a privilege, and not just a right—and we do not automatically say yes to any development that comes through. Basically, we try to squeeze developers as hard as [we] can.[2]

His approach, in many ways, is a classic socialist approach—growth is good, but it must serve the community, particularly low- and middle-income people; the creation of jobs is a primary consideration; business must pay their fair share; and there is little emphasis on environmental concerns.

Much of the progressive community felt that Sanders's approach to development was too limited. One administration insider said Burlington's progressive government lacked a comprehensive plan:

I think the greatest failure of the administration, as I look at it now, was not to have foreseen . . . the way that things were in flow in terms of development issues in Burlington and how early we needed to put brakes on a lot of the development, such as these incredibly tall buildings that are all over Burlington now . . . . All the condominiums being built, the whole development question, from individual housing to shopping centers . . . [to the] waterfront . . . and so on, needed to be dealt with [at] a much more comprehensive level and at an earlier time.

Sanders's emphasis on any kind of economic growth as long as it produced jobs, regardless of environmental or aesthetic concerns, was mentioned by several people, including one progressive critic:

When I look at his [Sanders's] identification of growth with jobs and welfare, I ask myself what's the difference in principle between that and some of Reagan's policies? The implication [of the CEDO's plan] basically is if you put the money through the big business end of the siphon, it will come out and benefit the people. What philosophy unites that report? It's a growth stimulant notion of what would produce things for the public welfare. We have growth taking place which is changing the whole landscape and intimacy of the city in forms that are not qualified by a popular or environmental interest, however much . . . rhetoric [you hear] in that direction.

One Progressive Coalition member was also critical of Sanders's approach to development:

I think the development of downtown Burlington has been something of a compromise. There are big office buildings going up [and] I think it looks like a mish-mash down there and . . . it's created traffic problems and parking problems. I think Bernie's . . . so anxious . . . to have building going on and not be anti-business and also create . . . new jobs and have the city be [economically] healthy, that he has maybe not been as watchful of the aesthetics of the downtown . . . and the traffic problems as he might have been.

Sanders escaped some of this kind of criticism on the issue of the Southern Connector, as we shall see.

Sanders's basic philosophy placed him at odds with many, potential friend and foe alike, and made for strange bedfellows at times. For example, his "honeymoon" with Antonio Pomerleau, "the city's largest individual taxpayer, [head of] a large insurance business, and own[er of] shopping centers and developments throughout the state," was a curious one that raised eyebrows in the progressive, not to mention business, community. The two seemed to strike a personal friendship early on in Sanders's first term. Said Sanders: "On a personal level, I have to say I'm fond of Tony. . . . He's a self-made capitalist, not a corporate capitalist, a man who is not afraid to think for himself."[3] This is not the sort of distinction one expects a socialist to make.

Although some progressives accused the administration of making too many compromises with developers, some saw the concessions won in a positive light:

Bernie's message to developers was pretty loud and clear for a long time—that you're not coming into the city to do whatever you want. You're going to have to be responsible to the neighborhood you're moving into and provide for amenities to the public. . . . It was a very sharp message, and it came . . . at a time when Burlington was booming and a lot of developers played along with that. It was probably a message that a lot of other mayors would not make.

Many developers, as it turned out, felt there were too many restrictions on their ability to do business in the city. According to the daily newspaper, "developers say many businesses are considering a move from the city to the suburbs, where land is cheap, parking free and government more welcoming."[4]

It also is true that Sanders's confrontational style and his socialist principles have made the business community uncomfortable. The mayor enjoys verbal sparring with the business community and likes to lay the blame for many problems at the door of big business. But rhetoric and action are two different things. One prominent Burlington businessman commented: "I think most of Bernie's initiatives around job formation and economic development have been very entrepreneurial and capitalistic, frankly." However, he admitted that before Sanders won office, a handful of businesses in town could railroad a development project through the mayor's office and the Board of Aldermen. Now, he stated, business has lost some of its influence and other interest groups in the city have more power. In any event, business fears of "nationalization" or real socialism in Burlington have proved unfounded.

Yet many businesspeople still intensely dislike the mayor and his socialist politics. They feel that, from the beginning, he was out to get them and soak them for everything they're worth. For example, one business owner said:

He [Sanders] has been very harsh on the business people in the community and he has not been helpful. He has attempted to harass many business members . . . thinking that they should pay a great deal more in taxes and that they should be giving a great deal more to the community. You won't see any business members agreeing to talk with him. . . . He just does not like us.

However, there is another side to this picture. Others in the business community were less negative, and in some cases, even positive about the Sanders administration's attitude toward business and economic development in the city. For example, one businessperson stated:

I don't know that it's [the administration's attitude] anti-business . . . it just isn't pro-business. I think there's a difference between the two. I'm not sure in my own mind that he [Sanders] has set out deliberately, in any form, to be anti-business, only to be pro a lot of other things [such as] social concerns and things he wants to accomplish, and he does it by going to where the dollars are generated, where he can get money, and that's from business. . . . [This] has a negative effect on business, but it's not an anti-business approach.

It is somewhat ironic that Sanders is accused of being anti-business. In fact, generally speaking, he has been very good for business in Burlington, helped in no small part by the city's excellent economic climate since he took office. (In September 1988, the unemployment rate was a mere 1.8 percent, one of the lowest in the country.) As a result, said a CEDO representative, development has boomed in Burlington, which put the Sanders administration in a good bargaining position with developers.[5] One city planner pointed out that such a situation made it much easier to control development. These factors led Sanders to comment: "Anyone who says we are anti-business or anti-growth is blind to what's going on in the city." Of course, if the city had experienced the effects of a recession during Sanders's years in office, the development scene would have been much different.

Since Sanders's election, a whole new spectrum of businesspeople now have insider status at city hall. Several real estate developers who were cut out of the old-boy network in the past have taken advantage of the change in administrations. They were willing to play ball with the Sanders administration and made off quite well as a result. Thus, there are still insiders and outsiders at city hall, only the players have changed.

For some in the business community, however, this does not mean that there is mutual trust or understanding between them and Sanders. Said one developer:

He [Sanders] kind of overreacts to the same extent probably that the business community overreacts to his socialist beliefs. He [Sanders] figures that the businessman is some greedy guy who is looking . . . to take the last dollar out of every deal—and that's not true—and the . . . business community probably thinks he's ready to run the hammer and sickle up the flag pole to city hall—which probably isn't true either. I think there's sort of a basic mistrust that's never really been overcome, though I think maybe he's tried a little harder, but I don't think he tries all that hard.

For others in the business community, it appears that the mayor's attitude toward the business community in general has changed over the years. A large real estate developer described how some of the barriers have broken down over time:

We were just these bunch of guys that he [Sanders] perceived were all Rockefellers and we were going to use the press to slander and annihilate him and we would buy whatever it took to get him out of office. Now, if we could have . . . obviously we didn't do such a good job.

The fact of the matter is we finally . . . sat down at tables many times and [we] realized he didn't have horns and [he realized] we didn't have fangs . . . and machine guns . . . and little by little we broke down the psychological barriers.

Sanders eventually became more willing to compromise. He conceded that there has been a "mellowing" on his part, in part because he dealt with people in the business community on a fairly regular basis and got to know them. Said the mayor: "After five years [in office], I think some of them [in the business community] understand that I'm not Joseph Stalin and I think after five years, I've gotten to understand and respect some of them."[6]

One academician offered a broader perspective on Sanders's relation to the business community and how that affected development:

He [Sanders] certainly has not detracted from economic development the way people feared he would. [However], I would have a very hard time saying he's actually contributed or accelerated development. He has maybe impacted the quality of debate about the direction of development and the acceptable parameters within which development must fall. But I think the compromises with the business community are hard to evaluate: who's taking the initiative, who's really getting things done, who's enabling things to happen? They [the business community] learned to work with him and he [Sanders] learned to work with them and I think that came with time.

Sanders and the people in his administration, through the CEDO and the Planning Commission, have played a very strong role in shaping the city's development projects in recent years. However, this doesn't mean a socialist development policy has been implemented in Burlington. Given the constraints of the capitalist economic system and who controls the flow of capital in the city, this would be unrealistic. The real question is whether the Sanders administration was doing everything possible to ensure qualitatively different, environmentally sound, and aesthetically pleasing development that takes into account the needs of low- and moderate-income people. The Sanders administration should be judged on whether it has promoted alternative kinds of development and/or stopped or at least tried to stop development that does not meet the above criteria. A closer examination of the creation of the CEDO and two important development issues—the waterfront and the Southern Connector—will help shed light on this important issue.

THE ORIGINS OF THE COMMUNITY AND ECONOMIC DEVELOPMENT OFFICE (CEDO)

The Community and Economic Development Office (CEDO) has had a major role in a number of important city planning and economic development issues facing the city of Burlington. In addition, the CEDO has been involved in many efforts in the city concerning housing, tenants' issues, community development, waterfront development, and citizen participation. These latter issues will be explored in detail in this and other chapters. To better understand the CEDO's role in Burlington, it is necessary to first look at the origins of this office.

In fall 1982, Mayor Bernard Sanders created the Mayor's Committee on Economic Development. The co-chairpersons of the committee were Jonathan Leopold, Jr., the city treasurer, and Harry Behney, director of the Greater Burlington Industrial Corporation. The task force was put together to improve the administration's connections with the city's business community. Relations between the mayor and the business community were in bad shape, and it was important "to reach some form of detente," according to Leopold.[7]

There were about thirty people on the task force, with the breakdown, roughly, as follows: one-third "sympathetic or open" businesspeople, one-third community activists, one-sixth academicians, and one-sixth city government bureaucrats. After a series of meetings, the task force proposed that "city government begin a much more active, aggressive, and creative role in fostering community development," aiding both business and the community at large. Furthermore, the task force suggested that the administration "establish a Community and Economic Development Office and take control . . . [of these activities] away from the Planning Department and Commission," explained Leopold.[8]

The reason for the recommendation to split community development functions off from the city's Planning Department and Commission, said Leopold, was that the department and commission were in conflict with the mayor and his administration on many issues. Also, the Planning Department was "responsible for regulating development in the city, and it is an inherent conflict that they [Planning Department officials] would also be responsible for it" [development].[9]

Winning aldermanic approval for the creation of the CEDO was a difficult task for the mayor and his Progressive Coalition supporters, but the strategy of working with the business community paid off, as this account from the daily newspaper indicates:

> With three Republicans joining supporters of Mayor Bernard Sanders ... Burlington aldermen approved Sanders's plan for a new agency to spur housing and waterfront development and attract new business to Burlington. The agency ... will strip the Planning Commission and Department of much of its development power, including over more than $1 million in federal development money. . . . The approval ended more than a year of tussles over the new office.[10]

The CEDO was formed in May 1983, with three Democrats and two Republicans voting against the proposal. One of the Democrats, James Burns, voted no because he felt "it would run counter to Burlington's citizen commission form of government ... [since] the new agency would be accountable to the aldermen and the mayor, not a commission." However, a number of prominent businesspeople in town spoke up in favor of the proposal, which swayed the majority of Republican votes on the board.[11]

A battle ensued several months later between Sanders and the board over his nomination of Peter Clavelle to the position of director. Some on the board saw Clavelle as a Sanders ally, while others were simply against the CEDO. Sanders and the Progressive Coalition prevailed, and Clavelle has been reappointed to the position every year, though some opposition to him on the board has persisted.[12] According to one administration insider, the residual opposition is due partly to the Democrats' dislike for the CEDO in the first place and partly because the CEDO has "been visible [and] controversial."

The creation of a Burlington Community and Economic Development Office apart from the Planning Department was a major accomplishment of the Sanders administration. It marked one of the first times the administration approached the business community on an issue and got its support. Even though Sanders himself did not make the contacts, a member of his administration—Jonathan Leopold, Jr.,—laid the groundwork for it.

Members of the Sanders administration and the Progressive Coalition generally saw the CEDO in a favorable light. For example, one progressive alderman said: "Getting a Community and Economic Development Office established within city government has had an immeasurable effect on development and the type of development that has gone on in Burlington."

Even those outside the Sanders administration had positive things to say about the CEDO. One of the businessmen who helped get the CEDO in the first place had this to say:

> I think that at times [the CEDO] has been used to our [the business community's] detriment, but ultimately the essence of it was to establish a pro-business environment. To a degree, it [has been] successful. I think it's been used a little more politically than we [the business community] had pictured it. . . . It's been a grass roots effort for 3,000 different things, and it's been a very politically based operation.

It was a significant victory for Sanders that the CEDO was answerable to the board and the mayor, not to a commission. Because of Peter Clavelle's competence and experience in the area of community development, his appointment to direct the CEDO was a real boost for Sanders. Most of the exciting, progressive, and perhaps even socialistically oriented initiatives of the Sanders administration, such as the Burlington Community Land Trust and the Burlington Local Ownership Development Project (see Chapter 6), have either originated with the CEDO or been fostered by it. Few, if any, community development offices around the country have been engaged in such progressive work, which was encouraged in the atmosphere that Sanders created at city hall.

One way in which the CEDO involved itself in development issues was through a federal program called the Urban Development Action Grant (UDAG) program. The CEDO's ability to bring in UDAG grants was impressive. According to one newspaper account, less than a year after its inception, the CEDO had brought in five times the UDAG money that the former Planning Department had in the years 1978 to 1983.[13]

Other CEDO initiatives include the Burlington Revolving Loan Program and the start-up of "incubator businesses." Both projects targeted small business development, which, according to one CEDO representative, was a high priority for the office. The CEDO helped secure almost $400,000 in federal funds for the Burlington Revolving Loan Program. From 1983 to 1985, the program helped ten small businesses keep or create about eighty jobs. Moreover, said the CEDO representative, the program has helped "leverage $1 million in private financing." Concerning the incubator businesses—buildings which house a group of businesses that share the costs—over twenty new, innovative enterprises have been started in one facility alone.[14]

Although the CEDO can be commended for its encouragement of large and small business development, the question remains as to whether it fostered a progressive approach to development, much less a socialist one. The CEDO's UDAG projects were very traditional, business-promoting projects that were good for the local economy, such as bringing a department store into downtown. The UDAGs also created jobs and tax revenues for the city. But there were few real concessions from the businesses benefiting from the grants, perhaps with the exception of Northshore Development's supermarket/parking lot proposal, in which the city had a two-thirds equity stake in the project's actual cash profits. However, the project never happened, according to CEDO representatives.

When it comes to local development projects, the CEDO's record in getting concessions from developers is somewhat better. (The major exception is the waterfront issue, which is taken up next.) CEDO officials talked about "private-public partnerships" formed through "pre-development agreements," and there were quite a few of them. The Village at North Shore and the Howe Meadows and South Meadow projects were prime examples of what CEDO officials described as "win-win situations" for the city and the developers. Concerning pre-development agreements, one CEDO official said:

> [We] established a process of negotiating pre-development agreements which established at the front end the quid pro quo for various developments. In situations when the developer is looking for public assistance, be it in the form of land or be it in the form of public financing ... we ... negotiate long and hard for public benefits which will be derived [from] that project. I think we've been able to create a win-win situation, where the developers achieve their objectives but there are also public benefits which are achieved by the projects.

One example of a pre-development agreement was the linkage between the Village at North Shore development and the Howe Meadows project. Developers John Varsames and Roderick Whittier of Northshore Associates agreed to develop forty affordable homes (nine lots of which were donated to the Burlington Community Land Trust) at Howe Meadows and donated a mile-long strip of beach to the city, which the developers pledged to improve, maintain, and provide with public access, in exchange for the city's blessing to build 220 expensive condominiums (priced from $75,000 to $120,000) on several acres of donated city-owned land near the lake.[15]

While the CEDO has been involved in many development projects in Burlington, none was as controversial and intricate or more clearly pointed out the difficulties of a socialist administration trying to work out development policy as the waterfront.

THE WATERFRONT

The waterfront issue epitomizes the complexities of development and the different political agendas of the various players in Burlington. The development of Burlington's waterfront has been on the drawing board for at least a decade. The Paquette administration was unsuccessful in pushing a development plan through, and so was the Sanders administration.

In early 1978, the Triad Corporation put forth "a $22 million community and residential redevelopment of Burlington's Lake Champlain waterfront." Triad's plan called for the phased-in development of over 400 condominiums and/or apartments, a number of stores and/or offices, a boat marina, and a walkway. While the corporation received a $3 million UDAG for the project, its financing scheme collapsed shortly thereafter.[16]

Next, Burlington developer Tony Pomerleau took charge of waterfront development. His initial plan was to build a somewhat scaled-down version of the original Triad proposal. In fall 1979, Pomerleau presented plans for a waterfront project that included over 300 condominiums, a one-acre park, and a pedestrian walkway. He too applied for a UDAG grant, but encountered problems and eventually decided to finance the project himself. The waterfront project was supposed to start in 1981 and cost over $25 million.[17]

As mentioned earlier, Sanders's 1981 mayoral campaign was run partially on a platform against the Pomerleau waterfront plan. It was clear then and it is equally clear now that Burlingtonians were not interested in seeing high-priced condominiums and/or expensive hotels and offices on their lakefront. Sanders sensed that, and he ran a campaign against massive development of the waterfront and for an unspecified "alternative waterfront development policy." After Sanders was elected, he continued to oppose Pomerleau's waterfront plan. Several months later he said he did "not oppose some private development on the waterfront," equivocating on his original position.[18]

Late in 1981, there was discussion within the administration as to whether or not to consider public ownership and development of the waterfront, but this idea was quickly dismissed, at least in part because of the recent reappraisal of the city's property, which increased the tax burden for many residents. Said Sanders: "In the best of all possible worlds, I don't want to see private development of the waterfront. I'd much rather see public development of the waterfront. . . . But if in this world I have to deal with private developers, I want a private developer who is going to be responsible to the needs of the people, one who will be willing to make some compromises."[19]

Early in 1982, Sanders made it clear that any waterfront plan should be approved by the people of Burlington and that a public referendum would be the best way to do it. Also, he indicated that he wouldn't support a waterfront project that would be "a rich man's paradise and an enclave for the wealthy," lashing out again at Pomerleau's plan for its lack of "public access" to Lake Champlain.[20]

In spring 1982, Sanders once again expressed interest in the idea of public ownership of the waterfront. Reported the daily newspaper: "Ideally, Sanders would like the city to purchase the land owned by the Central Vermont Railway. . . . If the city owned the land, city officials could control development on it. However, the city would have to purchase . . . [the land for] between $200,000 and $300,000 an acre . . . so the mayor would need a bond issue . . . to get public owner-ship."[21]

Sanders also was interested in seeing "large public parks" on the waterfront. He questioned the idea of building housing on the water-front but said: "Somebody could convince me it is needed." He men-tioned the desirability of housing for poor and working-class people, but "not necessarily on the waterfront."[22]

In fall 1982, Tony Pomerleau announced he would abandon his plan to develop the waterfront, claiming that the political climate in Burlington was unfavorable and that the bureaucracy was simply too much for him. Once Pomerleau backed out of the picture, Sanders was faced with having to put his own imprimatur on the waterfront. One way he and his administration tried to do so was to pass an interim zoning ordinance to put control of future development on the water-front in the hands of the Board of Aldermen rather than the Planning Commission, but they were rebuked not once but twice by the board.[23]

During winter 1982, Sanders and the CEDO decided to use the Neighborhood Planning Assemblies (see Chapter 5) "as a sounding board for waterfront development." The message came back from the meetings, especially in the Old North End, loud and clear: "Burling-ton's Lake Champlain waterfront should have marinas, fishing piers, ferries, restaurants and parks. *The shoreline should not have hotels, motels and condominiums*" (emphasis mine). Given this feedback, Sanders rearticulated his vision for the waterfront, which included a "water-front that . . . [was] open to the people" and "promis[ed] development that . . . *[would] not include condos or boutiques on Lake Champlain*" (em-phasis mine).[24]

Shortly into Sanders's second term, he and his allies on the Board of Aldermen attempted to have the city buy the Old Green Mountain Power building on the lakefront for public purposes. But after origi-nally giving the mayor the power to try to reach a deal with the electric company, the board, solely for political reasons, refused to authorize any deal.[25]

A new developer had appeared on the scene—the Alden Waterfront Corporation—by summer 1983. This time, Sanders and his administration, especially through the CEDO office, were involved in the waterfront development plans from the start. Alden appeared open to suggestions from Burlingtonians concerning the project. When the group finally unveiled its waterfront plans, it mesmerized many Burlingtonians, including the Sanders administration. It seemed to be a dream come true. Who could argue with a $100 million plan that included six or seven acres of park space, a harbor, a boat marina, an "inn," housing for everyone (including rentals for senior citizens and "moderate income" people), and even an "artists colony." Moreover, the city would share the wealth with Alden.[26]

Given the magnificent plan and its masterly presentation, who could be against it? Surveys from February 1984 Neighborhood Planning Assembly meetings on the plan showed 75 percent supporting the Alden plan. However, opposition soon began to mount against the plan. Some simply did not like it, feeling it was too grandiose a scheme for Burlington. But the real problem with the Alden plan was that it required a UDAG grant—and a big one—if it was to materialize in a form even remotely like the one presented. Because of the size of the grant application and Burlington's healthy economy, the UDAG was not approved. As a consequence, the whole project, as originally conceived, was in jeopardy.[27]

By this time, the Sanders administration was heavily invested in the Alden plan. To salvage the project, the administration and the CEDO worked up a scheme called tax incremental financing, which would allow the city to finance the infrastructural work on the Alden property without having to raise taxes. Essentially, this tax scheme would have seen a $6 million bond issue finance improvements to the Alden property, but it would be "paid back by the increased revenues created by the improvements to the property." The bond also would "provide funds to build a number of public facilities, including parks, a waterfront walkway, a portion of a city-long bicycle path, and a community boathouse."[28]

Yet the Alden waterfront project that voters were now asked to support was a different plan than first unveiled in 1983. According to Paul Flinn, a primary investor in the project, all Alden could "guarantee now . . . was a 200-room, five-story hotel and about 150 condominiums that may sell for as much as $300,000 apiece." Housing for low- and moderate-income people was to be put on hold until federal funding could be obtained for it.[29]

There was a public perception that Alden did not really need the bond money to do the project, a view that was reinforced by newspaper accounts concerning the financial background of the principals. It was revealed that the primary investor in the Alden project was "Elizabeth Flinn, . . . the great-granddaughter of Clarence Brown, who built up the *Wall Street Journal* and *Barron's National Business and Financial Weekly*. Miss Flinn is the daughter of Jane Bancroft Cook [who] was listed by *Forbes Magazine* last fall as one of the nation's 400 richest individuals with a personal fortune of more than $600 million."[30]

An interesting development concerning the bond issue vote was the alignment of political forces on both sides. On the one hand, Sanders and some of his Progressive Coalition members (others opposed the bond, but did not do so publicly), Republican aldermen, some prominent Democrats, and the business community (through the Chamber of Commerce and the Downtown Burlington Development Association), supported the bond and spent between $12,000 and $14,000 to pass it. On the other hand, a group called Citizens for a Better Waterfront, which was comprised of the Vermont Greens, Democratic aldermen, and someone from Citizens for America (a very conservative group), opposed it. Both sides made for very strange bedfellows. If nothing else, the Sanders administration appeared to be on the wrong side of the fence.[31] The bond issue was perceived by both sides and the public to be a referendum on the present Alden plan.

A spokesperson for the opposition group commented:

This project is everything Bernie Sanders said it would not be. We want something better. . . . When Bernie was first elected, . . . one of his campaign slogans was that the waterfront was not for sale and it would not be an enclave for the rich. . . . Now it seems Bernie's thinking is that the way to do the best for the people is to make the most money possible . . . [and treat the waterfront as] a cash crop.[32]

In response to this and similar charges, Sanders issued an angry rebuttal. Claiming that he had not sold out, he said that under the circumstances, he got "the best possible deal." The current plan, he said, did not make "an enclave for the rich" because of all the "public amenities" attached to the project. Said Sanders:

If we were fighting for condos and hotels, we wouldn't have wasted our time. The question is public amenities and how do we build them without raising property taxes. If park space, a community boat house, a bike path and a wide promenade along the lake edge, and the possibility of a major museum, is not a people-oriented waterfront, I don't know what is. There is an illusion that all we have to do is keep pushing a developer and keep pushing a developer. We feel we pushed him as far as we can go and we feel we got significant concessions.[33]

On election day, the news was not good for the Sanders administration and Alden. Bond supporters got about 53 percent of the vote, far short of the necessary two-thirds majority needed to pass it. Significantly, over half of the voters in Wards 2 and 3, that is, Sanders's base of support, voted against the bond issue. Election day fallout began immediately after the vote when Paul Flinn said that he would drop his effort to develop the waterfront.[34]

After the defeat of the bond issue, the CEDO commissioned a study to discover why people voted against it. Not surprisingly, the study found that people saw the Alden waterfront plan as "an 'elite development' with insufficient public access to Lake Champlain." Furthermore, people were concerned with gentrification, felt that the proposed hotels and condominiums were too near the water, and thought Alden would build even without the bond money. The report concluded: "The waterfront bond proposal was evidently defeated because a critical segment of the voters were opposed to 'exclusive' or 'elite' development that seemed disproportionately to benefit the affluent at the expense of the general public."[35]

A few days after the results of the study were made public, Sanders again spoke about the possibility of floating a bond issue asking the voters to support buying some or all of the waterfront land. However, for no apparent reason, the idea of public ownership suddenly was dropped again. Over a year later, though, the Sanders administration, with the approval of the Board of Aldermen, put forth another bond proposal. This $2.9 million bond would fund improvements to the waterfront property controlled by the city, such as "the construction of a boat house, a lakeside boardwalk, a boat launch, completion of the bicycle path and creation of several parks." In March 1987, the bond issue was overwhelmingly approved by Burlington voters, 73 to 27 percent.[36]

The Sanders administration also decided to pursue the "public trust" doctrine in the courts in 1986. This doctrine, which the Sanders administration supposedly used as leverage in its negotiations with Alden, said that all filled land by the waterfront, if no longer used for public purposes by the railroad, reverted back to public ownership. The city, along with the state of Vermont, asked the court to order the Central Vermont Railway and the Alden Corporation to hand over the filled land they controlled. After a series of fruitless negotiations between the city and the railroad to settle the issue out of court, a ruling finally was issued in the case. In its decision, the court ruled that the land belonged to the railroad, but that it had to be used for "public purposes." Railroad officials felt that the court's restrictions on the land's use (for example, the building of offices and housing did not meet "public purposes") were excessive and decided to take the issue to the Vermont Supreme Court.[37]

Another outstanding issue between the city on the one hand and the railroad and Alden (which still owned waterfront land) on the other hand concerned strict new zoning regulations adopted by the city to control the type of development on the waterfront. In essence, the regulations prohibited the kind of massive condominium development and hotel complex planned by Alden—at least on some parts of the waterfront land.[38]

At the same time, the Sanders administration once again raised the call for public ownership of the waterfront land, although this time it wasn't simply rhetoric. Several city departments were asked to explore possibilities for city purchase of waterfront land. In an unusual move, the mayor's announcement that the city might buy key parcels of land on the waterfront "to ensure that development of the land guarantees public access" was praised by The Burlington Free Press's editorial board.[39]

In early 1988, the administration proclaimed that it would condemn the the waterfront property owned by the railroad "through the process of eminent domain" if it refused to sell it to the city for a "reasonable" amount. Surprisingly, even this potential city action was approved in an editorial in the city's daily newspaper. Said The Burlington Free Press: "Central Vermont [Railway] officials should remember the public gave away the filled land to meet a need. Public needs have changed in 100 years. Maybe now the public should take the land back." Less than a month later, still another editorial read: "During 20 years of debate, Burlingtonians have demanded generous public access and green spaces when the downtown waterfront is redeveloped. City Hall now offers a direct solution: buy 23 acres for parks, promenades and recreation. That's such a good idea it's a shame the city didn't act 10 years ago."[40]

A short time later, the Board of Aldermen permitted certain city departments to discuss purchase of the waterfront land from the railroad. The city also began negotiations with the U.S. Navy to purchase one of its buildings on the lakefront. A multimillion-dollar bond would allow the city to buy the current building and relocate the Naval Reserve Center. It would be paid back by leasing the new space to stores and nonprofit organizations. The site also possibly would have "open-air markets, restaurants, bars, entertainment centers, an indoor playground, museums, galleries, [and] aquariums."[41]

Eventually, the city put together a $6.4 million bond issue for public improvements to the waterfront. It included $3.2 million to obtain and relocate the Naval Reserve Station, $2 million to purchase additional waterfront property for a park and a walkway, and $1.2 million to complete a bicycle path around the circumference of the city. While Democratic and Republican aldermen initially balked at the bond proposal, many city officials eventually came out in support of it, as did the Downtown Burlington Development Association. However, this wasn't enough; on election day in November 1988, only the $2 million bond for the park and walkway received the necessary two-thirds vote for passage, while the other two fell shy of the mark.[42]

Meanwhile, in light of the bond issue defeats and the pending Vermont Supreme Court decision on the "public trust" doctrine, the Central Vermont Railway began touting its own development plan for the waterfront. Its $170 million plan included a hotel, restaurant, 400 condominiums, 100 units of affordable housing, several marinas, and public access to the waterfront. The Sanders administration was less than enthusiastic about the proposal.[43]

But the railroad's plan was ill-fated. Shortly before Christmas Day, 1989, the city of Burlington received a gift from the Vermont Supreme Court. In a unanimous decision, the court ruled that "the trial court correctly concluded that Central Vermont Railway does not hold title to public land free of the 'public trust' doctrine." Central Vermont Railway, said the court, could only use the public land for "railroad, wharf, and storage purposes." Moreover, when the land is not being used for such purposes, it reverts back to the state. According to a CEDO official, Burlington is now in the position of reclaiming thirty- five acres of waterfront property for public use through negotiations with the state—which would be a victory for the city. The only recourse the railroad has is to appeal the Vermont Supreme Court's decision to the U.S. Supreme Court.

It is true that the scaled-down version of the 1985 Alden plan was different in form than the final 1982 Pomerleau plan, but in substance they were not too far apart. The final Alden plan called for 150 market-rate condominiums, a 200-room hotel, a little over four acres of park space, and several other public amenities, such as a boat house, promenade, and bike path. The final Pomerleau plan had called for 200 market-rate condominiums and a hotel, an acre of park, and a "pedestrian walkway." The major difference between the projects was in their design and the amount of park space, with the Pomerleau plan being less aesthetically pleasing and offering less park space than the Alden plan. Although there would have been more public access with the Alden project, it is questionable that this particular difference was significant enough to warrant the rejection of one and support of the other.

Sanders's original campaign theme, that the waterfront should not become "a rich man's paradise and an enclave for the wealthy," was violated as much by the Alden project as it was by the Pomerleau one. Sanders gradually deemphasized the "rich man's paradise" issue and instead argued that the important issue was now "public access" to a "people-oriented" waterfront, a switch that one critic found self-serving:

> His [Sanders's] line was: "It was a people-oriented waterfront." Well, will someone please define for me "people-oriented"? I mean that's one of those meaningless words—toilets are people-oriented [too]. . . . It was "rich" people-oriented; that's the word he leaves off it. That cost him a lot of support on his own team.

The key turning point for the Alden project was the rejection of the UDAG grant. If the grant had been approved, the project probably would have happened, and there would have been little, if any, objection to it since it would have been seen as giving a little of something to everyone—rich and poor alike. But the community perceived the revised Alden plan as an "enclave for the wealthy." Commented a critic:

> To hear the guy [Sanders]: "We're not going to [build] an enclave for the rich"—who railed against that, who struck a chord with people with that, to come back later with an enclave for the rich [and say]: "We won't call them high-priced condos, we'll call them neighborhood housing. We won't call it a high-rise [hotel]: we'll call it an inn." That was the height of sleaze.

The Sanders administration should have recognized this sooner. Following the rejection of the federal grant, the administration would have been wise to change its position to more accurately reflect the wishes of its constituency. While there was little long-term political damage to Sanders due to his pushing of the tax incremental bond issue to finance part of the Alden plan, it was not one of the administration's finest hours to so rigidly reject its constituents' needs and so tightly align itself with the business community and the Republican Party.

No other issue has more sharply divided the Progressive Coalition and members of the administration than waterfront development in general and the Alden plan in particular. Many coalition members saw the Alden plan as a compromise. One administration insider, for example, thought that it allowed for "too many Gucci bars, too many hotels." Although he thought that it was the only option available, he said it was like "making a deal with the devil." Other Progressive Coalition members who supported the project were more critical of Sanders. One said: "Maybe Bernie has gone a little too far in terms of pro-development. . . . The [Alden] plan is probably not in keeping in tune with what Bernie was talking about when he was first elected."

Others within the administration and the Progressive Coalition went further in their criticisms of the Alden plan, although this conflict between Sanders and some of his supporters never became public. Quite a few disagreed with the Alden plan, and some even worked against it. For example, one Progressive Coalition alderman was worried about the "resort aspect" of the plan and the potential "Bar-Harborization of the waterfront."[44] One administration insider explained that "Bernie decided this was a good plan, and there were a lot of people who didn't think it was a good plan, yet somehow you were being disloyal if you spoke against it because obviously it was the progressive [position]." A peace activist said that the Sanders administration formed a "truly unholy alliance" between itself, some progressives, Republicans, conservative Democrats, and the business community to try to pass it.

Sanders's opponents on the left probably attacked him more on this issue than on any other one. Some were upset that he did not pursue the "public trust" doctrine earlier, others were concerned about gentrification, still others believed he was selling out his socialist principles, and some thought he had manipulated the Neighborhood Planning Assemblies and/or falsely presented the Alden plan in publicity for the bond issue.

Sanders's response to this opposition to the Alden plan was:

When people said: "Well, this is not good enough [that is, the Alden plan]," well, no kidding. We understand that it is not good enough, but we also understand the very great limitations that we have on our options. Then you have some young people who are less than enthusiastic—as we are—about having condos on the waterfront . . . so they would prefer to see the land nondeveloped. And we understand that. But we think the land will eventually become developed in probably a worse way than what we supported.[45]

Ironically, but not surprisingly, Sanders's strongest supporters on this issue were the Republicans and the business community. If nothing else, this should have led Sanders to question his position. When your own constituency opposes you and your usual opponents support you, something is askew. It is revealing that one former Democratic alderman said: "The Alden plan was a Republican plan, it wasn't a socialist plan," while a businessperson commented that Sanders "was on the Republican side of the ledger on the last waterfront go around" [that is, the Alden plan].

From several perspectives, the Alden waterfront plan is Sanders's biggest failure. If it had happened, the Alden plan might have been an accomplishment, but definitely not a socialist one. Since it failed, Sanders cannot even claim it as a feather in his cap.

Sanders should have dropped the Alden plan as soon as the UDAG failed; perhaps the Alden plan, even in its original form, never should have been pursued. Instead, the administration should have addressed the "public trust" doctrine much earlier, ensuring a court fight that would have at least stalled (and in the long run blocked) any unfavorable development and helped clear the air on this issue.

The Sanders administration also could have pursued the option of a public bond to buy some waterfront property or go through the process of eminent domain to condemn it much sooner than it did. While Sanders is to be commended for finally exploring this approach, public ownership certainly should be a socialist's first choice. When the administration finally pursued this option in a serious way, the voters responded favorably in some instances.

If the city owned or at least controlled the waterfront property (which is now a distinct possibility, given the recent Vermont Supreme Court decision concerning the "public trust" doctrine), it could lease the land to worthwhile development projects. Said one Progressive Coalition member:

> In Los Angeles, they [the city] bought the waterfront, or a part of it, and they leased it out to private enterprises, and so in that sense they were able to control what went in there. It wasn't piecemeal development, and the city was . . . generating income, and it got to put some things it wanted down there [such as low-income housing]. I think certainly that there are a lot more options than what have been considered [by the Sanders administration].

In a similar vein, a Democratic Party official's idea of creating a public authority would have made it possible for the city to own the land and use it for public purposes. Such an idea is consistent with socialist principles and achievable at the local level. It is ironic that some cities without socialist mayors, such as New York, have pursued such options, while a city with a socialist mayor has not.

THE SOUTHERN CONNECTOR

The Southern Connector, which has been on the drawing board since the mid-1960s, is the most important (for some) highway and certainly a very controversial development project for the city of Burlington. The highway is the proposed solution to increased traffic and the lack of access to the central business district in the Burlington area in recent decades.[46]

In 1974, the original plan for the Southern Connector Highway called for a four-lane road or parkway, with 35-MPH traffic, that would hook up with a major artery near downtown Burlington. The state, however, had an alternate route for the road and succeeded in getting the original design changed. It was this latter version that was eventually adopted by the city's Planning Commission and Board of Aldermen. The major problem with the state's plan was that it took the road through the notorious Barge Canal, where toxic industrial wastes have been dumped for years.[47]

For a number of reasons, opposition to the road began to surface after this new route was proposed. First, environmentalists raised concerns about the canal's toxic wastes. Later, neighborhood groups opposed the road on the grounds that homes would be lost, that there were inadequate safety precautions, and that the road design was bad. The environmentalists' concerns were virtually ignored, and neither the Planning Commission nor the Board of Aldermen were very sympathetic to neighborhood residents' concerns. After much discussion of proposed design changes to the road, the board and commission did little to address residents' safety concerns.[48]

Infuriated with local government inaction, especially on the part of the board, South End neighborhood residents circulated a petition to try to delay, if not kill, the Southern Connector. Despite gathering more than 1,400 signatures on the petition, then Mayor Gordon Paquette refused to have the item put on the March 1981 town meeting ballot.[49] In retrospect, it appeared that this action on the part of Paquette was a contributing factor to his 1981 electoral defeat, since Sanders campaigned against the highway project and supported the petition drive.

Once Sanders took over as mayor of Burlington, he continued to oppose the Southern Connector—at least initially. At first, he attempted to help neighborhood residents kill the project, going so far as to ask homeowners in the South End to join him in developing a plan to stop the connector.[50] Shortly into his first term, though, Sanders began to change his mind about the road. Said Sanders:

> I think what led me to change is the feeling that the overwhelming majority of the people in the city of Burlington want a new road built. We have serious traffic problems, especially in the South End, and we have vehicular traffic going through neighborhoods which people object to. And I think if you did a poll today, you would find overwhelming support in the South End and in the city for the construction of the Southern Connector.[51]

Sanders then began to talk about a "scaled down" project and trying "to forge a compromise." His move was apparently supported by Joanne Beauchemin, a leading neighborhood opponent of the plan. Apparently, both Sanders and Beauchemin believed that at some point in time the highway was going to be built, so they might as well try to get the best road possible. Their reversal seemed justified on two counts: The Board of Aldermen was very close to completing all the necessary land deals, and neighborhood opposition to the road had lessened with time and increased traffic congestion.[52]

Sanders and various neighborhood residents then proposed a two-lane highway that was attractive and incorporated various safety features. They remained firm in their opposition to routing the connector through the Barge Canal, and they had several negotiating points in their favor, including a lawsuit filed by a supporter and the already-mentioned environmental problems. An attempt was made to negotiate a deal with the Board of Aldermen that would incorporate these concerns, but this proved fruitless, in part because of the business community's opposition to any meddling with the already-approved design for the road.[53]

Much maneuvering for position went on from the beginning of 1983 until early 1985. This included skirmishes with the board, legal wrangling in the courts, and arguments with the state Agency of Transportation and the federal government. However, after the March 1985 mayoral elections, a real possibility for reaching a compromise occurred. Not only had Sanders been reelected for a second time, but in fall 1984, Madeline Kunin, a Democrat, had been elected governor of Vermont. Her new secretary of transportation, Susan Crampton, said she would be open to discussing issues concerning the scale of the road, its design, and various safety features. At the same time, a group called the Burlington Urban Design Study (BUDS), an independent, federally funded architectural and planning group, was reviewing the Southern Connector plan and was expected to draft a new design proposal for the road.[54]

When the BUDS submitted its proposal, it proved to be much different than previous ones. The design called for "a landscaped two-lane design . . . that avoid[ed] the Pine Street [B]arge [C]anal." Moreover, the road would be "much narrower," and according to designer Peter Owens, form "a green-linked system, an emerald necklace" for Burlington. The new design created a "more attractive, human-oriented road." The road would be twenty-six feet wide, with no chain-linked fence on it. The new design was in sharp contrast to the officially approved plan, which called for "pavement 80 feet wide surrounded by [a] 6-foot-high chain-link fence."[55]

Sanders was clearly enthusiastic about the BUDS proposal. It seemed to offer the basis for a compromise between the city and the state. But there had been a period of tense exchanges between Sanders and Crampton, and even after the issuance of the BUDS report, two issues remained unresolved, standing in the way of reaching a solution. Sanders had reiterated his position that the Southern Connector could not be constructed as long as the contaminated tar deposits near the Barge Canal were still a problem. The state seemed less concerned about potential environmental problems. Moreover, the state was holding fast to the road being four lanes, while Sanders was strongly pushing for only two. Neither Crampton nor Sanders appeared willing to give any ground.[56]

In November 1985, an important event occurred. The Planning Commission passed a motion supporting the BUDS proposal. Sanders believed that now an important city agency had come out in support of the new design, but Maggie Green, chair of the Planning Commission, claimed the mayor misinterpreted the vote as meaning the commission backed fundamental changes in the design of the road.[57]

Another event unfolded that month that also had an impact on the eventual resolution of the project. According to the Burlington daily newspaper, "a monthly meeting of the Downtown Burlington Development Association (DBDA) erupted into a shouting match between Sanders and two businessmen over the Southern Connector." Several businesspeople attacked Sanders for "holding up construction of the road." From their perspective, as well as other businesspeople present, the highway was "essential to improve access to downtown and attract shoppers." One prominent businessperson explained the impact of that DBDA meeting and why the business community felt progress on the Southern Connector was so important:

It [the confrontation] had to happen, and it did. . . . That meeting showed everyone how big that issue is. I had guys say that if he would just let this thing be resolved . . . we'll work with him for a gross receipts tax [see Chapter 7] . . . but as long as he's holding that thing up, which we felt was holding up any development of the downtown,—unless that was resolved, there's going to be no cooperation.

A few days later, real estate developer Ernie Pomerleau published a piece in the daily newspaper saying it was time to resolve the issue. He said it was essential for the city and the state to reach agreement on three issues: the number of lanes, the road design, and whether it should go "through or around the [B]arge [C]anal."[58]

Whether by coincidence or not, slightly more than a week after the DBDA meeting, and a few days after Pomerleau's article, the city of Burlington and the state Agency of Transportation reached an accord concerning the Southern Connector. The agreement had these provisions:(1) "The U.S. Environmental Protection Agency and the state Agency of Environmental Conservation will be responsible for determining whether the road should pass through the canal, and if so, how and where"; (2) the state's transportation agency would abide by the BUDS proposals "to the fullest extent possible"; and (3) the person who had taken legal action to stop the state from condemning his land, Harry Atkinson, would withdraw his lawsuit. While the accord did not resolve the issue of the number of lanes for the road, Sanders commented that the BUDS report "mandate[d] an objective study of the number of lanes." In any event, Sanders referred to the deal as "a major breakthrough."[59]

In an analysis of the compromise, the daily newspaper reported that both Burlington and the state's Agency of Transportation won on some issues and lost on other issues. Said the newspaper:

> Specifically, Sanders gave up total opposition to a four-lane highway and a new traffic study, as well as several hoped for bonuses including improvements to Pine Street. . . .
>
> In return, he received a legally binding promise that the city's preferred method of construction [of] the road over the . . . Barge Canal would be given another look and that a series of design changes the city recommended would be added "to the fullest extent possible."[60]

The newspaper article also mentioned that the Sanders administration had agreed to drop a lawsuit by a property owner that was used as leverage in the case. The court date for the lawsuit was set for the week after the settlement. The mayor commented that the pending court hearing was the major reason for the compromise being reached, not "public pressure." Also, said Sanders, the agreement "allow[ed] the city to contest final design plans with which it disagree[d]." Neighborhood activist Joanne Beauchemin, in a commentary in the daily newspaper, praised Sanders for the compromise he reached with the state transportation agency. She said that the mayor "showed unique political courage" and that "Sanders certainly seems to have done extremely well in hammering out a compromise."[61]

Shortly after the agreement was forged, the federal Environmental Protection Agency (EPA) completed "the first phase of cleanup of the Burlington Barge Canal." However, the following spring, the city and state got some bad news. The newly appointed city project director for the Southern Connector, Bert Moffat, reported that the EPA decided that there must be another study of the Barge Canal, which would slow down, if not change, the building of the road. Moffat said that the study, which would take a year and a half to two years, was necessary "because the [B]arge [C]anal is part of the federal Superfund cleanup." Furthermore, Moffat said, "depending on the findings, the path of the road may have to be adjusted near the canal," maybe even going around it (as originally suggested in 1974)![62]

At a Board of Aldermen's meeting the following week, Moffat reported:

The [EPA] study is designed to see if putting the highway through or over the barge canal would force toxic contaminants to ooze out and possibly flow into Lake Champlain. If problems are found, the route of the highway may be altered to bypass the canal, which is on a list of sites being cleaned up under the federal Superfund program.

Moffat also told the aldermen that "the second phase of the road" probably would be slowed down and that it might not be funded "under the current formula."[63]

In January 1987, the bids went out for the construction of the first phase of the Southern Connector project. In fall 1987, the daily newspaper reported that the "second phase" of the highway project would not begin at least until 1989, primarily because of legal difficulties "with rights of way." It was mentioned that the Environmental Impact Statement had to be done before this phase of construction could start, and that "the highway will be detoured to Pine Street to avoid the Barge Canal toxic waste site."[64]

The plan for the Southern Connector has gone through many revisions in the last decade and a half. Yet, despite intense pressure from the various elements of Burlington's power elite, Sanders continued to champion certain issues around the Southern Connector, notably those of road design and environmental problems with the Barge Canal. Said Sanders:

> We battled [the Southern Connector] for four years in opposition to a superhighway type concept that in my view environmentally and aesthetically would have been very unfortunate for the city of Burlington. . . .
>
> We hung in there—and I think rather miraculously, to tell you the truth—we managed to get a very substantial compromise reached, which will in fact allow the street to be built in a way that is compatible with an urban street. And we got the city a lot more protection in terms of the environmental hazards associated with the Barge Canal than we . . . [had] . . . before. . . .
>
> Did we get everything we wanted out of it? No. But basically, given the opposition against us, I think we did very well.[65]

One Progressive Coalition member who was active on this issue had this to say about it:

> Is it my personal optimum solution? No, not necessarily. Is it an optimum solution for any specific aggregate of citizen constituencies who opposed the Southern Connector? [No]. I think it's a compromise that was dictated by the initiatives of the citizenry and the responsible officials in city government. It also confirmed . . . an architectural design plan—the BUDS—that we initiated at the city level.

According to this Progressive Coalition member, whether or not the road had two or four lanes was "not a critical issue." The important thing was that "it's designed with an interactive concept in mind so people can move across it and live with it . . . not as something walled off or tunneled through the city. That's what we didn't want," he said.

Most Democratic and Republican members of the Board of Aldermen had negative reactions toward the Sanders administration's handling of the Southern Connector, primarily because of the roadblocks thrown up by the administration to the building of the road. The business community, for reasons one can imagine, generally felt favorable toward the compromise, although they were dissatisfied with the process in getting there. One businessperson who worked on this issue said:

> [The Southern Connector], . . . I think, is the biggest single issue that divided the downtown business community and the administration. He ran opposed to that [road] . . . and then it got bogged down into details, and that's what tied it up. Our attitude was: "We don't care where you build it, you can build it on top of the trees, but we want access" [to the downtown].

Another businessperson highly involved in the Southern Connector issue commented on the process of reaching a solution to the problem:

We [Sanders and I] were sort of the buffer zone between the right and the left. If we were going to accomplish anything, we [Sanders and I] had to work [a solution out] in a compatible arena. . . . Although we differed vehemently on the approaches to dealing with the Southern Connector . . . we eventually . . . struck a deal. Ultimately, it will be a better highway for it.

Interestingly, many members of the business community were convinced that the timing of Sanders's compromise on the Southern Connector was related to the upcoming waterfront bond vote in December 1985. One commented: "We [the business community] were pretty sure he'd [Sanders] have to give in before the waterfront vote; I think he's pretty calculating." Because there were relatively few people fighting the road, and the Progressive Coalition didn't strongly oppose it, this businessperson said he "could never figure out why Bernie didn't abandon it [his opposition] long before he did." Another businessperson concurred that the timing of the deal was "absolutely" connected to the waterfront bond vote. The administration was almost forced to make a deal because "the waterfront couldn't exist without a Southern Connector."

Sanders and his supporters were vociferous in refuting these charges. He denied that the timing of the compromise was in any way related to the business community's support for the waterfront bond issue.[66] According to one Progressive Coalition member, Sanders "absolutely" did not compromise on the Southern Connector to get business support on the waterfront bond issue. This coalition member explained that the compromise came about only after the BUDS design had been approved by the Planning Commission and a couple of days before the Sanders administration had to decide whether or not to go ahead with a legal appeal before the Vermont Supreme Court. One newspaper reporter speculated that Sanders compromised when he did because "he realized they were not going to build it through the Barge Canal anyway so [he said]: 'Yeah, go ahead, build it, I'm not going to fight anymore.'"

It is ironic that after roughly fifteen years of arguments over the Southern Connector, the overall plan for the road will probably look very similar to the original 1974 design proposal, that is, a four-lane parkway with 35-MPH traffic that skirts around the Barge Canal! While Sanders is to be commended for fighting and probably winning the best compromise possible, he nevertheless reneged on his original opposition to the Southern Connector. While there are real traffic problems in the Burlington area—especially from South Burlington to downtown—a case can be made that the new road will only make matters worse. Said one progressive critic:

> The Southern Connector is going to bring in more cars; it will make it easy for the cars to come into a very congested downtown area. What you have here is an attempt to introduce another new highway into the city. The more highways you build the more cars you bring in; you [don't] reduce traffic, you encourage it.

Other alternatives—such as car pooling and public transportation from the outskirts of Burlington—were not seriously considered, according to this critic.

The long-term development consequences of building the road are unclear. It will certainly change the shape of the city in the very near future. One peace activist said:

> The Southern Connector is like an add-a-pearl necklace sort of thing. . . . Once you start urban renewal you have to make a hotel and you have to have a department store and you have to have the connector and you have to have the waterfront and it just has to all happen or else none of it thrives. And that [the Southern Connector] was one of the pearls that had to be added.

CONCLUSION

An analysis of the Alden waterfront plan and the Southern Connector highway project points up an overall weakness on Sanders's part concerning development-related issues. Although Sanders's rhetoric seems slanted toward a growth socialist perspective, there appears to be little clarity or consensus within the administration on what a nonreformist reform or socialist development policy would really look like.

We must ask how the Sanders administration's economic development policies differ from a traditional capitalist approach. If there is little or no difference, then we must further ask if this is due to the structural constraints in the system or to other factors. While decisions such as the construction of a highway and the development of waterfront property cannot necessarily be put along a socialist/nonsocialist continuum, the type of development and the kind of growth encouraged by municipal socialists is an important issue.

Sanders's statements on development, as discussed early in this chapter, would seem to indicate obvious differences between his approach and that of the unbridled capitalist. And in practice, the mayor had on occasion tried to do some things differently. In certain cases like the waterfront, though, there was little to distinguish his position from that of capitalist interests in the city of Burlington. Furthermore, it appears that the Sanders administration's position on this issue had little, if any, relation to the economic constraints imposed by the capitalist system.

The difference between the Sanders administration's position on waterfront development and that of some progressive critics seems analogous to the Red-Green split the West German Green Party faced on similar issues. Sanders, at least in his rhetoric, advocates a Red vision of growth socialism, stressing jobs for the working class and a healthy economy over other concerns such as the environment. The Green vision, on the other hand, stresses ecological concerns above all else and is anti-development in many ways. Said one progressive critic:

> There is a kind of Red-Green split—if you want to use that kind of vocabulary—in the sense that there are people who are fairly radical in their outlook . . . who are trying to bring in new social ideas that are beginning to emerge in our era.
>
> They [the Greens] don't exclude better living conditions. I'm not quarreling because he [Sanders] wants to see bread on the table. I'd like to see high-quality bread. Sanders seems to be content with white bread. . . .
>
> The Green perspective, which I would advocate, wants to re-empower people. The Red perspective of Sanders (and I wouldn't call it Red . . . I'd call it social-democratic), [is] frankly structured around bourgeois interests.

In response to these charges, Sanders replied:

> There are some people of the Green variety who are essentially anti-development and come up with a long philosophical position as to why almost any development is bad. . . . Some of them have a back-to-the-woods mentality that life should be simpler. . . . We [the administration] don't share that view, and there's opposition there.[67]

Any comprehensive answer to development issues must take into account qualitative concerns such as aesthetics, environmental impact, the quality and necessity of growth, public versus private ventures, and the impact on low- and moderate-income communities. Judged by these criteria on the waterfront issue, Sanders initially did well on aesthetic concerns, but later on, seemingly lost sight of some important ones. On most of the other concerns—the environment, the quality and necessity of growth, public ownership, and the impact on low- and moderate-income people—Sanders did not fare well.

Concerning the Southern Connector, Sanders rates fairly high on the question of aesthetics and environmental concerns, and perhaps the quality of growth. However, concerning the more fundamental issue of the necessity of growth, the question of mass transportation as an alternative to increased vehicular traffic, and the impact of the project on Burlington's low- and moderate-income neighborhoods, Sanders rates poorly.

Sanders and his administration have affected the nature of development in the city of Burlington. As we have seen, the Sanders administration accomplished some things, but in other cases, it fell short. We must ask whether there was a basic difference between the Sanders administration and a capitalist Democratic or Republican municipal administration regarding development issues. While the answer is a probable yes, it did nothing to threaten the capitalist economic order through nonreformist reforms to bring about "socialist" development in Burlington. Based on the two development projects examined here in depth, it would seem that the Sanders administration constrained the worst aspects of unbridled capitalist economic development. However, as evidenced by the critiques from various progressives, the administration certainly did not do as much as it could to limit undesirable development in the city, nor did it pursue, except perhaps at the end, a nonreformist reform or socialist strategy toward development projects.

Citizen Participation, Democracy, and the Neighborhoods

One of the guiding principles of democratic socialism is participatory democracy. By this is meant the active involvement of the citizenry in *all* decision-making processes, whether they be elections, city meetings, or access to city hall.

When we look at the Sanders administration's record in this area, there are certain places where an increase in citizen participation is quite evident. A sterling example is in the electoral arena. Here, as well as in the city's tenants' movement and the Neighborhood Planning Assemblies, low- and moderate-income people have been much more involved in the workings of local government.

But there are some troubling contradictions. For example, while the administration pushed for the creation of the assemblies, it also let some of them flounder and tried to impose its agenda on others. And while Mayor Sanders himself professed a democratic-socialist philosophy, his administration's internal decision-making processes tended to be limited and exclusionary, though perhaps not purposely, to certain progressives and women.

In this chapter, we will explore both the accomplishments and the shortcomings of the Sanders experiment in participatory democracy in Burlington and try to ascertain whether it makes a difference having a socialist in local office and if so, in what ways.

CITIZEN ELECTORAL INVOLVEMENT

Socialists holding municipal office clearly can effect change in the area of citizens' relation to local government. One measure of change in local politics is electoral involvement and voter turnout. Overall, Burlington has witnessed a dramatic increase in the number of candidates running for local offices and the number of people casting ballots since Sanders was elected mayor. Before his election, it was not unusual to see aldermanic races go uncontested in many wards. Now, uncontested aldermanic races are rare, and three challengers for one seat is not uncommon.

A more detailed look is revealing. For the mayoral races from 1971 to 1979, former Mayor Paquette faced only one opponent in most of the biennial mayoral races. Only once was there more than one challenger, and once he ran unopposed. Aldermanic races for the same time period exhibited an erratic pattern. In some years, the races were poorly contested, while in other years, they were actively contested. Right before the fateful 1981 election, there had been little activity in these local contests. Voter turnout for the years 1971 to 1980 fluctuated, too, ranging from a low of 22 percent both in 1976 and 1979 to a high of 36 percent in 1973. The average voter turnout from 1971 to 1980 was 28.7 percent, with the total number of registered voters going from 23,341 in 1971 to 29,053 in 1980.[1]

In the time period 1981 to 1989, some major differences are evident. All of the mayoral races, except the one in 1987, had at least three candidates. There have consistently been at least two, and very often three challengers, in almost every aldermanic race. There were no uncontested aldermanic races until 1986, when no one challenged the incumbent in Ward 6. Likewise, there was one uncontested aldermanic race in 1987 and 1988. In 1989, there were uncontested aldermanic races in two wards. Voter turnout showed similar increases as well for the years 1981 to 1989. It went from a low of 32 percent in 1981 to a high of 49 percent in 1987, though not in a linear fashion. The average voter turnout from 1981 to 1989 was 40 percent, while the number of registered voters decreased from a high of 32,893 in 1982 (there are no available figures for 1981) to 25,346 in spring 1989.[2]

Although on the surface it may seem paradoxical that the number of registered voters has decreased by about 7,500 since 1982, the explanation is reasonable. State law requires that voter registration lists be cleaned every two years. It is unclear whether the Paquette administration ever did so. However, once Sanders was elected, this task was taken seriously. Consequently, between 1982 and 1988, about 12,500 people were removed from the voter rolls.[3]

Even as it was cleaning Burlington's voter checklists, however, the administration also initiated several impressive voter registration drives. From 1982 to 1989, about 9,000 new people were added to the list. The end result is that the city's checklist has experienced a net loss of about 4,000 voters since 1980, when the number of registered voters was 29,053.[4]

Regarding electoral involvement and voter turnout, Sanders assessed the situation in this way:

One of the things that we were very concerned about was the whole level of democracy and political consciousness within the city of Burlington. Before I was mayor, you used to have mayoral elections in which the mayor himself would run without opposition—or with token opposition—where you had many on the Board of Aldermen running without opposition, or the School Board [members] running without opposition. Basically, you had a small political machine running the city without a whole lot of political participation. Voter turnout was very, very small. . . .

Voter turnout in local elections is now twice as high as it used to be. If we have accomplished nothing else but double the level of citizen participation . . . that is an enormous accomplishment. . . . I think the fact that we have educated people—empowered people—is the most important thing we have done . . . [and the] difference in the level of political consciousness . . . is a radical change.[5]

Clearly, there is no disputing that Sanders has had a significant impact on voter participation in Burlington politics. However, some questioned the importance of this contribution. Said one progressive critic:

The question is what it means. . . . Municipal activity that becomes exciting can arouse people into a more active political approach. I would not say it [increased voter participation] is a positive sign as such [because people are motivated for the wrong reasons]. It would be a far more positive sign if people created their own groups and organizations, not simply [that] they vote in great masses.

Sanders's role in increasing electoral participation—especially among the poor and working class—does deserve praise. But does increased voter participation in electoral politics necessarily mean that a city is further along the road toward socialism? Not at all. Increased electoral participation in itself certainly does not presage the dawning of a socialist era. Even when coupled with an increase in political awareness on important issues, all we can really say is that we are closer to a more participatory kind of democracy. Only if there is a specific nonreformist reform educational component to increased citizen electoral activity can we say that there is movement toward democratic socialism. At least one critic feels this has not occurred. Said a progressive critic:

> When Sanders does something, generally speaking, but not always, . . . that seems pretty radical, and he thinks he's going to arouse opposition, or he meets an impediment, he does not try to educate the electorate. And this is one of my biggest complaints against the Sanders administration.

But the arena of electoral politics is not the sole criterion by which to judge whether or not there has been movement in a socialist direction in Burlington. We must also ask if there has been an increase in citizen involvement beyond voting in local elections. Two concrete examples—the tenants' movement and the Neighborhood Planning Assemblies—should give us a better insight into this question.

TENANTS' MOVEMENT

According to a tenants' advocate in Burlington, renters comprise roughly two-thirds of Burlington's citizenry. Since much of Sanders's support came from tenants, his administration, especially through the CEDO office, has played an active role in many tenant-related matters. We will look at several issues—rent control, the antidiscrimination and security deposit ordinances, the antispeculation tax, and the condominium conversion ordinance—to see what was of concern to the Burlington tenants' movement and how the Sanders administration reacted to the issues.

Rent Control

The story of the relationship between the Sanders administration and Burlington's tenants begins with the mayor's first election campaign. As Sanders was running for mayor in 1981, the organization PACT (People Acting for Change Together) was busily organizing around tenants' issues. In winter 1980 to 1981, there was a battle brewing between PACT and the Board of Aldermen. PACT tried valiantly to get what they called a Fair Housing Proposal on the March 1981 city ballot. PACT had worked out an agreement with the landlords in town on a proposal, and it was up to the board to place it on the ballot. However, just before the deadline for putting items on the city ballot, the aldermen, by a vote of 7–5, decided to send the Fair

Housing Proposal back "to a committee for further study," thereby effectively killing the proposal.[6]

This affront to tenants by the aldermen encouraged PACT to collect the necessary signatures needed for a special election on a strengthened version of their Fair Housing Proposal in April 1981. In light of PACT's newer, tougher rent control plan, the Board of Aldermen, in an attempt to confuse the voters, decided by a vote of 6–5 to place a watered-down version of the Fair Housing Proposal on the ballot, too. According to the daily newspaper, "the plan, developed by a commission headed by alderman Maurice Mahoney, was vilified by both landlords and tenants before the board approved it."[7]

Both of the Fair Housing proposals "would have created a seven-member body with the power to lower rents on apartments after hearing complaints from tenants about excessive rent increases." However, the board's plan tried to balance things out by giving the proposed Fair Housing Commission the power to decide on tenant evictions, too, while the PACT proposal gave greater rights to tenants.[8]

Neither plan was destined to be approved by voters. The opposition to the Fair Housing plans, organized under the banner of "Citizens Against Rent Control," consisted of "a coalition of conservative leaders of the Democratic and Republican Parties, landlords, real estate agents, and homeowners." This group hired a professional consultant to run the campaign and spent an estimated $10,000 to defeat the measures. PACT, on the other hand, ran a weak campaign and spent twenty times less than their opponents on their proposal. On election day, the end result was that "Burlington voters rejected [the] two housing commission plans by overwhelming 4–1 margins. . . . The opponents of the proposals had been successful in portraying them as a form of rent control and scaring voters about what this would mean for Burlington." Even newly elected Mayor Bernard Sanders's endorsement of the PACT plan did not save it.[9]

One activist explained the 1981 defeat of rent control this way:

Partially it was bad timing. . . . We brought the thing forward right away, [and we] didn't realize [Sanders was] going to win. Sanders didn't really support it [the PACT proposal] enthusiastically, but even if he did, it probably would have been defeated anyway. We were out organized . . . by those people with lots of money. But then we let it drop [because we] got scared.

This activist went on to say that "the housing movement just was demolished and that's important to me because that was the root—one of the main roots—of the whole thing [that is, Sanders's election] and it was one of the areas that . . . got left behind."

A progressive critic of the administration commented: "He [Sanders] tried rent control—not exactly rent control but a form of rent control—and he's dropped the issue because people voted it down . . . [and has not tried] to educate the public." A newspaper reporter said that Sanders made a mistake in not pursuing the issue of rent control, "especially since Bernie's constituency is the renter class." Sanders explained his position this way:

> The idea of rent control is an idea that I am sympathetic to. . . .
> Four years ago, when we had two people on the Board of Aldermen, I supported [the PACT proposal] . . . very strongly. It got beaten 4–1. . . . Now, obviously things have changed. We now have six members on the board. . . . [But] is the tenants' movement necessarily stronger now than it was then? I don't know that it is. I don't see any particular sense to bring forth something which is unlikely to get passed by the voters, which will meet with tremendous legal opposition, unless there is a groundswell of support for it. . . .
>   Ultimately, the challenge [is]: How do you bring forth the several thousand people who are going to stand up and fight for their rights as tenants? You are not going to have any significant tenants' legislation unless there is a tenants' movement. . . . If there was a community movement to bring forth rent control, if there was mass support for rent control, the Progressive Coalition would have been more than delighted to carry the battle or to present it to the Board of Aldermen. There has not been . . . [so] it would be politically stupid [to do so]. . . . Would that be a benefit to the tenants' movement?[10]

One tenants' advocate agreed with Sanders. She generally felt that the administration's record on tenants' issues was good. Said this advocate:

> They [the Sanders administration] can't do it just as the administration, because if they could, I think they would have gotten a lot more done than what they've been able to get done. . . . I have not been in support of rent control—putting it on the ballot—because I don't think there is the groundswell of support that needs to be there to get that passed. I think what happened . . . the first time around [is that] it [the Fair Housing proposal] went to the ballot too soon, and the work wasn't done that needed to be done and the support wasn't there and it got slaughtered and the movement died because of that.

I think when you talk about getting things passed, laws in and of themselves are not ends in themselves because there [are] ways around every law we're going to get passed.... Going ahead with the ideal program [for example, rent control] ... at a time you can't use it as an organizing tool is ... a mistake because you're going to kill your movement instead of building it. I see it [rent control] as an option ... in the future.

Quite a few Progressive Coalition members, however, believed that if the progressives had been able to get that elusive seventh seat on the Board of Aldermen, rent control could have been passed by the board.

Antidiscrimination/Security Deposit Ordinances

While the Sanders administration was unable to do much on the issue of rent control, it did move, with eventual success, on several other renter initiatives. In summer 1984 the Progressive Coalition, with help from the CEDO, brought forth two proposals to the Board of Aldermen's Ordinance Committee. One ordinance would have dealt with discrimination against tenants. According to the daily newspaper, this proposal "would prohibit discrimination against the handicapped, children, people on public assistance and on the basis of sexual preference. Violators of the law could be fined $35 to $200 a day." In fall 1984, the Progressive Coalition succeeded in getting it approved. Reported the daily newspaper: "The Board of Aldermen, after nearly 3-1/2 hours of vigorous debate, voted unanimously [to approve the antidiscrimination ordinance]." A delighted Sanders said: "We passed, for the first time in the history of the state of Vermont, an ordinance which prohibited discrimination by landlords against women, against elderly people, against people who have kids."[11]

However, even passage of this "very mild fair housing ordinance" was not easy, according to one CEDO housing expert. This expert explained that the vote on the ordinance could have gone either way. What made the difference, she said, was that one of the aldermen, Republican Allen Gear, "changed his mind ... because he honestly believed it's not a bad thing to do ... [and he] vote[d] his conscience." Furthermore, once Gear switched sides, the Democrats, who saw they were going to be on the losing side of this issue, switched their votes, too. The housing expert thought the ordinance should have been "a real Democratic issue but ... a lot of their constituents are the landlords and property owners."

Regarding the effectiveness of the ordinance, the housing expert said:

> We haven't had one [complaint] go to court yet, but we've had complaints which are handled through the city attorney's office, and usually when the city attorney's office has called the owner and pointed it [the ordinance] out, the owner then has let the person at least see the apartment . . . and figure out if they could afford it.

She also said that the ordinance had halted the practice of landlords advertising apartments in the local newspapers with a "no children" stipulation in the ads.

The other ordinance implemented by the Sanders administration—again through the CEDO—concerned the issue of tenants' security deposits. The week following the yes vote on the antidiscrimination ordinance, the Board of Aldermen took up the security deposit issue. Reported the daily newspaper: "The Board of Aldermen gutted and then passed a proposed ordinance . . . to govern the handling of rental security deposits."[12]

Members of the Progressive Coalition, however, were unhappy with it. One administration insider explained that the original ordinance had the following provisions: "You couldn't charge more than one month's rent for security deposit, you had to give interest on the security deposit, you had to give it back within fourteen days, and if you have a dispute over it, the arbitration has to go to the Housing Board of Review [or you] go to court if necessary." The penalties are the same as any other housing code violation. The watered-down version, she explained, "ended up with three sentences that were meaningless, so Sanders vetoed it. We brought it [the original security deposit ordinance] back to the board, [and] again they voted it down."

It took over a year before the Progressive Coalition had recovered sufficiently to reintroduce the security deposit measure. This time, the progressives used the tactic of trying to get the Board of Aldermen to put it to a vote of the people in March 1986. However, the board still said no, claiming it "wanted more time to study [the ordinance]." Subsequently, Vermont Tenants Inc., a statewide, low-income tenants' advocacy organization, decided to launch a petition drive to force it onto the ballot. After a shaky start, the petition drive proved to be successful. On election day, the security deposit initiative won by 62 percent, or a vote of 5,380 for and 3,254 against. According to a tenants' advocate, the Board of Aldermen was not required to pass the measure after voters approved it because initiative measures are advisory and nonbinding. But, after the strong approval by the voters, the board found it politically expedient to implement a security deposit ordinance that was very similar to the measure the Progressive Coalition had tried to get passed more than a year earlier.[13]

Antispeculation Tax

During the same time period that the Progressive Coalition successfully passed the security deposit ordinance, the coalition also was working on another measure called the antispeculation tax. In early 1986, the daily newspaper stated:

Burlington officials want to tax real estate speculators who they say drive up rents by buying and selling rental properties for a quick profit. . . . The speculation tax would be an extension of the Vermont land gains tax and would apply only to apartment buildings sold within six years of their purchase. Profits from the sale of land and buildings would be taxed on a sliding scale. The larger the profit and the shorter the time between purchase and resale of the building, the higher the tax. Sanders and Clavelle estimate that the tax would generate $250,000 a year for a special trust fund that would help finance affordable housing, particularly for low and middle income residents displaced by rising rents.[14]

Rapidly increasing rents were a problem in Burlington. From the administration's point of view, part of the reason rents increased 100 percent in the decade from 1970 to 1980 and then increased another 100 percent in the five years from 1980 to 1985 was real estate speculation. Others in Burlington disagreed. There was a raucous public debate on the antispeculation tax issue at a meeting held shortly after the proposal was announced, at which time opponents to the plan strongly denounced it. A subcommittee of the Board of Aldermen also came out with a report that ripped apart the proposed tax. Two members of the board, one a Republican and one a Democrat, stated "that Burlington's housing shortage was caused by an undersupply and overdemand o[f] apartment units and that the anti-speculation proposal would not help the underlying problem, the need for more housing." On the other hand, two progressive aldermen commented that "they had come across 'hundreds' of cases of speculation within their wards."[15]

After the issuance of the aldermanic committee report, Sanders blasted its findings. Then the CEDO issued a rebuttal, which said "193 apartment buildings were sold in 1985, of which 88 were held less than seven years. Of those, 11 were bought and sold within a year and 32 were held less than two years. [Brenda] Torpy argues anyone who buys and sells within two years is a speculator."[16]

The debate on the antispeculation tax went on despite the Board of Aldermen's refusal to put the issue on the March 1986 city ballot. In addition to the petition drive to get the antidiscrimination ordinance on the ballot, Vermont Tenants Inc. also conducted a drive to get the antispeculation tax on the ballot. They were successful here, too. After the antispeculation tax was put on the ballot, a local realtor tried legal maneuvering to get it thrown off the ballot, but the court refused. In the March 1986 elections, the antispeculation tax was voted down on a 51 percent to 49 percent margin.[17]

The Progressive Coalition did not wait long to resurrect the issue. In fall 1986, the Board of Aldermen voted 7–5 to place the issue on the November ballot, thus staving off another threatened petition drive. Three Republicans who did not necessarily support the tax voted with the progressives. However, the antispeculation tax measure was modified to some degree, with a change in the definition of rental speculative property. Now, property sold within six years of purchase, as opposed to within two years, was considered speculative. Other minor changes also were made to make the measure more palatable, including permission for owners to deduct their "labor and material costs."[18]

Republican Sam Levin moved to add a provision to the tax "that would have required approval by the Board of Aldermen even if the tax were passed by the voters and the Legislature." (All city charter changes need the approval of the legislature: See Chapter 7.) Members of the Progressive Coalition saw this as a way to cripple the measure. While the board approved Levin's amendment by an 8–5 vote along party lines (Democrats and Republicans teamed up together to vote for it), Sanders vetoed it.[19]

On election day in November 1986, the revised antispeculation tax was approved in a 53 percent to 47 percent vote. The charter change thus went to the state legislature for its approval. Sanders testified in favor of the measure and told lawmakers: "Burlington may be wrong . . . [and if so,] we will pay the price. [But] don't tell the people of Burlington you know more about our problems than we do. Because, quite frankly, you don't." Legislators did not appreciate the mayor's comments. But even if Sanders had been polite about the matter, the outcome probably would not have been different. The day after Sanders's lobbying effort, the House of Representatives turned down the antispeculation tax in a 77–67 vote, thus effectively killing the measure.[20]

Just-Cause Eviction Ordinance

In summer 1988, the Board of Aldermen considered a just-cause eviction ordinance. Under this law, a landlord's ability to evict his or her tenants would be restricted. On the one hand, landlords would be able to evict tenants for not paying rent. On the other hand, landlords would not be able to increase rents as a means of forcing tenants to leave.[21]

Because of the controversial nature of this proposal, the Board of Aldermen decided to let the people of Burlington vote on the measure in the November 1988 election. Quickly, the campaign against the measure gained momentum. Democrat Rick Sharp, who is also a major landlord in the city, got the ball rolling by accusing just-cause eviction proponents of being "avowed socialists and communists." A short time later, an organization called Citizens Against Question 4 (the ballot proposition number of the proposed just-cause ordinance) held a press conference to proclaim that the ballot measure "is a scheme to impose rent control in Burlington and if enacted will worsen an already serious shortage of affordable apartments."[22]

Progressive Coalition members tried their best to respond to their opponents' charges. In response to Rick Sharp's comment, alderman Gene Bergman said: "It's disgusting and it has no place in the politics of our city. . . . I am a Progressive, and I am very proud of that." Meanwhile, alderman Terrill Bouricius accused Citizens Against Question 4 of running "the lowest and most loathsome" attacks against the just-cause eviction initiative. He also pointed out that about 10 percent of those tenants forced to move from their homes are unjustly evicted.[23]

Despite its attempts, the Progressive Coalition was unable to effectively refute its opponents' arguments against the proposed ordinance. One landlord stated that with 8,000 rental units in the city, only 140 Burlington tenants were evicted in 1987—less than 2 percent of the total. But the landlords' ability to portray the just-cause eviction measure as a "thinly veiled attempt at rent control" really turned the tide against the initiative. On election day, the proposed charter change amendment lost by a vote of 8,520 to 7,634, or 53 to 47 percent. However, the measure won by a 58 to 42 percent vote in Progressive Coalition strongholds (Wards 1, 2, and 3).[24]

The Sanders administration's record on tenant issues has generated some controversy among those both to the left and to the right of the mayor on the political spectrum. Given the administration's concern for low- and moderate-income people, one would expect tenants' concerns to be a big agenda item for Sanders. However, except in a few notable instances, this really has not been the case.

When one thinks of nonreformist issues that a local socialist administration could promote concerning tenants' rights, the issue of rent control immediately comes to mind. However, except for endorsing the original PACT Fair Housing proposal, which was a mild form of rent control, Sanders, who says he supports the idea, has not strongly promoted the issue.

Sanders's reasons for not doing so are clear. In his opinion, there is not the political base among tenants in the community or the political clout by the Progressive Coalition on the Board of Aldermen to do anything on this issue. One tenants' advocate agrees with the mayor's assessment. Consequently, the issue has never been seriously proposed during Sanders's tenure as mayor.

From a purely political point of view, Sanders and the tenants' advocate are probably correct. Given its composition, there is no way rent control would be passed by the Burlington Board of Aldermen. If nothing else, the difficult struggle to get city tenants an antidiscrimination ordinance and the security deposit ordinance is evidence that the board would not be receptive to the more radical idea of rent control.

However, this does not negate the idea being raised. One tenants' advocate points out that timing is important; one wants to bring up an issue when it is useful as an "organizing tool." But one progressive critic speaks about the educational function of an issue like rent control. Thus, we see a crucial question confronting socialist administrations: Should one be pragmatic and consider what is possible to achieve, and then work on these issues, even if they are only reformist reforms, or should one push a radical, nonreformist reform agenda even if it is very unlikely to pass? On the issue of rent control (as well as in other areas), Sanders opted for the former strategy.

One consequence is that there is a redirection of energy from issues like rent control to issues such as the antispeculation tax. This measure was another way of trying to deal with the problem of skyrocketing rents. By taxing real estate speculators, the measure would have set up a trust fund to help build low- and moderate-income housing. While this proposal was approved by voters as a charter change on the municipal level, it failed in the state legislature.

Quite a bit of criticism has been leveled at the administration, especially by Democrats, for having done little or nothing for low-income renters. Meanwhile, the Democrats praise the former administration for having done much more. On the surface, such allegations are true. That is, Paquette was responsible for a lot of new low-income housing projects. Of course, what is not mentioned by the Democrats is that during the Reagan presidency, federal funds for the construction of low-income housing projects virtually dried up. Not only in Burlington, but in all other cities across the nation, housing for low-income people has become an issue of critical proportions.

The Sanders administration, primarily through the CEDO, has tried to develop innovative proposals to help meet the housing needs of low- and moderate-income people in Burlington (see Chapter 6). Their efforts have been predicated, to some extent, on perceived political viability, and what progress has been made must be partially at-tributed to the tenants' movement in Burlington. Vermont Tenants Inc., in conjunction with the CEDO, has put forth some important proposals to deal with tenants' concerns, some of which have passed. Given the constraints on the city and the up-and-down nature of the tenants' movement, the administration has made some significant gains in tenants' rights, though in at least one important area—rent control—they made no progress.

NEIGHBORHOOD PLANNING ASSEMBLIES (NPAs)

The Neighborhood Planning Assemblies (NPAs) began on a very optimistic note. The idea, according to one activist, originated at a conference of neighborhood groups in fall 1981. One of the groups presented a proposal for the creation of a grass-roots neighborhood network to the conference, and it was greeted with enthusiasm. It was decided that the group should pursue the idea with the newly elected Sanders administration. According to the activist, however, Sanders "came up with this proposal to have planning assemblies in the different neighborhoods to discuss planning issues," thus usurping the original proposal.

At an aldermanic meeting in fall 1982, there was "a resolution passed by the Board of Aldermen and signed by Mayor Bernard Sanders to promote citizen participation" through the creation of the assemblies. Besides the solicitation of ideas on waterfront develop-ment, the assemblies also were intended to have "the task of helping to decide how to spend $782,000 of Community Development money."[25]

Over the next year, there were scheduled assembly meetings in every ward of the city, where neighborhood concerns, the spending of com-munity development funds, waterfront development, and bylaws and structure were discussed. About a year after the resolution, the daily newspaper reported that "every neighborhood in Burlington has had ... meetings to discuss ways of improving their community, to gripe about a housing project, parking problems or traffic signs. ... The gatherings are the ultimate in participatory democracy. Anyone who shows up gets to talk and vote on every decision."[26]

The assemblies could only make recommendations and had no formal powers, the article went on to say. Regarding the waterfront, at a citywide meeting of the assemblies, they had "voted a preference for public access, parks, marinas and restaurants." Concerning neighborhood issues, the assemblies had received a $90,000 Community Development Block Grant ($15,000 for each of the city's six wards) "to spend on projects that will stem urban blight, employ youths, upgrade housing or preserve historic buildings." Michael Monte, whose job at the time was to help organize the assemblies, was quoted as saying: "The assemblies are a hybrid of a neighborhood group and an arm of city government. . . . They allow people to come out and interact with city government." Sanders commented in this same article: "The Neighborhood Planning Assemblies are the very best vehicles by which one can give input and criticism."[27]

Over the years, some assemblies discussed a wide range of problems, from baseball to the waterfront plan, from pollution problems to crime and police protection. The assemblies also experienced varying levels of activity, with those in Wards 5 and 6 being dormant until recently.[28]

An article in the daily newspaper in fall 1987 presented a fairly positive view of the assemblies. Calling them a "qualified success," it pointed out that they have improved communication between the neighborhoods and the city and brought about positive, concrete changes in various parts of the city. In wealthier parts of the city, however, the assemblies have done little.[29]

According to one CEDO official, since 1988 all the assemblies are active again. Some are meeting monthly, while other are meeting quarterly. One CEDO staff person is devoting most of her time to working with them. Recently, all the assemblies chose representatives to sit on a citywide environmental conservation board (though technically the Board of Aldermen is supposed to appoint people to these positions). Moreover, the CEDO office, in conjunction with the assemblies, is working on a charter revision that would formally incorporate the assemblies into the city's governmental structure. Under this proposal, the assemblies would meet yearly, town meeting style, to decide certain issues, such as the election of city commission members.

Many people interviewed, however, viewed the NPAs as disappointing, if not a failure. Moreover, this impression cut across the political spectrum. One administration insider said that while the assemblies are a "good, progressive idea [permitting] citizens' input and citizens' planning activities," in actuality their functioning has been only "mediocre, based on people's energy and input." This insider explained that the assemblies were "only as progressive as the neighborhood is . . . [and since] we don't control the[ir] agenda or issues as much as . . . community organizers [do with neighborhood groups] . . . [we] can only bring [them] . . . so far." He also said that while a few of the assemblies were progressive, a number were not. Moreover, unless there was an exciting issue, few people tended to show up for assembly meetings. In this insider's estimation, until recently only the assemblies in Wards 1 and 3 have been successful.

A few members of the Sanders administration and the Progressive Coalition felt positive about the assemblies, but most thought they had not lived up to their potential. One offered this analysis of their failure:

The NPA is an issue of democracy that has created tension . . . especially the way they [the administration] dealt with the waterfront. . . . They [the administration] didn't put the energy into the NPAs—the Progressive Coalition didn't attempt to build them as institutions, they attempted to build them as conveyer belts. That's because they were seen as substitutes for their [the Progressive Coalition's] own organization.

One progressive alderman commented that with the decline of the neighborhood movement in Burlington, an attempt was made to substitute the assemblies for them. His assessment was that although a few of them worked, a number didn't, including the one in his own ward. Another echoed the previous comments, adding that some of the assemblies took negative stands on progressive development issues. One Progressive Coalition member was very critical of them, saying they were a "flop." Furthermore, she added, the assemblies "turned out to be regular mouthpieces for the opposition, or in our wards, mouthpieces for us. [They have] no real power in making decisions, except [with] Community Development Block Grant monies." She cited the waterfront development issue as an example of their giving input with no ability to decide on the final plans. Moreover, she stated, the assemblies had no real money to hire staff. In some cases, she concluded, they came out against progressive initiatives, such as the South Meadow housing project (see Chapter 6).

Another Progressive Coalition member was pointed in his assessment: "The Neighborhood Planning Assemblies didn't work worth a shit." He went on to say:

I think things could have been done differently. . . . [We could have] take[n] some of the CDBG [Community Development Block Grant] money and hire[d] a couple of full-time organizers

... and then let them be completely independent and put pressure on the administration in various areas. . . . Basically the administration is trying to . . . be progressive without having a feedback loop and they need some outside pressure. . . . The fact that they haven't done that is . . . a real serious problem.

Other progressives critical of the Sanders administration were generally disappointed with the NPAs, too. One activist saw much of the original enthusiasm die on the vine:

[The] assemblies started off with a lot of expectations of people getting together, figuring out [the] priorities and needs of different neighborhoods. Over time, it just became clear that Sanders was reluctant about [them], felt threatened by them, and over time tried to make them more and more just an arm of the Community [and Economic] Development Office. . . .The first few Neighborhood [Planning] Assembly meetings started off well and instilled people with confidence. . . . Unfortunately, there really wasn't the follow-through and commitment [on Sanders's part] to really make community control a priority.

Still another progressive commented:

The Neighborhood [Planning] Assemblies didn't work out as I thought. They were intended to . . . be the grass roots expression where a lot of these issues (for example, the waterfront) would be debated. What seemed to happen was that they would be used by the administration to present their points of view of what they were going to do, to explain policy rather than inviting people to create policy. . . . There's been a top-down element involved with the way they worked.

One progressive critic reflected that

the Neighborhood Planning Assemblies are quite often summoned together to give a patina of democratic support to a proposal that Sanders has—the most striking example being the way the Neighborhood Planning Assemblies were manipulated by Sanders [o]n behalf of the waterfront issue.

The reactions from several Democrats also were mixed. One alderman felt that because people went to these gatherings and were able to bring up their issues, the assemblies were a good thing. "I think it's been a benefit to the citizens of each of the wards," he said. But another was less enthusiastic:

> I think when the Neighborhood Planning Assemblies were in-
> itiated, I had great hopes for them, but I think they've really been
> neglected more by city hall—certainly financially—. . . in terms
> of neighborhood development money. . . . I thought they were
> going to be a way of the neighborhoods sending information up
> to the bureaucrats in city hall, saying these are the problems and
> this is what we want. More than anything else, what I've seen is
> city hall sending stuff down and using the Neighborhood Plan-
> ning Assemblies as a vehicle to push their own ideas (for ex-
> ample, the waterfront).

What happened to this bold experiment? Essentially, the role envisioned for the assemblies just never materialized. They were to be an
experiment in democratic neighborhood empowerment and citizen
participation, encouraged by city hall. In their execution, however,
they did not function in this way. Several barely got off the ground
because of lack of interest. In several other wards, assemblies turned
out to have conservative politics, thereby thwarting the implementation of a progressive city hall agenda. In those wards where assemblies
were organized and were progressive, attendance and participation
were spotty, depending on the issues at hand. And, in at least one of
the wards, the assembly was competing with an existing neighborhood group.

The other major problem stemmed from how the assemblies were
organized. The city's role in their creation meant they became, either
by design or by default, a perceived organ of the administration, at
least in the wards where Sanders had his power base. This was
especially true on the waterfront issue. But the attempt to set up a
network of independent neighborhood assemblies in Burlington was
fraught with potential problems. On the one hand, their perceived
status as an extension of city hall generated a lack of faith in their
independent status. On the other hand, if the assemblies had become
a countervailing power base, they might have proved embarrassing
to the administration. Thus, it may have been in Sanders's self-interest
to let them flounder.

The formation of the assemblies in Burlington did *not* lead to the
demise of the previously existing network of neighborhood organizations in the city, as some observers have claimed. Nor was the demise
of the neighborhood groups in Burlington directly linked to Sanders's
election (although Michael Monte, former director of the King Street
Youth Center, which supported several of these groups, did take a job

with the administration). Although the attempt to complement the neighborhood groups in Burlington with the assemblies was a noble effort, for the most part it was unsuccessful. While it is true that Community Development Block Grant money was made available for various neighborhood projects, by not helping to secure the resources to hire organizers to work for them, the Sanders administration shoulders some of the blame for their ineffectiveness.

What seems certain is that without independence from city hall and their own funding base, the assemblies will never live up to their full potential. Although it is unrealistic to expect them to have replaced the neighborhood groups movement of the 1970s, the Sanders administration could have done more to foster effective assemblies. Their inability to act as independent entities, and when appropriate, to criticize or oppose administration policies and development plans, reduced their usefulness.

There are signs, however, that the NPAs may yet fufill their stated intentions. The recent proposal to formally grant the assemblies certain powers now reserved for the city council, such as commission appointments, is a step in this direction. While such a change in the city's governmental structure would have to be approved by the voters, the ensuing discussion could empower Burlington's citizenry. The assemblies could eventually become one of the vehicles for citizen empowerment.

GENERAL CITIZEN INVOLVEMENT IN CITY POLITICS

In Burlington, there has been a strong revival of citizen involvement in the political life of the city, as we have seen from the previous examples. Most people credit Sanders for this accomplishment. For example, at the beginning of 1982, the daily newspaper said that the new mayor's "greatest accomplishment . . . has been to increase citizen interest in city government and involve more citizens in the process." One year later, Sanders himself said "his top accomplishment since being elected in 1981 is bringing new people into City Hall and reawakening an interest in city government."[30]

Sanders's election has had a positive impact on the electorate and created an atmosphere conducive to discussion and debate on important issues. Almost everyone spoken to seemed to corroborate this impression, regardless of political persuasion. There also has been greater involvement from groups that had, in the past, been left out of the political process in the city.

Those involved in the Sanders administration were excited about the changes they had seen as a result of the mayor's election. One spoke of a "new spirit," of a "city hall there for the people," of "get[ting] people excited . . . [and] infus[ing] them with a sense of participation and enthusiasm for the community." Another said the administration had enlivened the political process, raised "conscious-ness," and fostered the "empowerment" of Burlington's population. Still another stated that the "biggest thing Sanders has accomplished is a change in atmosphere, . . . a change in the basic tone in the com-munity in terms of involvement."

Past and present Progressive Coalition alderpeople also felt strongly that Sanders had had a positive impact on the attitudes, perceptions, and involvement of the average Burlingtonian, as well as influencing events further from home. One spoke of the new "open-ness of city government." Another said: "People feel they can go down to the Board of Aldermen meetings and talk to politicians," and that there also was "access to city hall for a lot of people who previously had no access." For still another, the Sanders administration had instilled a heightened "awareness of issues" among the local citizenry and acted as a "catalyst of change" for other cities around the country attempting to model Burlington's example. Yet another mentioned the increased "interest and hope" that exists, a heightening of "people's expectations," and a change in low- and moderate-income people's perception "that government might actually try to do something in the interest of ordinary people."

One Progressive Coalition member stated: "They've [the Sanders administration] increased the hope that government can make a difference in what happens to people . . . [and] raised the awareness that it's possible to make significant change in the city of Burlington." Another said that it was no longer "politics as usual" in Burlington. He observed that now

> city decisions are widely discussed. . . . You don't have a democracy without an informed electorate. People talk politics seriously instead of just delegating that to someone else. . . .
> I think there's a great sense of pride. . . . People feel proud of a city that does new things. . . . People feel excited about living here. . . . They've [the Sanders administration] just changed [the] values of people in the city, of what's important and how to live in a small city. It's a wonderful, much more dynamic city because of the progressives and what's been happening here.

Still another Progressive Coalition member commented: "If you look at the operation of the city, it's much more democratic. There are many, many more people involved in things and [they] repre-sent all classes." He continued: "I think . . . [the] major accomplishment [of the Sanders administration] is to politicize the city. Getting politics injected back into the city has made the city a much more alive place."

Others close to the Sanders administration also had positive comments. One union official explained that Sanders's "getting people involved was a big thing. . . . I guess the main thing I appreciate is . . . see[ing] the government opened up to the people [and having them] really not be . . . intimidated to take part."

Even those usually critical of the Sanders administration acknowledged his accomplishments in this area. One activist said the major achievement in this area was "creating, . . . for a period of time, a sense of enthusiasm around city issues and [a] feeling that working on city issues was a positive thing. . . . That spirit for a couple of years was an incredible thing." He then added: "I guess there was a real opening up of city hall in terms of people with specific grievances being able to really come in and feel that there were people in control of the different agencies whose job it was to actually talk to them and deal with things that came up." Another progressive critic put it this way: "He's [Sanders] made city hall open to certain kinds of people . . . [and] as much as I disagree with him on lots of stuff now, I'm more comfortable . . . walking in there [city hall] than when Paquette was in there."

But at least one progressive critic felt otherwise. He felt that "in terms of changing political consciousness in the city of Burlington, I don't think much has really been accomplished in that area because there's no real consistency to where he's [Sanders] coming from."

Democrats, in general, felt that Sanders had increased citizen participation in local government. One alderman said: "People are more interested in what's going on in Burlington city government [and] that's . . . very good." Another commented that during the "last four or five years, [there has been] a greater community involvement, which I think is a plus [and attributable] to the Sanders administration." However, another said:

One of the biggest accomplishments was to change public perception towards government; that it [city government] should not be a closed group of people in city hall that make decisions behind people's backs, but instead the decisions should be made out in the open. In practice, I don't think they fufill that, but in public perceptions, I think they do.

Yet, even this Democrat admitted that there was now "a lot more interest in city hall."

Republicans were no less enthusiastic—and perhaps a little more so—because they have benefited from the participation explosion as well. One alderman said:

I think that he [Sanders] has shaken up politics in Burlington and made everybody more active and more aware of the fact that there are constituencies out there who you've got to stay in touch with and that demographics are changing and that political leaders have to change and stay in tune with their electorate, because if you don't, Gordie Paquette can be you.

This alderman added that the Sanders administration "has opened the government to a lot of interest groups who now feel that they have somebody to talk to, . . . for example, the tenants' organizations and social groups who now feel there is someone in power who will listen to them. They felt shut out of that process in the past."

Other past and present Republican aldermen concurred. One said: "There's no question that what he's [Sanders] been able to do is to bring in a whole group of people, who in the past have been (or felt they have been) disenfranchised—the low-income people, the elderly, some of the students, and disaffected Democrats." Another reflected that Sanders "really revitalized people's interest in politics in Burlington . . . [and] there's a chance for almost anyone to participate." Still another commented: "They have definitely stimulated participation and debate . . . so you have more people involved."

Other Republicans also noticed the contribution Sanders had made in this area. One observed that the "involvement in politics" has increased and there is a "high level of interest . . . [and] opening the door to young people." She also added that there was "involvement of a different level of social and economic [classes] in politics." Another said that "the revitalization of political . . . involvement is a tremendous benefit to the city."

Members of the business community also were positive in their assessment of Sanders's opening of the political process. One said: "The [caliber] of the [Republicans and Democrats on] the Board of Aldermen . . . has improved . . . since Sanders has been in office [because it has] awakened the Republicans and Democrats . . . to work harder . . . to get out the vote."

Another praised the "involvement versus the apathy [that existed before]." Still another felt that the "mobilization of voters is a strong positive feature. Sanders created a three-party system that's quite viable, and we have many candidates running for elections, and I think that's a tremendous credit to him." Yet another commented: "I think they've [the Sanders administration] tried to get more of the community involved than the previous administration. I think they've been more open." Finally, one business owner whose politics are diametrically opposed to the Sanders administration said: "They've [the Sanders administration] certainly made people more interested in city government [and] I think that's an accomplishment."

Several academicians also had favorable comments regarding Sanders and increased citizen involvement. For example, one said: "The level of interest in community affairs and the level of participation by people who had not previously had a real interest or stake in city activities is enormous. . . . That's part of his leadership."

Another commented: "There's been a major participation explosion in the city." He then asked:

So has Bernie had an impact on the city? Absolutely. The city is a different place . . . and it will never again return to the sleepytime town of yesteryear where a handful of old-boy members of French and Irish families sit down around the table and do the city business. The participation portion of the Sanders revolution is permanent.

This academician also expressed positive feelings about the role of the administration in fostering a new attitude in the community:

There's a greater awareness of the plight of poor people in the city. . . . People in Wards 2 and 3 [now] have a . . . real say in city government. Sanders's major impact has been . . . on the soul of Burlington's underclass. . . . He's [also] had a tremendous impact on the way Burlingtonians see themselves.

There was no general consensus among the news media regarding Sanders's overall impact on citizen participation. One editor remarked: "I think he's reawakened the interest in politics among the people of the city and that is all to the good." However, one news reporter felt that while the Sanders administration claimed to have gotten people "involved in the political process," this trend seemed to have reached its zenith and was now on the downswing.

Given the overwhelmingly positive impressions that people of different political persuasions had concerning Sanders's role vis-à-vis citizen involvement in Burlington's political arena, it is fair to say that the mayor has been responsible for presiding over an unprecedented increase in the level of political involvement and awareness in the city. And while increased citizen involvement in the day-to-day affairs of the community—especially among low- and moderate-income people—is not in itself indicative of a nonreformist reform, it is surely one of the goals of a new democratic-socialist society. For this accomplishment Sanders deserves credit. However, not every attempt by the Sanders administration to increase citizen involvement met with such success.

LACK OF ACCESS TO THE SANDERS ADMINISTRATION AND QUESTIONS CONCERNING INTERNAL DEMOCRACY

Although the Sanders years have brought an increase in citizens' participation in local government, there has been a concurrent strengthening of the mayor's power and role in Burlington in a variety of ways. This has led to greater centralization of the mayor's powers and resulted, at times, in having important issues decided by either Sanders himself or the mayor and a handful of close, mostly male, advisors. Such characteristics are common among politicians on any level of government, which is precisely the point. There appears to be little difference between Sanders, a socialist mayor, and any nonsocialist mayor regarding the issues of who has access to the mayor's office, decision-making processes within the administration, and the centralization of power.

When those interviewed addressed the issue of access to and participation in the decision-making process within the administration, as well as the issue of the centralization of power, criticism was the watchword from almost everyone. Many women inside the Sanders administration raised concerns about the mayor's style and his decision-making process. One administration insider, speaking from personal experience, said that women sometimes were "overlooked" or "cut out of the decision-making process." While Sanders "has a lot of respect for individual women," said another administration insider, he does not get enough "input" from women, who "would like to have more influence" in his administration (see Chapter 8).

One progressive activist criticized Sanders's style on other grounds:

Because the movement is so diffuse, and Bernie's particular style is so individualistic and anti-organizational, . . . you have [a] problem. . . . Bernie is like an anarchist, in that he does what he wants to do. . . . He's going to do what Bernie Sanders thinks is right, that's all he's going to do, and if you don't like it, tough; he's going to do it anyway.

This activist's criticisms went further. In addition to the anarchist streak, he also spoke of what he labeled "authoritarian" tendencies:

I don't think he has a real commitment to internal democracy. Again, it comes down to having people run and do what his tight-knit inner circle want to have happen, and then if you don't buy it, you're out and he'll direct a lot of wrath and a lot of . . . energy to stop your initiatives. He won't support you. . . .

There is [also] the sense of ostracizing people. I know a number of people who feel burnt because they can't deal with Bernie, they can't get through to him, they can't work with him; it's all on Bernie's terms.

Another activist said of Sanders:

He's viewed as having a circle of people around him that he relates to—a pretty small circle . . . that he consults—sometimes—and listens to sometimes and sometimes doesn't.

If you've been written out of that circle, either actively or passively, that is, if you've either been ignored and not solicited for your views or if you've been turned down, [you have no access to Sanders]. There are people who have tried to gain access to his closest advisors (that is, Terry Bouricius, the Clavelles, Jonathan [Leopold, Jr.] . . . who are just not allowed in—they can't get their calls answered and they can't get invited to meetings, or if they come to meetings, they're treated poorly.

Progressive critics of the administration leveled similar criticisms. One said:

He just meets with two or three people and that's who decides what's going to happen, and he just really doesn't care what anybody else thinks.

I think he or somebody like him could have gone a lot further in actually accomplishing things that he set out to do if instead of operating in this mode of being—. . . the lone individual who's gonna legislate reforms from the top down and get people what they need—if he was more part of a movement and more in touch with people at the grass roots and not just the people he could get political support from.

Another felt that while city hall was more open, it was only more open to a certain group of people. Thus, only the players have changed, not the style of government:

Here's this guy [Bernie] who's saying he's a democrat, [that] everyone should participate, but he's very isolated, and he doesn't want an organization to which he should be accountable. That's becoming more and more well-known. The more people work for him, the more people find out what the style really is and they become a little disaffected and drift away.

Still another charged that Sanders's style works against democracy:

The most fundamental thing that's wrong with the administration is that we have personal paternalism here—we don't have municipal democracy. I'm not saying that he's built a machine like Daley, . . . [but] he is the center of government in Burlington.

His identification of his destiny with the political future of the city—its economic future—in fact the whole socialist future of Vermont (he might be the first Jewish president of the U.S.) . . . has led to a degree of personal paternalism that vitiates democracy.

Bernie Sanders functions like a black hole; all that energy which existed on the base level, which hopefully could have been coordinated through a movement that encouraged it, has now been absorbed into city hall and would have otherwise gone into the development of genuine popular groups.

This "paternalism," according to the critic, was that

his [Sanders's] politics thus become intensely personalized— with personal paternalism you have personal politics—so if you criticize him, you're in the dog house. You cannot co-exist with Sanders—either you're with him or against him. There's no way of . . . really trying to criticize him without him taking it very, very personally.

Yet another progressive critic, who used to be a Sanders supporter and split with him over the waterfront bond issue, unleashed the harshest criticism by referring to the mayor's "totally undemocratic administration. . . . It's less democratic to me than the Democrats and Republicans." The reason, according to her, was that while voters knew when and where the Democratic or Republican Parties were meeting because they printed their meeting time and place in the newspaper, the Progressive Coalition was undemocratic because "nobody knows when it meets, or where, . . . [it doesn't] have primaries, it's just his [Sanders's] thing." She added that someone could only run as a Progressive Coalition candidate with Sanders's approval, and that once elected, the aldermen vote together all the time. She then likened the Progressive Coalition to "a communist party."

One Democratic alderman also criticized the supposed open nature of the political process in Burlington:

He [Sanders] doesn't want an open process. He started off with an open process, which I respected, [but] he has since closed the process completely. The waterfront is a classic example; . . . no more public input, you react to what he presents, and that's it. He doesn't give you information—you have to research the information and then try to react to what he's presented. He's done that in almost every phase of government.

In response to such criticisms, Sanders responded angrily:

Sure, criticism can be made, but I get really disgusted and very, very angry at the cheap-shot criticism . . . and ultimately I think many of the people think it doesn't make a damn bit of difference who's in government anyhow—what difference does it make? They [the critics] have some kind of utopian scheme for the world. . . . That's some of the opposition that we have—that we haven't yet created utopia and we've been in Burlington government for four years.[31]

However, on the issue of the centralization of decision making, Sanders commented:

That's a good point . . . and I don't know the answer to that; the criticism may be valid, but it's very difficult. We work simultaneously in ten or fifteen different areas and how you can involve large numbers of people in all of the debates and discussion, when ultimately the vote takes place at the Board of Aldermen level, is not easy.
   I think we have not done as good a job as we can do, I would say that frankly, but it really is not easy. . . . One of the things we did is establish NPAs where all the issues of importance to the city are debated and discussed, so I think we have a lot more than used to be the case.
   The real issue is how you maintain the involvement of people in any kind of political process. The truth is, we have a very difficult time. . . . How do you get them to come out to meetings? I think anyone who says our intent is not that is not telling the truth. . . . Have we gone about it always in the right way? I'd be willing to concede that we haven't.[32]

It is ironic that while Sanders has opened up the democratic process within the city as a whole, within his own administration, there is a clear tendency to concentrate power and limit access to internal decision-making processes to an inner circle of advisors, most of them men. Those labeled as outsiders, for whatever reasons, have a difficult time getting a fair hearing by the mayor or his close advisors. And Sanders, who is known for being independent, often makes decisions with little or no input from the people around him. This may be an admirable trait in some circumstances, but it certainly is an impediment to developing a nonreformist reform strategy toward a democratic-socialist society. As many people as possible must be included in both internal and external decision-making processes if we are to move away from the hierarchical, authoritarian, and centralized models of society that are inimical to the long-term interests of the vast majority of people.

Sanders's commitment to democratic socialism stands at odds with his decision-making process—and it is this inability to put into practice his beliefs that is so disappointing to many progressives. As has so often been stated by the women's movement, "the personal is the political." Consequently, the quality of individual actions, whether in interpersonal relationships or in public office, influences the movement toward a new society.

CONCLUSION

While Sanders did much during his four terms as mayor to increase general citizen participation in Burlington politics, he also acted to alienate a number of progressives in the community—and even in his own administration—through his personal style of politics. Ironically, many of those that one would expect to be the mayor's closest allies turn out to be Sanders's harshest critics.

There is no doubt that the general citizenry of Burlington is more involved in local government and the political process than perhaps at any time in the past. All of the electoral data examined clearly indicate this. And many special interest groups that had a difficult time gaining access to previous administrations—such as tenants, low- to moderate-income neighborhood groups, artists, youths, and others—were supported in one way or another by the Sanders administration. In general, those who often have trouble having their interests represented by city hall, that is, poor and working-class people, were much more fairly treated by Mayor Sanders. This isn't surprising, as this group forms the backbone of his political support.

However, as we shall see in more detail in Chapters 8 and 9, other interest groups, such as women and the peace movement, did not have such an easy time gaining access to the Sanders administration. Thus, progressives whose political agenda is somewhat different from that of Sanders often found themselves at odds with the mayor—and often left out of the decision-making process. This seems especially true among those on the left who have anarchist tendencies. Clearly, Sanders operates on the principles of centralistic socialism (though his own style is very individualistic), and his administration occasionally used high-handed tactics. For those who profess a more decentralistic kind of socialism, Sanders's actions sometimes bordered on the intolerable.

The situation becomes even more difficult for Sanders when analyzed from a feminist perspective. His frequent retreat to an old-boy style of making decisions indicates that he has incorporated few of the principles that guide the women's movement today, all the more disappointing to socialist feminists that see his administration as more of the same old patriarchy.

For those who value empowerment from the bottom up, the Sanders administration presents a mixed record. On the one hand, increased voter participation by low- and moderate-income people and greater involvement of certain interest groups normally left out of the political process gives cheer. On the other hand, the centralization of power in the mayor's office, the presence of a small in-group and a much larger out-group, the inability of some interest groups to have their concerns aired, the difficulty of women's voices being heard at city hall, and the difficulties in creating viable Neighborhood Planning Assemblies in most wards are a cause of concern. Some of these are clearly related to Sanders the man; his personality and style make it hard for some to work with him. Other problems are attributable to Sanders the politician and the political system in which he must maneuver.

This is not to let Sanders off the hook, as it were, but to acknowledge the difficulty—in analysis and practice—of separating Sanders's accomplishments and failures from the capitalist system in which he operates. But there can be little doubt that Sanders bears the responsibility for running the city like a hierarchically run business instead of creating a democratic-socialist polity, where *all* people have a voice and are truly empowered.

The Question of Ownership under Municipal Socialism

The issue of ownership often is considered a central theme in socialist societies. To many, socialism means state ownership of vital industries, transportation, and services, as well as nationalization of banks. Simply put, the state produces and distributes the goods and services and helps generate and control the flow of capital in society.

Under the U.S. capitalist economic system, state ownership of banks and businesses is rare and clearly unattainable on a large scale.[1] No municipal socialist administration in the United States is going to take over the financial centers and private industry in its city or town. However, traditional capitalist ownership patterns can be challenged through nonreformist reforms, such as the municipalization of utilities, co-operative housing ventures, public ownership of land, and worker-owned and worker-controlled businesses. This is exactly what the Sanders administration tried to do.

THE BATTLE FOR MUNICIPAL CABLE TELEVISION

As a bona fide socialist mayor, it is not surprising that Bernard Sanders would want to municipalize something in the city of Burlington. Part of the historical legacy of socialist administrations on the local level in the United States has been the municipalization of utilities. Burlington has a history of municipalization, too. Ever since its incorporation in 1865, the city has had a publicly owned sewer system. The city created a municipally owned water system in 1866 when it bought the Burlington Aqueduct Company. In 1904, the progressive Democratic administration of Mayor Burke took over the Burlington Electric Light Department.[2]

During the 1980s, the local privately owned cable television company—Green Mountain Cable (a subsidiary of Cox Cable in Atlanta, Georgia)—became a clear target for Sanders. Amidst customer dissatisfaction (for example, the lack of access to certain popular cable channels), Sanders appointed a committee in spring 1983 to explore the feasibility of the municipal ownership of the cable television company in Burlington. No doubt one of the factors motivating the mayor's action was to improve the quality of cable television programming in the city, since only the basic networks (CBS, NBC, ABC, and PBS) were available without cable reception in Burlington. The high percentage of elderly people in the Burlington area (one of Sanders's more important constituencies), many of whom watched cable television, made it even more important for the city to play a role.[3]

After a lengthy fight with the privately owned cable company, *The Burlington Free Press*, and the state's Public Service Board, Sanders lost his bid to municipalize Green Mountain Cable. But the effort produced a $1 million out-of-court cash settlement and a 5 percent franchise fee on cable company income starting in 1991. During the battle, the issue over the ownership of cable television was defined as "free enterprise" versus "government control" by the daily newspaper. But that was a distorted view, because in Vermont cable television is considered a public utility and falls under the jurisdiction and regulation of the state's Public Service Board. Presently, Vermont is one of only a few states in the country where the state, as opposed to the city itself, grants cable licenses.[4]

Sanders made clear from the start of the struggle between his administration and the cable company that he wanted to construct an entirely new cable television system for the city of Burlington, with the Burlington Electric Light Department in charge of it. Said the mayor: "In terms of a monopoly . . . if somebody has to make money on it [cable television], I'd rather see it be the city rather than a corporation in Atlanta." Given that the city already owned the electric company, it made sense to allow it to coordinate a municipal cable television system. Not only would the city benefit from the management expertise at the Light Department, but it would be able to use some of the cable technology to improve its own performance, such as in the area of "electric load-management."[5]

In mid-summer 1983, Sanders's cable television committee came out in support of a Light Department request to the Public Service Board for permission to build a new, state-of-the-art cable television package with fifty-five channels. The committee also felt that if an outside consultant's feasibility study was positive, then the Light Department should attempt to gain control of Green Mountain Cable's license to do business with the city.[6]

When the consultants, Rice Associates of Washington, D.C., issued their report, it excited members of the Sanders administration and generated controversy in the Burlington community, particularly among business leaders. According to the report, "Burlington could save between $1.5 million and $9 million of the cost of various city services over the next 15 years by constructing and operating a municipally owned cable television system." Moreover, the consultants' report showed that about 50 percent of Burlingtonians approved of the idea of municipal cable television, while only about a quarter of them disapproved of it.[7]

The editorial board of *The Burlington Free Press* didn't take kindly to the Sanders administration's attempt to go into the cable television business. In several editorials that summer, the daily newspaper ripped apart the idea. In one, the editors stated:

> The idea [of a city-owned cable television system] is so ludicrous as to exceed the bounds of common sense. It is not only unreasonable but it also is impractical. It is, plainly and simply, one of the most harebrained proposals to emerge from the Sanders administration since it first occupied City Hall in 1981. . . .
>
> Do they now want to control the airwaves so that they can bring their message to a larger audience about the utopian paradise they have fashioned in Burlington? Will watching city-owned cable television be the panacea for the other ills that beset the community?[8]

Sanders found himself in an unfamiliar position in spring 1984 when the Board of Aldermen unanimously supported a city resolution to apply to the Public Service Board for the right to run a municipally owned cable system. While the aldermen's resolution was not binding on the city, it did pave the way for the city's ownership of the system.[9]

The Rice report and the city resolution combined to put pressure on Green Mountain Cable to negotiate with the city. During summer 1984, talks between the Light Department and the cable company seemed to bear some fruit. On the initiative of the Light Department, a tentative agreement was reached whereby the city would no longer pursue the option of "municipal ownership" if the cable company would drop its ongoing fight with Burlington over the excavation fee (see Chapter 7) as well as make other concessions. When the proposed settlement made its way to the mayor's desk, he commented: "If Cox came around with an agreement that met our minimum requirements, it's conceivable that we could forgo the municipal route."[10]

However, an agreement was not forthcoming. Sanders felt that the proposed cable company concessions were too meager, and he pushed the private cable company for more. However, a series of political maneuvers between Green Mountain Cable, the Light Department, and the Board of Aldermen eventually combined to undermine the mayor's negotiating position. The management of the Light Department, as it turns out, was more interested in reaching a suitable compromise with the cable company than it was in running a city-owned cable television station. As for the Board of Aldermen, the Democrats and Republicans once again decided to play politics with the mayor by reversing the previous resolution vote that allowed the city to file an application with the Public Service Board to run a city-owned cable television system. In response to the aldermen's maneuvering, Sanders promised to veto the board's action.[11]

The administration's strong bargaining position had suddenly collapsed. Not only did his former allies—that is, the Light Department and the Board of Aldermen—switch sides on the issue, but the Public Service Board ruled against the city in fall 1984. Without ruling on Burlington's application to run its own municipal cable system, the Public Service Board acted favorably on a Green Mountain Cable rate increase request to rebuild their system, thus apparently making the city's application a moot point. Said Sanders: "If Cox is allowed to rebuild, then the game is over."[12]

But in winter 1984, the assistant city attorney handling the case, John Franco, made a startling discovery: "According to the city charter, there is no valid cable franchise." It appeared that a previous city contract with cable companies only granted a cable franchise from 1952 to 1982, and therefore at the end of the contract period, the city regained control over the franchise. The discovery gave the Sanders administration much-needed leverage over the cable company. In light of the Public Service Board's ruling in favor of Green Mountain Cable and Franco's discovery of the expired thirty-year contract, the Sanders administration went to the Vermont Supreme Court to block the cable company from rebuilding its system and asked for a ruling on the city's claim to have control of the cable franchise.[13]

The Sanders administration and the cable company had reached a legal stalemate. In a surprising development months later, Cox Cable of Atlanta decided to sell Green Mountain Cable. Cox agreed to settle out of court with the city to pave the way for the sale to the new group of investors at Mountain Cable Company. In spring 1985, shortly after the city had filed its appeal to the Vermont Supreme Court, Mountain Cable agreed to give the city $1 million if it would drop its appeal, forgo its plans for a city-owned cable system, raise no opposition to the sale of Green Mountain Cable, and agree to let the new cable company use the city's poles to put up cables.[14]

The money offered by Mountain Cable was in part a settlement with the city on the excavation fee issue. The payment was to cover any excavation costs the new company would incur as a result of reconstructing the cable system. Mountain Cable "also agreed to pay the city an annual franchise fee of no more than 5 percent of its gross revenues in the city, beginning in 1991." Finally, the new company would have an office in city hall and pay an annual rent of $35,000. There was little opposition from the Board of Aldermen to the deal between Mountain Cable and the city. A few days later, the deal was passed unanimously by the board.[15]

When the check for $1 million finally arrived in Burlington, the mayor was ecstatic. Not only would Burlingtonians be getting a "modern, state of the art cable television system in the city of Burlington," but, commented Sanders, the deal with Mountain Cable was "in every way superior" to the one previously offered by Green Mountain Cable. Robert McGill, Mountain Cable's new president, remarked that Cox and the city reached an agreement "because Cox . . . was eager enough for cash to knock $1 million off the purchase price." Furthermore, said McGill, "it became very clear to Cox that the city of Burlington has been very successful in building legal machinery that was going to grind away at Cox."[16]

Despite losing his battle to municipalize cable television in Burlington, the mayor obviously was pleased with the deal worked out between the city and the new cable company. Said Sanders:

> On two occasions, I vetoed legislation [from the Board of Aldermen] which would have negated our negotiating position regarding the establishment of a new cable system in Burlington. By holding tough on that, we ended up getting a $1 million dollar settlement from the cable company, plus in 1990 . . . [a] 5 percent franchise fee.
>
> Would a municipal system have been better? The answer is: I think so. But the fact that we went forward with the municipal system and could have tied up the new company in court for a long, long time was one of the reasons we got a $1 million cash settlement.
>
> In retrospect . . . I would have liked to have seen a municipal system in the city. [But] what we have accomplished in our battles, I would say, have been pretty successful.[17]

Several others who were intimately involved in the cable television issue had some insightful comments. "I don't think that's one of the great triumphs [of the Sanders administration but] I think it was a good deal," reflected one Progressive Coalition member. While he felt that it "might have been possible" to get a city-owned cable system, interference from the Public Service Board and the courts was significant. Moreover there was no guarantee that either Burlington voters or the state legislature would have gone along with a required charter change permitting municipalization. "Given that none of those [potential obstacles] were likely to be easy . . . the choice was: Should one just go down the road to possible disaster . . . [by taking a] small chance of triumph, or compromise?," asked this Progressive Coalition member. Obviously, Sanders made the "political decision" to do the latter, he said.

One administration insider called the $1 million deal with Cox Cable a real victory for the administration. "We were pounded up and down by the press, by the Democrats and Republicans because they were trying to give away the store," he said. Despite this opposition, the Sanders administration prevailed because it stuck to its guns and the new cable company was in a jam. He explained that because the company was trying to leverage funds on Wall Street and was having a difficult time, the city was in a strong bargaining position.

This administration insider admitted that Sanders compromised by taking cash instead of fighting for a municipal cable television system, but said it would have been nearly impossible to bring municipal cable television to Burlington. The reason, according to him, was the combined opposition of the Board of Aldermen, the Light Department, and the Public Service Board. Even if the Progressive Coalition had had a majority on the Board of Aldermen, he said, the Public Service Board's "complete hostility" to the idea probably would have prevented municipalization.

Sanders's effort to municipalize the cable television system in the city clearly raised the ire of *The Burlington Free Press* and the hackles of the business community in Burlington. This is evident from the nature of the attacks appearing in the daily newspaper and the comments issued by the private cable company in response to the administration's efforts. The newspaper accused the Sanders administration of seeking to "control the airwaves"; the cable company raised the issue of "government control versus free enterprise." Both issues were red herrings, the former because the city wouldn't have directly controlled the programming of a municipal cable television system, the latter because the cable television industry already was regulated by the state Public Service Board.

The Sanders administration used the threat of municipalization to force Green Mountain Cable to make more and more concessions. As assistant city attorney John Franco said: "The city's saber rattling, even if it goes nowhere, was making the cable system [that is, Green Mountain Cable] more responsive to the public good." When the Sanders administration sought to municipalize Green Mountain Cable, the cable company decided to improve its programming and provide a public access channel. But it also sought and won a rate hike to justify expanded programming to compete with the administration's municipalization plan.[18]

By publicly raising the advantages of municipalization, Sanders garnered support for the idea, which was reflected in public opinion polls. However, it is doubtful that the Sanders administration could have won on the municipalization issue. There were simply too many local, state, and legal constraints. While the effort to get municipal cable television failed, it did result in a $1 million cash settlement for the city and better programming (though at higher rates) for Burlington viewers.

Sanders once again showed himself to be the consummate politician by forcing a settlement with the cable company. The old adage that "politics is the art of compromise" seems applicable even for a socialist like Bernard Sanders. Yet if municipal ownership is a cornerstone of socialism on the local level, then city-owned cable television may have been a nonreformist reform worth pursuing, even though victory was unlikely.

SOUTH MEADOW PROJECT AND NORTHGATE APARTMENTS

Providing affordable housing was always a major priority of the Sanders administration, given that much of his constituency is renters. The mayor and the CEDO therefore undertook the South Meadow Project, a federally funded housing development that provides a mixture of rental and cooperatively owned apartments for people across the income spectrum.

A long-term goal of the South Meadow Project is to make it possible for some low- and moderate-income tenants to eventually own their own apartment unit. One CEDO official, who spoke at length about this project, said that the project allows tenants who now lease to build up equity as owners in a nonprofit, limited equity co-op twenty years down the road. This would be accomplished by setting up a housing trust fund allowing the tenants to purchase the building and land at the time of its sale.

The cooperative apartments at South Meadow are a "step better than rental housing" because "tenants have the security of tenure, . . . more say, more control, . . . [and] it will be perpetually affordable," said this CEDO official. She distinguished between the various forms of cooperative housing arrangements. First, there are leasing cooperatives, which she described as a lot like rental housing but with one important difference: "The thing that makes it different from rentals is just [that] the structure of management is [partially] in the hands of the residents [and partially in the hands of developers] and [it] give[s] them the possibility of owning it in the future and buy[ing] at a much reduced price."

By contrast, according to this CEDO official, ownership cooperatives are full equity co-ops where "people just band together to buy real estate and make money off of it" (such as Co-op City in Brooklyn, N.Y.). In between leasing co-ops and owner co-ops, she said, are limited equity co-ops: [They are] "housing cooperatives that form a cooperative corporation which owns real estate, and then every resident has a share in that corporation and own[s] it based upon the residency and the project, and their monthly payment goes not only to monthly costs but toward the equity share [for] the whole project." Under this arrangement, explained this official, "you get back what you put in."

The CEDO had to set up South Meadow as a leasing co-op rather than a limited equity co-op because the Vermont legislature, at the time, did not legally recognize the latter. The CEDO official was hopeful that the legislature would provide "enabling legislation" for "nonprofit housing co-ops," primarily as a result of the CEDO's lobbying efforts. During the 1988 legislative session, the state legislature passed the co-op housing bill, formally recognizing limited equity co-ops.

Through a federal program known as the Housing Development Action Grant (HODAG), the CEDO was granted $3.8 million in fiscal 1983 to help subsidize the building of the South Meadow Project by local developers. According to the CEDO's initial plan, one-half of the units (eighty) were to be rented apartments while the other half were to be cooperative apartments. Furthermore, of the 160 apartment units, three-quarters were to be "market rate units," while the other quarter were to be federally subsidized. Therefore, a total of forty units—twenty rentals and twenty co-ops—would be available to moderate-income people through a rent-subsidization program.[19]

In the beginning, the South Meadow Project did not go over well in the neighborhood where it was to be built. The original application for the project called for 200 units, but at a fiery aldermanic meeting, the board decided to reduce the number to 160 to appease angry neighborhood residents. But even this wasn't enough for the South End residents. At a subsequent neighborhood meeting with the two developers, they made further concessions. While residents were pleased with the developers' proposed changes, they also wanted the number of units cut roughly in half because, in their opinion, the project's density was too great. It wasn't until over a year later that the developers and neighborhood residents were able to agree on a compromise, which saw the developers drop twelve more units from the project, making the total 148 units. In exchange, residents of the area agreed to end "an appeal of [the] Planning Commission's approval" of the project. The Board of Aldermen also agreed to the compromise proposal.[20]

One administration insider believed that South Meadow was an "excellent project," but like other CEDO projects, it ran "into a firestorm of opposition." He explained:

This is an area where sometimes we run into conflicts relative to our philosophies of community and citizen participation. In [a neighborhood] meeting, by a vote of 63–1, they [the residents] told us they didn't want the [South Meadow] project in their neighborhood. This is a situation where we had to balance the neighborhood needs and desires with the broader community needs, and there are those who argue that we have ignored the will of the people and we are shoving this project down their throats. It's been a difficult process and one which has really raised the ire of many residents.

One member of the business community familiar with the South Meadow Project explained the financial intricacies of the development. The city of Burlington won a $3.8 million HODAG grant, which it then lent to the developers at "very low interest" to help construct the project. In return for this loan, the developers gave a long-term lease to the South Meadow cooperative association, that is, the tenants living there. The lease stated that the original HODAG grant of $3.8 million plus about $1 million in accrued interest would be given to the cooperative association in twenty years to help it buy the land and building from the developers when the lease expired. While the project's total current value was about $9 million in 1985 (the HODAG grant is included in this figure), in 2005, when the tenants purchase the property, it will be worth at least $15 million. Over the twenty years, the housing cooperative association will have built up about $4.8 million in equity to make the purchase. Meanwhile, the developers will profit to the tune of at least $6 million—the difference between the 1985 value and the expected value of the project in 2005.

This arrangement, said the businessperson, provides "some of the benefits of home ownership, [being] . . . sort of a cross between an apartment and a condominium." For the tenants, there is the dream of owning a share of the co-op in twenty years and the protection that the building will not be turned into condominiums at that time. The businessperson said that South Meadow is important to Burlington since "the city's goal primarily has been to try to set something up so that . . . [the project] perpetually will assure the affordability of these units."

A CEDO official agreed with the above analysis. In the past, she said, federally subsidized housing programs had proven to be primarily beneficial to their developers. The major difference between South Meadow and other federally subsidized housing projects is that once the developers sell the project to the tenants, they will then own it, not some other developer or investor. In contrast, said the CEDO official, one of the federally subsidized housing projects in Burlington, Northgate Apartments, soon will be sold because its twenty-year federal subsidy is up. The low-income people there face a difficult time if the apartments are turned into condominiums.

Northgate Apartments is Burlington's (as well as the state's) largest subsidized low-income housing complex, with 336 apartment units housing 1,500 people. Built in 1968, it is located in the city's New North End near Lake Champlain, making it a prime real estate site. After 1988, the owner of Northgate could pay off his forty-year federal government mortgage and convert the units into market-rate condominiums, or choose to sell the apartment complex. In a worst case scenario, most, if not all of the current residents of Northgate would be forced out of their homes. One-fourth of the city's "rent-subsidized housing" is represented by the Northgate development, and the Sanders administration felt obliged to help out an important part of its constituency.[21]

In late 1986, the city's Affordable Housing Task Force suggested a condominium conversion ordinance to protect beleaguered tenants in the city, with an eye toward Northgate. The Sanders administration drafted and won passage of an ordinance that put the brakes on condominium conversions and required developers to make a contribution to a special city housing trust fund.[22]

Specifically, the ordinance, which was soundly passed in March 1987, assessed "a transfer fee of four percent on the sale price" of apartments turned into condominiums that will be used to help find housing for displaced tenants and produce more "affordable housing." In addition, landlords would have to give tenants two years' advance warning (four years' warning for senior citizens and tenants with disabilities) of any condominium conversion plans. Most importantly, though, the law requires landlords to give tenants' groups or the city the "right of first refusal," that is, the first option to buy, before the units could be sold or made into condominiums.[23]

Needless to say, administration supporters and the city's tenants were pleased, while Burlington real estate developers, in general, reacted unfavorably to the new ordinance, saying it would negatively impact housing investment in the city. While it is very difficult to judge the ordinance's overall impact on the housing market, its effect on condominium conversions is clear. In the period between 1981 and 1987, before the ordinance was passed, about sixty units a year were turned into condominiums. Since the ordinance became law in March 1987, not a single landlord has notified the city about an intended condominium conversion.[24]

The city's ability to get a condominium conversion ordinance passed was also an important victory for tenants, especially those at federally subsidized, low-income housing projects like Northgate. In this case, tenants who might be displaced will now have the option to buy their units as part of an association. Residents at Northgate formed a nonprofit corporation called Northgate Non-Profit Housing to negotiate with the owner about purchasing the property.[25]

To accomplish their goal, Northgate tenants had to raise almost $22 million—$11 million to purchase the property and another $11 million to rehabilitate the apartments. The Department of Housing and Urban Development (HUD) agreed to loan Northgate Non-Profit $2 million toward the deal, and in March 1989, the Vermont Housing and Conservation Board, a state agency working on housing issues, kicked in $3 million. Through its new affordable housing fund, approved by city voters in March 1989, Burlington also loaned Northgate Non-Profit $50,000. On 28 December 1989 Northgate Non-Profit had raised the necessary funds to close the deal. Initially, Northgate will be a tenant-managed, nonprofit organization, but within fifteen years, it will become a tenant-run and tenant-owned building.[26]

Both the South Meadow Project and Northgate Non-Profit are clear efforts by the Sanders administration to provide permanent affordable housing for low- and moderate-income people in the city. Giving tenants a greater say in the collective management of their own housing units and allowing them the eventual option of purchasing their apartments lays the groundwork for creating new options of housing ownership for tenants. These projects are an important step toward changing the usual housing ownership patterns under capitalism, especially for those whose prospects of owning their own home are typically only a dream, and could be nonreformist reforms toward a democratic-socialist society.

THE BURLINGTON COMMUNITY LAND TRUST (BCLT)

The lack of affordable housing spurred other efforts by the Sanders administration as well. In late 1983, over fifty people—including bankers, realtors, lawyers, city housing specialists, members of the religious community, and tenants—packed a Burlington conference room for the first official meeting of the Burlington Community Land Trust (BCLT). In an effort to provide more affordable housing for its low- and moderate-income citizens, Burlington—with a $200,000 grant—became the first municipality in the United States to fund a community land trust.[27]

The purpose of a land trust is to make home ownership a reality for low- and moderate-income people by removing the price of land from the cost of buying a home. Instead, the land is owned "in trust" by the BCLT, which then leases it to homeowners at a very reasonable cost. The legal separation of the home from the land allows "people to get into housing that they couldn't ordinarily afford to buy," according to one BCLT board member. Since land usually amounts to 20 percent of the cost of buying a new home, said a CEDO official, home ownership becomes more of a possibility under the land trust arrangement.

Tim McKenzie, the administrator of the BCLT, best expressed the long-term significance of the community land trust:

> [The ultimate goal is to] remove a significant portion of the land in Burlington from the speculative [real estate] market forever, so that the cost of the land and its increasing value will never ever be factored into the purchase of the shelter that's built on the land. . . . [In this way], there will also be an adequate and affordable stock of housing for Burlington's low- and moderate-income people without further public subsidy.[28]

As of July 1989, the Burlington Community Land Trust had a total of eighty-five living units sitting on thirty-seven parcels of land, according to Pat Peterson, associate director of the BCLT. This amounts to less than one percent of the city's housing stock of 13,500 units. Fifty-nine of the living units are currently rentals in multifamily buildings, six of which are scheduled to become cooperatively owned in the near future. Twenty-three single family units are also part of the BCLT's housing inventory. There also are three nonprofit commercial spaces among the land trust's holdings, including its office and the Community Health Center in the Old North End.[29]

According to McKenzie, by the year 2004, the BCLT would like to own 25 percent of the residential property in Burlington. That goal is achievable, he said, if the land trust can acquire about 200 residential units per year between 1987 and the year 2004. He cautioned that his figures assumed no growth in Burlington's housing market (an unlikely prospect, he admitted). Even if this optimistic goal was realized, he stated that the land trust wouldn't meet the needs of all of Burlington's low- and moderate-income residents because 40 percent of the city's population can't get housing without having to pay out more than 30 percent of their income in housing costs.[30]

The operating philosophy of the land trust, said McKenzie, is that some amount of affordable housing should be available to the Burlington community in perpetuity. Housing should be viewed as a basic right and not a privilege, according to this philosophy, and therefore land should be seen as a "community resource" rather than something from which to make a profit. "Land itself was not created of any human effort, there's no equity anybody put into that land in the first place, so it's fundamentally wrong to be taking all this equity out of the land, and doing it over and over and over again," he said.[31]

The idea for the BCLT began germinating toward the end of 1982. Initially, it was hoped that the land trust would be funded through the Community Development Block Grant program, a federal government program that gives money to community projects aiding low- and moderate-income people. Land trust officials made a request for $400,000 to the city's block grant committee to provide for initial funding. The proposal went through a detailed review by several different groups, including the Neighborhood Planning Assemblies and various aldermanic committees. Although the land trust proposal had cleared these hurdles without major problems, it turned out that in the 1983 Community Development Block Grant funding year, there were simply too many good proposals to fund the land trust out of this pool of federal money. So, to get money for the land trust, it was necessary to secure both Sanders's and the Board of Aldermen's support for it from general city revenues, specifically the recently discovered $1.9 million in surplus funds.[32]

Doing so initially proved difficult. According to McKenzie, the mayor was skeptical of the proposal. The reason, said McKenzie, is that Sanders at first didn't quite see the long-term implications of the land trust. "Bernie wants something that's going to help a lot of people—and tomorrow," McKenzie explained.[33]

The Sunday before the scheduled aldermanic vote on the city budget, McKenzie had a discussion with Peter Clavelle, director of the CEDO, about the land trust and Sanders's reluctance to support it. Both Clavelle and Jonathan Leopold, Jr., then spoke to the mayor that afternoon. Their persuasive arguments convinced Sanders to support the land trust idea. They also decided that $200,000 would be taken from surplus money in the general fund. The Board of Aldermen agreed to go along with this proposal, but because some of the board members had reservations, the CEDO was put in charge of the project and the money.[34]

The BCLT purchased its first piece of real estate—a single-family home—in summer 1984. According to the daily paper, Kathy Nielson bought the home for $40,000, though the market value of the home was $60,000. In addition, she was able to secure a below-market-rate mortgage through the land trust. (The land trust also provides a potential homeowner access to bank financing for their new home.)[35]

If Nielson ever sold the house, the amount of profit she would make could not exceed 25 percent (it used to be 10 percent) of the increased value of the home (no profit can be realized from the increased value of the land). Furthermore, the next purchaser of the home must be someone in similar economic circumstances or the land trust itself. McKenzie said that while "it's substantially cheaper to own [a home] through the land trust . . . there are substantially less economic benefits should you ever decide to sell."[36]

The land trust has targeted Burlington's Old North End neighborhood for the bulk of its activities because of the area's low- and moderate-income population and the problem of gentrification. McKenzie said that the land trust "tries to give preference to long-term residents of Burlington . . . that are in danger of displacement."[37]

The BCLT has taken the original $200,000 grant from the city and leveraged about twenty times that amount to do its work. This has been accomplished with some Community Development Block Grants, loans at low-interest rates or with no interest from various church groups and socially responsible investors, and donations and support from a wide range of sources, including banks, businesses, churches, and realtors. The net result, said McKenzie, is that "as we acquire properties, the corporation [that is, the BCLT] is acquiring assets, against which [we] can . . . borrow . . . to get more money."[38]

In May 1987, the BCLT received $150,000 from the city's block grant program to augment its property acquisitions, said McKenzie. At that time too, it received a $1 million credit line from the Burlington Employees Retirement system when the Board of Aldermen instructed that all city funds be divested from corporations doing business in South Africa and instead be invested in the local community.[39] As of June 1989, the land trust had about $3.7 million in assets and $2.8 million in liabilities, according to one BCLT official.

The BCLT has had its share of controversies. Some realtors in Burlington were suspicious of the land trust, although almost all of the BCLT's property transactions have gone through the realty community, according to McKenzie, and some individual realtors have been supportive of the idea. "I think the general realty community is

very apprehensive of the land trust [because] . . . it's [in] . . . their inherent best interest to see property [values] continue to rise," he said.[40]

For example, Janet Dunn, a realtor in Burlington, wrote *The Burlington Free Press* and said:

> If I believed that there should be no private ownership of land, I
> would be bragging to the world that in Burlington, VT., my
> wildest dreams had come true. I would proclaim that a vehicle
> designed to remove a substantial quantity of land from private
> ownership is operational in Burlington, called the Burlington
> Community Land Trust. . . .
>
> If you believe that one of the most precious rights we, as
> individuals, have in our country is the right to own land, a right
> protected by our Constitution, then you should take a long, hard
> look at this land trust.[41]

Homeowners also have opposed the idea of a land trust. "Some
Burlington homeowners . . . have written letters and picketed land
trust meetings, denouncing the trust as socialistic and as likely to
undermine land values," according to *The Burlington Free Press*. For
example, the BCLT was planning to develop and manage forty homes
on land donated by two developers in Burlington, John Varsames and
Roderick Whittier. The land trust worked out a complex deal between
the CEDO and the two developers, who would build 200 high-priced
condominiums on land (part of which was donated by the city) close
to the lake. In exchange, the developers would build forty affordable
houses, known as the Howe Meadows Project, in the city's New North
End (see Chapter 4).[42]

The plan, however, met with strong neighborhood protest. New
North End homeowners near the Howe Meadows site organized a
group called Homeowners Against the Land Trust (HALT) in opposition to the project, fearing it would drive down their property values.
One evening, about twelve HALT members staged a protest before a
meeting of the Board of Aldermen to discuss the proposed project. The
BCLT decided to compromise, agreeing to develop and manage only
nine of the donated lots.[43] According to one progressive alderman, it
required a coalition of "Republicans and progressives working together" to finally pass this compromise measure at a Board of Aldermen meeting.

There is a small right-wing element in the Burlington community
who "are rabidly against the land trust [because they feel that] . . . this
is the communist revolution . . . right here in our own back yard,"
McKenzie explained. He then added: "We get red-baited every day by
those folks," but added that "when you get a chance to sit down and

talk to people on a one-to-one basis, they understand what we're doing."[44]

McKenzie admits the land trust is a "very radical" and "socialist" concept because "its primary goal is social benefit as opposed to individual gain." And while it involves engaging in some "unholy alliances" (that is, with the banks), he said: "It's a definite challenge to the way we think about a very fundamental thing" [that is, land]. He concluded by stating that "land reform is where most revolutions start." Given McKenzie's remarks, it is surprising that the land trust hasn't drawn a more negative reaction. In fact, the BCLT enjoys almost unanimous support across the political spectrum.[45]

Mayor Sanders viewed the land trust as a cutting-edge initiative.[46] One administration official commented: "What we attempted to do [with the creation of the land trust] is to achieve long-term structural changes in our whole model of home ownership." One CEDO official also was enthusiastic: "By far and away, the most exceptional thing that we've done in housing and the most lasting effect that it will have on city housing is the Burlington Community Land Trust." One Progressive Coalition member stated that "the community land trust . . . is probably the best [housing initiative] . . . and probably one of the most revolutionary ways of providing housing for low- and mod- erate- income people." She continued by saying that over the long haul it "has the biggest potential for socialist change in the city." Among progressives, only one was less than enthusiastic. He said: "The land trust . . . is nice . . . [but] the problem [of housing] is really a structural problem [and thus the land trust approach] . . . seems to be Band-Aids."

Burlington's Democrats, who often criticized the Sanders admin- istration on housing issues, had fairly positive things to say about the land trust. For example, one party activist said that the land trust would not have much of an effect on the housing problem in Burlington because so few units were involved. But he said that it was "a very good idea . . . to create more affordable housing." Moreover, he added: "Over the long term, the land trust may have a big impact" and it is "definitely a . . . socially enlightened idea or socialist idea."

Even Republicans and members of Burlington's business commu- nity had favorable reactions. One party official called it "a good idea," saying that "it's a better relationship to one's home than perhaps being a renter." He also said he had no "philosophical problems" with the concept. Most members of the business community also were suppor- tive of the land trust. One banker saw the BCLT as a "very progressive type of concept" but didn't "really see the land trust as being the epitome of socialism." He commented: "Across the board, we've gotten some very good cooperation from the bankers in town." He also added that the BCLT would not "destroy the marketplace" and would "have [only a] marginal impact on property values." Two Burlington realtors also expressed some support for the BCLT. One said he backed it even though the land trust wasn't in his "self- interest," while the other commented that he supported the idea of the land trust.

However, one business analyst expressed some reservations. He said that while the idea sounded good and might even "create afford-able housing," a major drawback for homeowners was that they would only lease the land, not purchase it. Consequently, since a homeowner only built up limited equity, it would be difficult for them to buy a more expensive house later on.

The reasons for the relative lack of opposition, compared to other administration initiatives, are three-fold. First, the fact that Burlington is the first city in the country to fund a land trust out of its treasury makes it notable, and because of the way it initially was financed, the opposition on the Board of Aldermen was unable to effectively block it. Second, the land trust is so small at this stage that it doesn't really threaten the interests of the city's "power elites." In other words, most of those one would expect to be opposed to the concept of the land trust have not been directly affected by it. Finally, many people recog-nize the difficulty average Americans are having in securing homes, and that it is in the self-interest of groups like bankers, for example, to explore other financial arrangements for home buyers.

Of all the initiatives fostered by the CEDO, the BCLT has been one of the most successful, and probably the most radical, nonreformist reform in both conception and execution. Success can be credited to the personal drive and motivation of McKenzie. He took early charge of the BCLT and committed the time and provided the necessary direction to make the project work.

In many other cities, people have had to fight their own city hall to get support for local land trusts. Nevertheless, over the past fifteen years, land trusts have formed in about a dozen states as diverse as California, Connecticut, Maine, Massachusetts, New Jersey, Ohio, Ten-nessee, and Texas. Often, churches take the lead in their development. Now that the Sanders administration has funded and promoted a land trust, many municipalities across the country are looking to Burling-ton for information, guidance, and inspiration, said McKenzie. In September 1986, the BCLT was recognized by the United Nations as having made a unique contribution to helping solve the housing problem faced by poor people. As part of the 1987 "International Year of Shelter for the Homeless," the BCLT was one of seventeen out of 180 projects studied by HUD that received the U.N. award.[47]

In addition to serving an important social goal—decent housing for everyone—the land trust is in stride with the socialist theme of public ownership. The land trust's property is not subject to market forces, and the necessity of privately owning a piece of land (which in our society is the sine qua non of owning your own home), is removed. As a result, the possibility of home ownership is open to low- and moderate-income people. Because housing should be a fundamental right, any endeavor that helps make it more affordable for low- and moderate-income people can be viewed as a step toward socialism on the municipal level.

However, by McKenzie's own admission, the land trust has fallen short in providing affordable housing to the poor. The recent move toward purchasing and selling apartments to renters in multi-unit dwellings was an attempt to address this issue. No longer would low-income renters be at the whim of landlords or threatened with eviction from public housing units once the federal subsidies are gone.

While the BCLT strives toward affordable housing, it does nothing to challenge the notion of the private ownership of living space. The next step must be to proclaim housing as a public good, provided, for example, by a local housing trust, the state, or the federal government. Of course, the massive public housing projects created by the federal government in the 1960s and 1970s were an attempt to do this, but they failed in many ways, most notably in that they weren't a permanent arrangement for many of the renters. Under a capitalist economic order, the goal of public housing for everyone will never be achieved. But at the very least, a mixture of the three possible options—private ownership of home and land, private ownership of home but public ownership of land, and the public ownership of both home and land—should be available, based on people's needs and desires.

WORKER OWNERSHIP AND WORKER SELF-MANAGEMENT

In an effort to "turn corporate hierarchy upside down,"[48] the Sanders administration initiated a city program—the Burlington Local Ownership Development Project—that encourages worker ownership of small businesses. In summer 1984, the CEDO formed the Burlington Local Ownership Advisory Board. From this, the Local Ownership Project was born. One of its goals was "to start up locally owned and controlled businesses . . . [with] job creation strategies . . . specifically targeted to low-income female heads of households and working class youth." Furthermore, the project was intended to help existing Burlington businesses become worker-owned if they so desired.[49]

Though Burlington's overall unemployment rate was among the lowest in the United States in 1988, one CEDO official said, there are several groups of people—poor, single women who are raising families, young adults from a working-class background, and "frustrated yuppies"—who either have no employment or only part-time employment. The issue for Burlington, he said, was therefore the "quality of jobs." To deal with this issue, the CEDO "developed a range of strategies which attempted to address the unique problems of those groups."

Worker ownership, according to this CEDO official, means "talking about structural reform of the economy . . . [and] promoting a new model for [the] ownership of businesses." There weren't many city governments across the country supporting such nonreformist reforms, according to another CEDO official. It wasn't until the 1985 legislative session, said Bruce Seifer (who is in charge of the Local Ownership Project), that the CEDO successfully lobbied in a quiet way to make it legally possible for worker-owned businesses to be recognized under state law. With this accomplished, it became much easier for worker-owned businesses to operate, and the CEDO began to actively explore this option with several business enterprises in the city.[50]

With a lot of community education and outreach, including several community forums, Seifer was able to interest a lot of businesses in the possibility of restructuring themselves as worker-owned cooperatives. The idea behind worker ownership is to encourage "economic democracy," according to Seifer. Having workers exert collective control over the management and the operation of their own businesses should at least theoretically make them more productive, responsible, and happy. Seifer was not surprised at the interest expressed in this alternative form of business ownership. "There are 8,000 companies [in the United States] that have some form of worker ownership . . . [and] 10 million people that work for these companies . . . so it's a growing trend [and] every major magazine in the country had a cover story on it in the last year and a half," he said.[51]

Since 1983, more than seventy-five businesses have shown interest in the idea of worker ownership, from a computer consulting firm to an auto repair company. While two businesses (Wild Oats and Leading Energy) converted to worker ownership, they eventually failed. As of December 1989, one business (Data Systems) is in the process of converting to worker ownership, while two others are exploring the possibility of conversion.[52]

It is instructive to look at why one of the worker-owned businesses failed. In fall 1986, Wild Oats, a retail store specializing in maternity clothes, officially became the first worker-owned and worker-controlled business in Burlington. But according Seifer, this venture was short-lived; by June 1987, one-half of the business was sold back to the owner, and the other half was sold to a Canadian investor to raise more capital to expand the company. However, by 1988 the business folded for lack of capital, said Seifer.[53]

Seifer, however, was optimistic about the long-term prospects of the Local Ownership Project: "We're trying to restructure the way people do business . . . and it's a long-term development project. It's a long-term strategy of the Sanders administration and I think it's going to work; it takes years and years and years to change the way people do business." He did say, though, that the CEDO was now looking at a "broader approach" to the concept, including democratic and non-democratic Employee Stock Ownership Plans (ESOPs) and profit-sharing arrangements between owners and workers. While the conversion of existing business to worker ownership was still a viable strategy, the start-up of new worker-owned businesses was no longer a major focus of the project's work.[54]

Surprisingly, the banks in Burlington have been more than willing to cooperate with the city in helping to finance and support the local ownership project. Seifer said:

> It's advantageous for them [the banks] to work with us because we can access public funds to help bring good projects that they want to do [but] are a little risky for them . . . so if they can marry or work [in] a partnership with the public sector where the public sector comes in and also provides some of the financing, it reduces the risk, it helps with the collateral coverage they're worried about, . . . and it's profitable for them. . . . They realize that by working together, it will be good for everybody; it's a win-win situation.[55]

There have been quite a few inquiries from around the country on the Burlington experiment with worker ownership. "It's unique," Seifer said, "because there's no place else [no other municipality] in the country that's running a local ownership development project and we have been recognized in national publications as being a unique program to look at." In 1987, the Local Ownership Project received a national award from the U.S. Conference of Mayors for its innovative approach.[56]

The worker ownership project has received somewhat mixed reviews in Burlington, even among Progressive Coalition members. Sanders said that the project "is clearly a radical socialist initiative that you're not going to find in too many other communities."[57] One

Progressive Coalition alderman said it was a good project, while a Progressive Coalition member said that she wasn't "sure how successful it's been . . . [but that it] potentially could be [important]." The most negative comment came from another coalition member, who simply said: "I don't think that the worker ownership project has done a lot."

One activist said it was one of the administration's "major accomplishments." Another felt that "the emphasis on workers' cooperatives will pass by the wayside" in light of plans to develop the waterfront because there simply won't be enough capital to finance both types of development. One progressive critic, while in favor of "municipal ownership," believed that locally owned businesses would simply foster "a more capitalistic spirit."

In addition to the South Meadow Project, Northgate Non-Profit Housing, and the Burlington Community Land Trust, worker ownership had the potential to be another one of the nonreformist reforms pursued by the Sanders administration. In this case, traditional forms of business ownership are challenged. This CEDO program is an attempt to eliminate the internal hierarchical management structure through the workers' collective ownership of their enterprises. A company where workers have equal investment in *and* control over operations (that is, one worker, one vote), is progressive. Under this scenario, workers participate in and make decisions on all the issues affecting their work lives, a radical departure from the way business tends to operate today.[58]

Of course, worker ownership has taken different forms around the country in the past decade or so—with some forms being less progressive than others. For example, promoting worker ownership through worker buy-outs like ESOPs, especially in ailing companies, is not particularly progressive, and certainly is not socialistic, since the workers, even if they have a majority interest in the stock, usually have little direct control over the company. In most of these cases, management controls things as usual, and the company's board of directors is not accountable to nor representative of the workers.[59]

Some would argue that worker ownership is not socialistic, but instead "workers' capitalism." However, if this is true, then the Yugoslav economic model (which is based, to a large extent, on worker ownership of industry) would be capitalist rather than socialist, an argument few socialists would concur with. Although Burlington's attempt at worker ownership occurs in a capitalist economic system, it is still a nonreformist reform since the workers own the means of production and may even decide how the productive capacity is utilized and what kinds of products are manufactured and sold.

Of course, the means of production are not publicly owned and managed by the state, and perhaps the products being produced are not in the best interests of society as a whole. But this isn't necessarily bad. Under worker ownership, the owner-employees certainly have more of an investment in their work and their products when they own the company and make the important decisions concerning its welfare. Experience shows that public or state ownership of the means of production does not guarantee either worker control or public control over what is produced, as seen in Eastern Europe and the Soviet Union, at least until recently. Moreover, even if state ownership of large industry was possible and could be made beneficial to workers and society, there would still be room for worker ownership of small business enterprises.

In Burlington, the model of worker ownership fostered by the CEDO has encouraged movement toward more humane methods of organizing and controlling work. Given the nonreformist reform character of worker ownership and control, it is understandable that things would move slowly. However, the worker ownership project has recently faltered.

Unlike the land trust, the Local Ownership Project is still formally tied to the CEDO, and is therefore dependent on it for staff time and financial resources. The disadvantages of this dependency point to the need for a community development-type corporation outside of the CEDO. The CEDO made a step in that direction when it contemplated the creation of the Burlington Local Development Corporation in 1987. As a private, nonprofit corporation, the Local Development Corporation could have promoted worker-owned businesses and could have raised its own capital.[60] While the city attorney's office is looking at the possibility of setting up a separate nonprofit Local Development Project, its future is uncertain, given probable staffing and funding problems. In the meantime, the Burlington Community Development Corporation (which is really the city's Finance Board) has tried to play this role, but with limited success, said one CEDO official.

Worker ownership does not seem to threaten the Burlington business community and has faced little opposition. The business community's lack of concern over the worker ownership project is perhaps the strongest evidence of its small impact on the community. For the most part, the program is invisible and does not seem to compete for existing capital resources. The recent trend of the Local Ownership Project indicates that unlike the BCLT, it is not likely to raise the ire of the business community in years to come. The primary function of the worker ownership component has been educational; many people and businesses in the Greater Burlington area are now aware of it and see it as a resource. Also, the state of Vermont now recognizes worker cooperative corporations as a legal entity, according to Seifer.[61]

CONCLUSION

Clearly the Sanders administration attempted to alter ownership patterns in the city of Burlington, and in some cases, succeeded in adopting innovative forms of homeowners', tenants', and workers' ownership. While none of these potentially radical reforms is socialistic in and of itself, the pattern that emerges is one of challenging the existing order of things, both in terms of consciousness and of practice. It is too early to tell whether these attempts are sufficiently strong to create a ripple in the sea of capitalism—at least in Burlington. In what was perhaps his boldest initiative, Sanders lost the fight to municipalize cable television, an obvious blow to his socialist aspirations. However, his administration, primarily through the work of the CEDO, did successfully challenge the prevailing modus operandi in housing and employment, thereby realizing some of the possibilities of local socialism.

Taxes and the Redistribution of Wealth

During his tenure as mayor of Burlington, Bernard Sanders probably championed tax reform—and having big business pay its fair share of taxes—more than any other issue. No other issue so clearly strikes to the heart of city-state relations and the disproportionate tax burden of different classes.

Despite Vermont's tradition of town meeting, cities and towns are literally creatures of the state and therefore beholden to it in many ways. Perhaps most importantly, the only taxing power that most cities and towns in Vermont have is the property tax, which, by many accounts, is a regressively based tax, hurting those who can least afford it the most. Since Vermont is not a "home rule" state—that is, its towns and municipalities cannot alter their own charters without the approval of the state legislature—there are constant tensions between local and state interests over taxing powers, as most municipalities are entirely dependent on the property tax to fund most local government activities.

It is within this context that we must look at Sanders's battles over taxes. As the mayor of the state's largest city, he was one of the major advocates of changing the power relationships between towns or cities and the state and of the redistribution of wealth between rich and poor. Thus, battles over reappraisal, the gross receipts tax, payment in lieu of taxes from tax-exempt entities, property tax reclassification, and the excavation fee all could have been anticipated. That Sanders was able to win on several of these issues, which has redistributed the tax burden between the haves and the have-nots to some degree and fundamentally changed the dialogue between local and state government in Vermont, was certainly to his credit.

GENERAL PROPERTY TAXES AND PROPERTY TAX
REBATE PLAN

Steve Jeffrey, head of the Vermont League of Cities and Towns, has stated that "nationally . . . the property tax accounts for 30.7 percent of all state and local taxes, but the figure in Vermont is 43.2 percent."[1] Thus, the property tax burden hit hard at Vermonters, especially low- and moderate-income homeowners.

Sanders has opposed "the property tax as a viable way for local government to operate either for education or for municipal services. It's a regressive, absurd tax," he said, because low- and moderate-income people who own property have to pay it regardless of their ability to do so. As it is currently structured, the property tax proportionally taxes those with different income levels at the same rate.[2]

Because of Sanders's strong position on this issue, Burlington taxpayers have not really experienced a property tax increase for general city government expenditures since his election in 1981. That year, he requested and got from Burlington taxpayers a 25-cent property tax increase for local government costs—40 cents less than former mayor Gordon Paquette's proposed tax hike. Moreover, in 1983 Sanders implemented a 7-cent property tax decrease for city government expenditures. There was a slight property tax decrease for cost associated with city government in 1987, but this was offset by an equivalent tax increase in 1988.[3]

Sanders's ability to hold the line on property tax increases has made him a popular politician in Burlington. Keeping property taxes steady or even decreasing them has traditionally been a Republican theme, but often at the expense of limiting city services and social programs. Sanders, on the other hand, has kept taxes down while increasing city services. In the process, he has built a base of support that cuts across traditional political lines, forging a new model of municipal government.

Although the property tax as a primary funding source for local government is widely disliked, holding the line on increases has limited the administration's options. Because municipalities lack "home rule," cities have to request permission from the state legislature to levy additional taxes not granted in their city charter. If Burlington had home rule, it could implement any tax it desired within reason.

One administration insider explained that "the relationship between the municipalities and the state is one of the most subordinated and centralized in the country." He lambasted the Vermont legislature for claiming that "local control" existed in towns and cities in Vermont. Said this insider: "You get local control to decide whether you're going to raise regressive taxes or fire teachers. . . . You have local control as long as the range of decisions is essentially meaningless and are really . . . housekeeping decisions." He argued that the state legislature ran interference with local communities when it came to the big decisions around money. He said: "We're going to be talking about tax reform until we're blue in the face. It's not there in the political equation right now because it's basically a politically conservative mood out there."

One newspaper reporter said that Sanders had done a lot to raise the issue with the state legislature, showing how the state relied too heavily on the property tax. He commented: "He [Sanders] has been at the forefront—it's been an accomplishment of his—he has changed the focus of the debate in Vermont over how towns can pay for what they do . . . [and] the unfairness of the property tax."

Although Sanders received high marks from many for refusing to raise property taxes, the praise has not been unanimous. A newspaper editor voiced a criticism heard from several Democratic and Republican aldermen as well:

Even when people talk about "Well, he's [Sanders] held down taxes,"what he's done is [find] a back door approach . . . in lieu of taxes. . . . Very few people even understand that [when] . . . you have indirect taxation (for example, utility fees go up and the utility then pays the money to the city) . . . it allows the city not to ask for a tax increase.

And at least one critic chastised Sanders for his position on the property tax because it benefited the wrong people. Said this Republican:

The [Sanders] policy of holding down property taxes has benefited that group [yuppies] more than it's benefited the low-income people, in my opinion. A lot of his policies are focused on the property tax as not a reasonable choice for funding city services. When you look at . . . his alternatives, [they] are less progressive than the property tax. . . .

Bernie should be utilizing programs available, for example, property tax relief, and raise property taxes to increase revenues—[this is] a better strategy. His taxes are 20 to 30 percent below most other cities in the state, including . . . Montpelier; in some cases, 60 percent lower than places like Springfield. . . .

I just think he's stupid with respect to his own interests. . . . He could have a much bigger tax base today than he has and he can have his low-income folks much better taken care of than they are. . . . He could have a high quality, high property tax, high relief strategy that was very good for the city and didn't hurt the low-income people. But he didn't have the political courage to do that, so he's crippled services, he's let things decline, and he always looks like he's fighting the right fight.

Those in the business community definitely felt that Vermont's rebate program made the property tax at least neutral, if not progressive in nature. For example, one business analyst said:

With the rebate program . . . for people with incomes under $20,000, the property tax becomes a progressive tax . . . because the percentage of income that's going to pay taxes is less for lower income [people] than for the higher income [people].
Now a regressive tax is considered any tax that takes a larger proportion of income from the low income as against the higher income. Basically, it [the property tax] is a regressive tax if you don't have a rebate plan.

One critic had this criticism of Sanders's neglect of the property tax rebate program:

The current property tax relief program, which they [the state of Vermont] just expanded, is really geared to the people he's [Sanders] talking about—poor people, working people, and elderly people who are renters or who own their home. There is quite a program—and there has been for ten years in this state—a property tax relief program for those people that gives you the money right back on your tax form. . . .
It's one program Bernie would not publicize [and] . . . the progressives ignore it because it was passed by the dirty Democrats. . . . They've [Sanders and the Progressive Coalition] always downplayed it because they can't take credit for it and they don't want to point to a good thing Democrats have done.

One academician said that studies have been inconclusive on whether or not the property tax is regressive. Some indicated that it was a regressive tax, others said the opposite. She was unaware of any data base concerning the number of people who seek property tax rebates, but added that given the state's rebate program, it was debatable whether the property tax was regressive. In her opinion, holding down property taxes was probably beneficial to the poor and rich alike.

The mayor's views of the property tax rebate program was that it was vastly underfunded, with minimal increases in funding over the years, and that it provided relief to only about 2 percent of the population. While it might adequately take care of the "lowest-income users," said Sanders, it does little to help moderate-income people. He did admit, however, that if the program was significantly changed, that is, if less restrictive eligibility requirements were passed and a lot more money was put into it, that it was possible to "neutralize" the regressive nature of the property tax. But he thought this was unlikely to happen.[4]

While property taxes are regressive in nature, it is unclear whether they adversely affect low-income people in Burlington because of the state's rebate plan. Clearly, though, not everyone who is eligible for the plan takes advantage of it. It is more certain that the property tax system does not benefit moderate-income people, since their income is too low to ignore its bite but too high to qualify for a rebate. Given these considerations, Sanders's refusal to raise property taxes and his attempts to find alternative sources of funds can be understood.

REAPPRAISAL

Burlington homeowners, who saw only one general property tax increase during the Sanders years, did experience other increases in the property tax due to reappraisal. Soon after Sanders took office, Burlington faced a citywide reappraisal of all city property for the first time in twenty years. Burlington stood to lose over half a million dollars in state aid to education if it did not reappraise its property to comply with a new state law mandating reappraisals at least every ten years. The daily newspaper reported that those who owned homes in Burlington's newer developments (for example, the New North End) already had their property valued at much higher rates than did people who owned their homes in the older parts of town (such as the Old North End).[5]

Eventually, a deal was worked out with the Burlington School Board whereby it "would lend the city money for the reappraisal," which was to take two years. This action was approved by the Board of Aldermen. It was anticipated that "the effects [of reappraisal would] be felt most sharply by low-income and elderly residents." As a result, the Progressive Coalition devised a charter change to help mitigate the worst effects of reappraisal on poor and elderly residents—one which would allow the city to provide local tax breaks to senior citizens. Said one Progressive Coalition alderman: "We [the Progressive Coalition] want to allow reappraisal to take place and minimize its impact on low- and fixed-income owners." However, the state legislature refused to allow Burlington to change its city charter to ameliorate the new tax burden on poor and elderly homeowners.[6]

As the date for the implementation of reappraisal approached, members of the Progressive Coalition were anxious. Alderman Terrill Bouricius, whose constituency was from the Old North End, commented: "Because reappraisal will cause the tax burden to shift from commercial to residential properties, more than half of the city's residents could pay more taxes even with no increase in the tax rate."[7]

When the reappraisal results were released, the impact on low- and moderate-income people was worse than expected. Three of four homeowners in Burlington saw the value of their homes substantially increase. According to assistant city attorney John Franco, the biggest jump was in the Old North End, where the average rise was almost 100 percent. "Taxes on a third of those homes [rose] more than 150 percent," he said. Even the New North End was hit hard—about three-quarters of the houses saw increases in their property valuation averaging over 50 percent.[8]

As a consequence of reappraisal, there was "an average increase for residential taxpayers of 20 percent and a decrease for businesses of 15 percent." Some businesses in town experienced significant property tax decreases due to reappraisal. For example, General Electric saw its property tax bill drop "from $253,883 to $197,711—a reduction of $56,172 or 22.1 percent."[9]

Mayor Sanders was incensed about the reappraisal's effect on the majority of Burlingtonians. According to Sanders, "preliminary figures show commercial and industrial taxpayers will bear about $1.9 million less of Burlington's tax burden during the coming fiscal year, and residential taxpayers will pay that much more." He accused the state legislature of "intentionally shifting the tax burden from wealthy and powerful corporations to poor and working people" by mandating reappraisal.[10]

In assessing the reason for reappraisal and its impact on the city, one administration insider reflected:

> The reappraisal was supported and mandated by the Democrats and Republicans all the way down the line. We were forced to do it; we were going to lose substantial hunks of state aid money if we didn't do it, plus there were threats of class action suits and taxpayers' action suits.
>
> From a policy point of view, reappraisal was a disaster. It shifted tax burdens away from large commercial and industrial taxpayers onto residential taxpayers and hurt poor and working-class neighborhoods the most.

This insider also commented that reappraisal was "local Reaganomics: You take the burden off of corporations and you put it onto residential taxpayers in the most regressive form of taxation [that is, property taxes] that exists."

Most critics of Sanders's position on the property tax fail to mention the adverse effect of reappraisal on low- and moderate-income homeowners and the benefits reaped by the more wealthy homeowners of Burlington and the business community. Reappraisal, then, served to reinforce the regressive tendency of the property tax.

ALTERNATIVES TO THE PROPERTY TAX

Background

Sanders has spent much time and energy championing alternatives to the property tax. During his 1981 campaign he raised the possibility of a city income tax, but quickly dropped the idea after his election, realizing that the constraints on municipal taxing power in Vermont made it an unrealistic option. Said Sanders: "Taxing wealth and income is the most progressive [alternative]. . . . I can do neither, we don't have the power."[11]

Sanders set up a tax study committee shortly after his first election to explore possible tax alternatives. This committee, headed by Jennie Stoler Versteeg, an economics professor at a local college, recommended a citywide reappraisal and suggested that Burlington look at "new ways of raising money to support city government." The committee proposed three different ways to help fund local government: (1) taxing the city's bars, restaurants, arcades, and cable television (that is, a gross receipts tax); (2) getting payments from the University of Vermont in lieu of taxes; and (3) requesting permission from the state legislature to implement a tax classification scheme so that businesses paid more and homeowners paid less property taxes.[12]

Gross Receipts Tax / Rooms and Meals Tax

The gross receipts, or rooms and meals tax, was probably the most important and hardest-fought tax proposal put forth by the Sanders administration. The administration's gross receipts tax proposal was often referred to, mistakenly, as a rooms and meals tax. The difference between the two is important, said one administration insider, because the former is a tax permitted by the city charter while the latter is a "rider on the state sales tax" (thereby requiring both a charter change and legislative approval). Part of the confusion stems from the fact that the second phase of this alternative tax battle was in the form of a rooms and meals tax.

The long battle for the gross receipts tax began in early 1982. At that time, Joseph McNeil, the city attorney, issued a legal opinion saying "Burlington has the power to become the first Vermont municipality to raise local taxes with a room and meals [sic] tax." The city attorney stated that a 1949 provision in the city charter permitted Burlington "to tax restaurant meals, tavern drinks and hotel rooms." However, he also pointed out that since Burlington only existed as a legal entity through the grace of the Vermont legislature, it could decide to take that taxing power away from Burlington.[13]

Sanders was quick to move on this issue. He asked the Board of Aldermen to immediately implement the gross receipts tax provision of the city charter, which he saw as a major alternative to the "regressive" property tax. Assistant city attorney John Franco calculated that for every 1 percent increment in the gross receipts tax, the city could bring in about $300,000.[14]

From the time the idea was first raised, it met with stiff opposition from state officials. R. Paul Wickes, legal counsel to then Governor Richard Snelling and head of Burlington's Marketplace Commission, warned against implementation of a tax which "could hurt downtown business." Then Republican Governor Snelling publicly stated his opposition to the tax, too. Peter Guiliani, a state representative in charge of the powerful House Ways and Means Committee, said: "I think the Legislature will be very reluctant to establish a precedent for allowing a local tax the state already levies."[15]

While lobbying at the statehouse to prevent the revocation of a charter provision allowing the tax, Sanders told lawmakers:

I think it's perhaps time that there be changes in the way cities and towns raise revenue. We're asking your help in providing the city of Burlington and other towns and cities in the state [a chance] to stabilize or lower their property taxes by bringing in revenue from additional sources they don't have right now. . . . We think, in general, it is right for cities and towns to have that freedom.[16]

In the meantime, Sanders was courting support in Burlington. First, he got approval for the idea from the Burlington Finance Board. He then told the Board of Aldermen that if it approved the measure, he would lower the city's general tax rate by 3 cents. If not, it would be necessary to increase the city's tax rate by 34 cents to bring in the necessary revenues to offset an anticipated half-million-dollar deficit in Burlington's finances for the coming year, the mayor said.[17]

The city's restauranteurs soon began to organize against the proposal, citing the administration's "anti-business" attitude. Eventually,
the restauranteurs, with the support of the city's hotel owners, formed
the Burlington Restaurant and Hotel Association to help fight the
proposed tax.[18]

But Sanders was not alone in his effort to get Burlington to pass
alternative methods of taxation. Municipal officials from ten other
cities endorsed Burlington's plan, as did the Vermont League of Cities
and Towns. Robert Stewart, the head of the league at the time, pointed
out that Burlington's proposal was a step "toward the establishment
of home rule in Vermont." He commented that many communities in
Vermont felt constrained by the state legislature's restrictions on their
taxing powers. Said Stewart: "What you saw . . . [in the legislature]
was a confrontation where one level of government was basically
nicely asking for its financial freedom, its ability to stand on its own
two feet and establish its own method of taxation." Sanders said in a
statement that "municipalities in 30 states presently have various
forms of local sales or gross receipts taxes." Furthermore, one study
indicated that forty-one states allowed their cities "home rule authority" in various matters.[19]

The daily newspaper reported that since "support for local control
has always been deep-seated in Vermont, [it was] an attitude that
could convince lawmakers that a hands-off attitude would be best."
However, if Burlington did implement a gross receipts tax, it "could
shake Vermont's government structure to its foundations, because it
would disrupt the balance of power that exists between the state and
local concerns," said the daily paper.[20]

When the state legislature took up the issue of Burlington's implementation of a gross receipts tax in accordance with its own city
charter, Sanders proved victorious. Said the daily newspaper:

> In a decision that stunned onlookers and legislators, the House
> overwhelmingly rejected a charter change that would have foiled
> plans for a city rooms-and-meals [sic] tax. The voice vote was
> interpreted as a victory for home rule. Conservatives and liberals
> teamed up to back Burlington on the grounds the Legislature
> should not amend a community's charter against their will.[21]

While Sanders was pleased with the outcome, he clearly realized
that the fight was only half over. Now, he had to push and win
approval for his plan before the Board of Aldermen. This proved to
be a much tougher and longer battle.[22]

Sanders's plan to raise almost a million dollars through a 3 percent
gross receipts tax came at a good time, it seemed, since the important

1982 municipal elections were about to happen. As it turned out, the election of three additional Progressive Coalition aldermen to the board (for a total of five supporters) was not enough to get it to consider the gross receipts tax proposal.[23]

Sanders and the Progressive Coalition then devised a strategy to indirectly force the Board of Aldermen to address the issue. Members of the Progressive Coalition started a citywide initiative measure calling for a special election on an "advisory question," an idea the board had previously rejected. Within several weeks, they gathered over 1,600 signatures (about 1,400 valid signatures were required) to place the measure on the ballot.[24]

One administration insider commented that the "advisory vote" for the gross receipts tax in the special election was "an attempt to break a political logjam that had developed in front of the Board of Aldermen" (the board refused to report the tax out of committee). With their five board seats and a strong showing at the ballot, the Progressive Coalition and the Sanders administration hoped they could muster the necessary political leverage to get the board to pass the measure. However, as the insider pointed out, even if it had been approved by the electorate and the Board of Aldermen had passed an ordinance to that effect, the measure most likely would have been tied up in the courts for years.

Meanwhile, organized opposition to the measure began to mount. Not surprisingly, the Chamber of Commerce came out against the gross receipts tax proposal. The organization issued a statement calling the tax "regressive" and said that it might do "long-term harm to the city." The newly formed Burlington Restaurant and Hotel Association said it would run a campaign against the gross receipts tax and raise over $5,000 to defeat it. The group planned to pay a California consultant, Bernie Walp, to organize the effort. (Mr. Walp had gained notoriety in some quarters of Burlington in 1981 when he ran the successful campaign against rent control.) However, opposition from restaurant owners was not unanimous. Dick Bove, an unsuccessful mayoral candidate in 1981 and owner of a popular restaurant, came out in support of the gross receipts tax, saying that it was a "tax on luxury."[25]

The opposition was charged with running a deceptive campaign. Two days before the election, one administration insider claimed that information put out by the gross receipts opponents was "purposely misleading." She said, for example, that the symbol the opposition used on their "vote no" literature gave the impression that the tax would be on all food and beverages.[26] A Progressive Coalition alderman also was upset with the opposition's "big lie campaign" against the measure. He charged them with running a campaign that confused people—leaving the impression that groceries and drinks were going to be taxed in the manner of a sales tax rather than taxing only those who ate at restaurants and drank at bars. The opposition's symbol—a "circle with a red line through the product code"—clearly conveyed the message that food would be taxed.

On election day, Sanders and his supporters were disappointed. The gross receipts tax measure lost by only forty-eight votes. While those in the Old North End (Wards 2 and 3) passed it by a healthy majority, the more well-to-do wards turned it down by significant margins.[27] One administration insider commented after the defeat that the gross receipts tax lost on the ballot because "they [the opposition] brought in the hired gun [that is, Bernie Walp] and we didn't even work for it as hard as we should have." A Progressive Coalition alderman admitted it was a serious defeat for the administration but said that "we want a rooms and meals tax [sic] of some kind . . . and we're probably going to get something sooner or later."

Sanders accused the opposition of running a campaign of lies and of spending more than $10,000 to defeat the tax plan. However, he also admitted that supporters of the measure did not work hard enough. "We did not wage a good campaign," said Sanders. The mayor commented that he still planned to fight for his proposal. However, he was willing to cut the proposed tax in half, and asked the Board of Aldermen to consider the new plan as soon as possible.[28]

Shortly after the election, the aldermanic Ordinance Committee, comprised of one Sanders supporter and two members of the opposition, sent the gross receipts tax to the full board without its blessing. In fall 1982, the board rejected it by a 7–5 vote. The mayor was willing to lower the tax even further to 1 percent, but the issue died with the vote.[29]

There was a hiatus of several years between the first and second rounds of the fight for this alternative tax in Burlington. Phase two began in earnest early in 1985. This time the measure was in the form of a rooms and meals tax, which would be used to help finance Burlington's financially troubled schools. One administration insider said that while it would have been easier, on one level, for the Sanders administration and the Progressive Coalition to try to again use the city charter provision allowing the implementation of a gross receipts tax on "innkeepers, saloons, victual houses, billboard parlors and amusement parks," even if it had passed at the board level, the administration would "then [be] in court on [a] taxpayers' action suit for three or four years." To avoid these legal complications, the administration came up with the rooms and meals tax plan the second time around. "The way we tried to cut through that," explained the insider, "is rather than doing an ordinance pursuant to our existing authority in the charter, [we wanted] . . . to piggyback onto the state rooms and meals tax, figuring [we'd] get it approved by the legislature [and] then it wo[uld not] be assailed in court."

The Burlington School Board was in a financial crunch, facing the prospect of having to ask voters for a general property tax hike of 28 cents. Instead of taking the usual route, the school board's Finance Committee suggested to the whole school board that it look at a rooms and meals tax to raise the money to offset a substantial part of their $1 million debt. The Finance Committee reasoned it was merely asking the state legislature to fufill "promises to find alternatives to property taxes" for local communities.[30]

This time, the Board of Aldermen was more receptive to the idea. The board decided to allow a citywide vote on a 1.5 percent rooms and meals tax in March 1985, assuming the school board wanted the electorate to do so. But several aldermen questioned whether the state legislature would approve the charter change even if Burlington voters passed it.[31]

Shortly after the Board of Aldermen approved the ballot item, some opposition arose. But the opposition was more muted than last time, at least on some levels. For example, restaurant owners were evenly split over the rooms and meals tax this time. Both the governor, Democrat Madeline Kunin, and the state's lieutenant governor, Republican Peter Smith, came out against the measure. The daily newspaper reported that "their reluctance highlights what appears to be growing opposition to the city's attempt to use the gross receipts [sic] tax as a way to ease its dependence on the property tax."[32]

Opposition to the idea did not prevent the school board, on a close 6–5 vote, from asking voters to approve the 1.5 percent rooms and meals tax rather than face a 28-cent general property tax hike. The Board of Aldermen abided by the school board's wish and officially placed the measure on the March 1985 ballot. Once on the ballot, there was little organized opposition to it. Most restaurant owners were convinced that even if the measure passed in Burlington, the legislature would never approve it. City and school officials campaigned hard for the rooms and meals tax proposal. Given their strong campaign and the lack of an organized opposition, the measure passed easily.[33]

While the first hurdle had been passed, the second and much tougher one had yet to begin. Said the daily newspaper:

Burlington's proposed charter changes [there were several others on the ballot, too] are controversial and their outcome is expected to be precedent-setting because they challenge the legislative mandate which regulates the revenue-sharing activities of towns and cities. In Vermont, municipalities may levy only property taxes.

However, some members of the legislature hinted that they would discuss the rooms and meals tax proposal with Burlington if the city was willing to give up some of its state educational aid. The city refused and continued to lobby hard for the tax, saying that the legislature "should respect the will of the people of Burlington." The city, however, was butting heads with the Kunin administration, which was strongly opposed to the proposed charter changes that would grant the city the power of home rule in the area of taxes.[34]

Despite a massive outpouring of support from many Burlingtonians for the charter changes, the House Municipal Corporations and Elections Committee, on an 8–2 vote, turned down the request. Said Sanders: "How can people in Vermont be asked to respect the laws passed by the Legislature when the Legislature is threatening to ignore the democratically voiced opinions of the people in the largest city in the state?" The committee did, however, refer the rooms and meals tax to another committee for its review.[35]

Even with persistent lobbying, the House Ways and Means Committee voted 11–0 against the proposal. When it came up several days later for a vote in the full House, the daily newspaper reported that "the House . . . reaffirmed its long opposition to increased local taxing powers by crushing charter changes which would have given Burlington the authority to tap new revenue sources." The reason was clear: State legislators were unwilling to relinquish control of taxation.[36]

Sanders, obviously annoyed with the state legislature, commented: "The Vermont Legislature told the people of Burlington . . . that their wishes and their views as to how they want to run their government are meaningless and the only solution to their problems is higher property taxes."[37]

One administration official assessed the fight for the rooms and meals tax in the following way. While avoiding the potential court challenge, this official reflected that "we underestimated the resistance" [in the legislature]. He used this analogy to convey his point:

When we went down there [to the legislature], it was sort of like that scene in Annie Hall where Woody Allen goes to dinner with Annie in the Midwest (she comes from a very WASP[ish], Protestant background), and they're all sitting around the Sunday dinner and looking at him and they're seeing a rabbi with a beard, hat and whole bit, but he's not wearing any of those things.

When we were down there, they [the legislators] were looking at us and seeing Fidel Castro. . . . It didn't matter what you said— they weren't hearing us.

A Progressive Coalition alderman commented that the whole idea behind the rooms and meals tax was to "get people paying taxes who can afford paying it . . . versus low-income people who have to pay it [that is, the property tax]." He said that he was surprised by the degree of resistance in the legislature since a lot of municipalities around the country have taxing powers: "It's not the most radical thought in the world."

The third round in the fight for an alternative to the property tax, again as a gross receipts tax, began in fall 1985. Burlington, like many other cities across the country, was anticipating revenue shortfalls—as much as $1 million—due to the cutback in federal revenue sharing funds. In response, Sanders set up a business committee in the city to explore different alternatives for raising money. Sanders declared that he wanted to prevent antagonism from the business community concerning his alternative tax ideas: "We no longer accept the situation where we will be opposed and opposed and opposed. . . . We will initiate a dialogue to see in what ways [we can] develop new sources of revenues." Pat Robins, a prominent member of the business community, immediately praised Sanders's action.[38]

After several meetings, the business task force was ready to make its recommendations. Surprisingly, one of the committee's proposals was a 1 percent gross receipts tax on Burlington's eating places, amusement arcades, and theaters, and a 2 percent gross receipts tax on Burlington's hotels. The new tax would bring over half a million dollars a year into the city coffers. A sunset provision also was built into the proposal; if an equally lucrative alternative to the gross receipts tax was found, it would be dropped. In addition, two other alternative tax proposals—a property tax classification system and the removal of the tax-exempt status of the University of Vermont and the Medical Center Hospital of Vermont— also were proposed. These combined proposals were almost identical to those suggested by Sanders's 1981 tax study committee. The administration speculated that the three initiatives combined would bring over $2 million into city coffers, while the removal of the inventory tax (another committee proposal) would drop city revenues by over half a million dollars, bringing a total increase in city revenues to about $1.5 million dollars.[39]

Sanders had persuaded the business community that the city faced an impending financial crisis unless something could be done to prevent it. Said one businessman on the committee: "If we had walked in the first day [we met] and been presented with these alternatives, we would have emphatically rejected them. But as a committee, we have been sensitized to the needs of the city and the budget shortfalls." A Republican alderman also on the committee said: "The mayor convinced us we needed more than belt tightening." Pat Robins, another committee member, reflected that a "gross receipts tax has merit as long as it's not too high and does not hurt business."[40]

Once Sanders got the support of the business task force for his gross receipts tax, the rest was easy. Just a few weeks later, the entire Board of Aldermen, with the exception of Republican Will Skelton, voted in favor of the measure. Skelton justified his no vote this way: "The proposal is a direct attack on the future development of certain types of businesses." Sanders, of course, was absolutely delighted to finally get the measure approved. He told the board: "What you've done is historic. . . . This is a major step forward in breaking the dependence on the regressive property tax."[41]

A daily newspaper analysis of why Sanders succeeded in implementing the gross receipts tax in 1986 but failed in 1982 mentioned the following reasons: (1) it was about one-half the amount of the original proposal, (2) it would be removed if a different alternative tax was implemented, and (3) it was a response to the loss of federal revenue sharing money. Sanders made a politically smart move by setting up a business task force, which neutralized potential opposition. He chose, in this case, "cooperation" over "confrontation," said the newspaper. And it worked.[42]

For the most part, the business community was remarkably cooperative in implementing the tax. The daily newspaper reported that "some restaurants have added 1 percent on the bill, in essence raising the state's room and meals tax from 6 to 7 percent. Others are listing the 1 percent separate. Restauranteurs also are allowed to not show the 1 percent and to roll it into their price structure."[43]

The city did experience one legal challenge to the gross receipts tax. Food catering services at the local colleges, which felt they should be exempt, were not excluded from the tax, so Saga (a food catering service), the University of Vermont, and Trinity College filed suit against the city. The city filed an antitrust countersuit against the university (claiming the food caterer, Saga, did not bid against other companies when it won a new contract with the university), but the court ruled against Burlington on this point.[44] As of early 1991, the matter still had not been settled.

Certain members of the state legislature also made another attempt to limit Burlington's ability to impose the gross receipts tax and other special city taxes. Sanders, in testimony before the House Municipal Corporations and Elections Committee, told legislators that the city would be "devastated" if this happened, since special taxes bring $2 million yearly into Burlington's coffers. Once again, though, the legislature thought better of tampering with Burlington's home rule prerogative, and did not repeal the sections of the city's charter that allowed for the levying of special taxes.[45]

Concerning this phase of the alternative tax battle, Mayor Sanders had this to say right before it was approved by the Board of Aldermen:

> We think we have . . . neutralized a good deal of the business community's opposition to it, but you never know. If one person and a good lawyer wants to take it to court, we're not 100 percent convinced that they can't win. . . .
>
> We've come in for a smaller amount . . . and with the loss of revenue sharing many people in the business community and the Board of Aldermen say: "Hey, yeah, reappraisal has knocked the hell out of this city, people are not going to vote for property tax increases, this is the way to go."
>
> [The gross receipts tax] . . . will be the most significant alternative to the property tax ever passed by any city in the history of the state of Vermont.[46]

Sanders felt a key reason for the success of the gross receipts in the third round was the business task force. He admitted that creating the task force and attending the meetings was a "change of tactics," but believed it was the right thing to do given the city's financial predicament.[47]

As might be expected, those people within the Sanders administration and Progressive Coalition thought passage of the gross receipts tax was a major victory. One union official commented that it proved the point that when Sanders brought forth an innovative idea, at first there was stiff opposition, but over time people accept it.

Although the gross receipts tax was supported by Democrats and Republicans alike, it was not without its critics. One business analyst, though acknowledging that some in the business community supported the mayor, felt they did not really represent any business organizations like the Chamber of Commerce. Those that had supported the tax were being short-sighted, in his opinion:

> Traditionally, if you look at tax structures in New England, none of the New England states have gone very heavily into local option taxation. They traditionally use the real estate tax as a fundamental basis for financing local costs. The problem with local options is that you create competing situations which can upset your system. . . . Sound taxation ought to be based on

trying to prevent any kind of internal upheaval in your economy if you can do it.

One final round in the gross receipts tax battle was a March 1989 effort by the Sanders administration to expand the tax to "beer, wine, and tobacco products" in order to fund a city child-care proposal. A year before, Sanders and the Progressive Coalition had been unsuccessful in getting voters to approve a charter change that would have allowed the city to "create a $600,000 fund for child care by placing a special [property tax] on businesses and non-profit institutions." Because this measure was defeated by a 2–1 margin, the Burlington Child Care Council was established in order to come up with a proposal which made sense for Burlington. After much debate, the council proposed that the city set up a $1.2 million child-care fund to be paid for by "taxpayers, businesses, and tax-exempt institutions."[48]

The funding mechanism for the child-care fund, however, could not be agreed upon by the council. Consequently, assistant city attorney John Franco suggested that the gross receipts tax be used to raise revenues for the fund. Known as the "sin tax," this proposal would have raised $560,000 by placing a tax of "2 cents on beer and wine in containers 16 ounces or less and 5 cents on larger containers. A nickel tax would be levied on every pack of cigarettes." An additional $465,000 would be collected by imposing a $32 "tax" on city businesses to pay for "non-resident employee[s] who need . . . child care," while another $200,000 to $250,000 would be raised from tax-exempt institutions such as the Medical Center of Vermont and the University of Vermont. The "sin tax" and the other tax proposals were written as two separate ballot items.[49]

Not surprisingly, Burlington grocers opposed the so-called "sin tax," claiming it would force Burlingtonians to do their shopping elsewhere. They organized the Burlington United Retail Grocers group to actively fight the "sin tax" ballot measure. While a poll conducted shortly before the March 1989 election suggested that the vote was too close to call, election day proved otherwise. On town meeting day, city voters turned down both ballot measures by the same 2–1 margin that had defeated the 1988 child-care fund proposal. In summing up the results of the election, assistant city attorney John Franco commented: "I think that the voters have said in the last two election[s that] they don't want to spend local tax money on child care," and that the state and federal governments should pick up the tab.[50]

The gross receipts tax was one of the fiercest battles and sweetest victories for Sanders. Through sheer persistence and deft political maneuvering, the mayor eventually got this measure passed by the Board of Aldermen, albeit in a weakened form. The failed attempt to extend it to beer, wine, and cigarettes, however, indicated the potential limitations of this local taxing provision.

Sanders acknowledged that the gross receipts tax was not a radical proposal; many communities have similar taxes. But for Burlington, and especially Vermont, it was something innovative and novel. Given that Vermont is one of only nine states in the country that has no home rule provision on taxation, it was truly a step forward. This progressive initiative eased the tax burden of low- and moderate-income people and put it onto the more well-to-do—especially the out-of-towners—who dined out, went to the movies, or stayed in hotels.

Property Tax Classification

Besides the gross receipts tax, the Sanders administration proposed several other alternative tax ideas. One of these was property tax classification. In March 1985, a ballot measure to give Burlington the power, pending future voter approval, to implement a plan to mitigate the negative consequences of reappraisal was introduced. The idea behind this proposal was to establish some form of property tax classification in the city. Such a scheme would have permitted the differential taxation of residential property versus business property. The measure passed, 60 to 40 percent, but lost badly in the state legislature that year. The Sanders administration tried again in 1986, putting a more specific property tax classification plan on the ballot. The voters approved the new charter change by a 58 to 42 percent vote.[51]

During the 1986 session of the state legislature, the property tax reform measure fared better. Late in the session, the property classification system got the approval of the House Municipal Corporations Committee by an 8–3 vote, though lost 6–5 in the House Ways and Means Committee. When the vote came before the full House, Burlington (and Winooski) were victorious in their effort to implement tax classification. An ecstatic Sanders proclaimed: "This is a major victory for progressive taxation." The mayor felt the measure passed in the House because it "did not interfere with the state's taxing powers and because legislators were more likely to approve alternative taxes the second time around." Under the plan, the city would tax businesses at 120 percent valuation while residential and other properties would be taxed at 100 percent valuation. The Vermont Senate went along with the House and approved the measure by a landslide. The tax was expected to generate over $1 million in extra revenues, which when coupled with the revenue losses from the repeal of the inventory tax (which was part of the proposal), would provide a net yield of about $600,000 for the city.[52]

About a year after the implementation of the property tax classification plan, several of the businessmen who had sat on the mayor's business task force began to question the wisdom of their actions. Patrick Robins claimed that classification conveyed a "negative signal" to businesses interested in Burlington. Patrick Burns, a restauranteur, thought that the business committee had not scrutinized the plan closely enough. Shortly after their comments appeared in the daily paper, one of the businesses in town filed a suit in court "claiming that the Vermont Constitution requires that property in a municipality be assessed at a uniform rate." The city attorney's office countercharged that the state of Vermont permitted not only tax classification but tax-exempt status, too. A few months later, a judge determined that the city's tax classification scheme was constitutional.[53]

Administration officials and Progressive Coalition members were strongly in favor of property tax reclassification. Democrats and Republicans supported it as well. In fact, one Democratic alderman thought that the Democrats, even before Sanders's time, favored reclassification, and that even though Republicans had some difficulties with it, they also would support it. A Republican alderman confirmed this by saying he supported reclassification and getting rid of the inventory tax as a "compromise" proposal. A Democratic state official commented that reclassification was eventually approved by the legislature "because it was an eminently reasonable approach which had implications . . . beyond the city of Burlington."

Those in the Burlington business community were mixed in their assessment. One prominent businessman said that "120 percent classification isn't a big deal in dollars and cents" but that he's "always reluctant to add one more layer" [of taxes]. Nevertheless, he supported it. A business community representative explained that while the business interests in town strongly opposed the property tax classification scheme in the 1985 legislative session because "it was like a carte blanche," the story was different the following year:

Philosophically, the Chamber has a tax policy that is opposed to classification. . . . [However], this year [1986] . . . it was 120 percent for . . . nonresidential as opposed to 100 percent for residential. I do know there's some members of the business community who don't feel terribly, terribly . . . uncomfortable with that . . . mainly because they do recognize that the city's in one ring ding of a financial position. It's a lot more palatable because it's concrete.

There may be some grousing as to why the city's in the position it's in . . . [but] nobody wants to see the city go bankrupt or down the tubes.

However, a business community analyst thought that reclassification was "dangerous to the extent that once you start it, there is always somebody looking to change it—to increase it, revise it. Once you open the door, . . . there's no limit as to how you could classify."

One real estate developer also was against the classification scheme:

If there's one thing that hasn't been done as well as it could have been done I think it's the method in which Sanders has tried to raise tax dollars. He hasn't increased people's property taxes; I think he hangs his hat on that as being his major claim to fame. I think he's done that somewhat at the detriment of the business community in that he really looks to the business community to solve all the city's problems.

While the tax reclassification plan saw businesses pay more of their share, it was not a radical change in the city's tax burden. Because of reappraisal, which saw most Burlington businesses' tax burden decrease substantially, property tax reclassification at best had Burlington businesses paying taxes equivalent to their pre-reappraisal levels. The most far-reaching impact of property tax reclassification was not the higher taxes that some businesses now paid (it should be remembered that in exchange for property tax reclassification, the inventory tax was repealed, thus producing a washout for some businesses), but that the property tax formula was modified to make it a less unfair tax for the city's property owners, especially low- and moderate-income homeowners.

Payment in Lieu of Taxes

Another Sanders initiative during his tenure in office has been to get various tax-exempt institutions in the city—most notably the University of Vermont and the Medical Center Hospital of Vermont—to pay taxes or make payments in lieu of taxes to the city. Forty to fifty percent of Burlington's land and buildings is tax-exempt, putting the city in a difficult position, according to one progressive alderman.

When Sanders first ran for mayor in 1981, one of his campaign promises was to force the university to make tax payments to the city. By his second term, he had backed off from this promise and instead talked about getting the state to reimburse the city for the university's tax-exempt status, but the university and the state legislature success-fully blocked Sanders's attempts to collect taxes from tax-exempt institutions. For example, in the 1985 legislative session, a charter change approved by Burlington voters in March of that year to miti-gate the damage done by property reappraisal was voted down by a House committee. If passed, it would have opened the door for the city to tax the university.[54]

At the start of 1986, the tax-exempt status of various institutions once again became an issue. This time, the Sanders administration had some unlikely allies. Several aldermen were frustrated by the univer-sity's failure to negotiate with the city on the issue. Republican Sam Levin, for example, publicly suggested that both the university and medical center should "pay the city for fire protection service." Levin said they should do so because "the two institutions caused a drain on city services and should be required to pay something in return."[55]

Calls from the aldermen and the business task force for the univer-sity to reimburse the city forced the university to defend itself. The president of the university, Lattie Coor, publicly called on the mayor to show him that the university was a drain on the city. In light of its continued stonewalling, the administration and the Progressive Coali-tion sought a charter change to force the university and medical center, as well as other tax-exempt properties, to pay taxes on one-quarter of their "assessed value." Sanders explained the move this way: "For the last five years, we have sat down and talked with Dr. Coor and the Board of Trustees about the university making payments, as well as building more housing. . . . They say they are going to study it and they study it and they study it. Well, they're still studying it [and] I'm tired of this nonsense."[56]

In the March 1986 local election, Burlingtonians approved a charter change that would allow the taxation of properties like the university and medical center. Sanders's delight with this result was tempered by the state legislature, which once again rejected Burlington's efforts to amend their charter.[57]

The administration's efforts were not completely wasted. Because of pressure from the Board of Aldermen and the citywide sentiment in favor of the charter change, the university decided to open negotiations with the city officials "to discuss payments by the school for fire protection." While the city wanted the university to make "a payment based on its appraised value and the percentage of the city budget that is spent on fire services," the university wished to pay only based on use, that is, for each time the city's fire department had to be called out. Eventually, a deal was worked out between the administration and the university concerning payments for fire protection during tense negotiations about its proposed business school expansion.[58]

Once an accord was reached by the city and the university, Sanders shifted gears and decided to go after the medical center. The mayor, who was invited to speak to the medical center's board for the first time, said he would ask for payments in lieu of taxes for city services used by the hospital. But his administration did more than simply ask. In late June 1987, Sanders "dropped a financial bombshell" on the medical center when Burlington sent it a tax bill for almost $3 million. The hospital also was informed that the city would legally question its tax-exempt status. The hospital refused to pay the bill and took on the city by filing a legal injunction to stop Burlington from demanding tax payments from it. Much to the hospital's surprise, the court would not grant the injunction.[59]

There was a lot at stake in the battle between the medical center and the Sanders administration. Said the daily newspaper: "The hospital is banking on almost 200 years of tradition where hospitals have been considered, legally speaking, 'charitable institutions,' providing a vital public function." On the other hand, the Sanders administration was hoping the court would take a new look at the issue of what constituted a "charitable institution," given the hospital's purportedly poor track record in a number of areas.[60]

During the court proceedings, the hospital claimed that it was a "charitable" organization providing "free medical care" to the community. However, the city called witnesses who refuted the medical center's claim to be a "charitable institution, because it has posted profits, offered too little free care, and paid its top administrators too much."[61]

In fall 1987, the court declared that "the hospital was tax-exempt on the grounds that it operates as a charity, and not as a profit-making business." Thus, the city's tax bill to the hospital for $2.8 million was invalid. Burlington's socialist mayor vowed to carry the legal battle to Vermont's Supreme Court. The Board of Aldermen agreed to the mayor's request. Not surprisingly, however, the city lost its appeal.[62]

Regarding the payment in lieu of taxes issues, the Sanders administration did not achieve its goals. Other than forcing a few minor concessions from the university, Sanders was unsuccessful in getting two of Burlington's largest public, tax-exempt institutions to make significant financial contributions to the city, either in the form of tax payments or through other payments.

However, the administration's efforts should not be viewed as completely ineffective. Sanders mobilized both the Board of Aldermen and public opinion to his side of the issue, perhaps setting the stage for further progress. He also forced the university to the bargaining table, something it refused to do in the past. With the hospital, Sanders was able, through the legal apparatus, to force it to defend its tax-exempt status.

Right-of-Way and Excavation Fees

Another alternative to the property tax explored by the Sanders administration was a proposed fee on utility companies that dug up city streets to install and repair their equipment. Sanders's first foray in this area was called the "right-of-way" fee or the "street rental" fee. In fall 1982, Sanders announced a plan to impose on utility companies "a rental fee for use of city property, similar to fees paid by other companies using city property—and similar to the fees utilities pay for stringing lines across private property." Sanders said his idea was not new, and that many towns and cities across the United States had already done so. The mayor also claimed that his proposal was not a tax. Sanders hoped the new fee would bring in close to $1 million per year in revenues for the city.[63]

The new right-of-way fee was to be charged to New England Telephone, Vermont Gas Systems, and Green Mountain Cable. The telephone and gas utilities would "pay the city 4 percent of their gross receipts collected in Burlington each year for the privilege of using the streets," while the cable television company would pay out only 3 percent. Sanders said that the utility companies probably "would seek a rate increase to pass the cost along to ratepayers," but still felt it was important to hold the utilities "morally" accountable for the damage done to city streets through their digging operations. City Treasurer Jonathan Leopold, Jr., added that Burlington residents had "been unwittingly subsidizing the utilities" since the utilities had not been paying their fair share to keep up the streets.[64]

Few people questioned the need to repair Burlington's streets and sidewalks, as well as repave and recurb them. The former city street superintendent, James Ogden, said that 1,200 street excavations had occurred in the city from 1977 to 1982. Sanders commented that "a recent Chittenden County Regional Planning Commission study concluded that Burlington should spend $1.2 million on street repairs each year to keep the road system up to par." Without the street rental fee, said Sanders, it would require a property tax hike of 50 cents every year in order to repave and repair the streets and sidewalks of Burlington. A tax hike of this magnitude for the Street Department was not a reality, said the mayor, since a 32-cent property tax hike for repairing the streets was overwhelmingly turned down at a special election in 1982.[65]

Sanders faced an uphill battle to get the right-of-way fee passed. Said the daily newspaper: "Burlington Mayor Bernard Sanders' plan to charge telephone, gas and cable television utilities city fees faces a long haul before aldermen, city voters, state regulators and Vermont courts." The plan, according to the newspaper, was expected to cost New England Telephone and Vermont Gas Systems about half a million dollars each, while Green Mountain Cable would pay only about $25,000 a year. Attorneys for the companies promised a very long battle in the courts, since with few exceptions, street rental fees were not in place anywhere else in Vermont. However, assistant city attorney John Franco thought the city had a good legal case, given that the state legislature, through the city's charter, had empowered Burlington to levy such fees on utility companies.[66]

In spring 1983, Sanders's proposal for a right-of-way fee on utility companies was examined by a subcommittee of the Board of Aldermen. An early indication of the board's sentiment was evident on a vote to charge the telephone company for ripping up city streets while installing underground lines. This measure lost on a split vote between Sanders's supporters and Democrats/Republicans. At the same meeting, James Ogden reported to the board that the utility companies' combined total damage to city streets was a half-million dollars per year.[67]

The telephone company worked hard to defeat the street rental fee. In a mailing to their Burlington customers, the company said that if the fee passed, customers would see a 4 percent raise in their rates. Then, in summer 1983, at a public meeting of the Board of Aldermen's subcommittee studying the fee, a parade of utility attorneys and managers testified against the measure, claiming that the fee "would be passed on to Burlington customers" and that it was a regressive tax on the utility companies. John Franco, on the other hand, said that it was a fair fee, and "compared the utilities to other Burlington businesses which must pay rent for city streets or for use of city-owned property." *The Burlington Free Press* editorial board also disliked the street rental fee proposal. In an editorial, the daily newspaper attacked the idea, primarily because it thought the cost would be passed on to the utility companies' customers.[68]

Faced with strong opposition, Sanders withdrew his original proposal to levy a right-of-way fee on the utilities. In its place, he proposed levying on the utility companies "an excavation fee that would reflect only the damage they do to streets when digging them up to move underground pipes or cables." While the municipally owned Water Resources Department and Burlington Electric Light Department were not included under the original right-of-way fee, they were included under the new proposed excavation fee. Sanders said one reason he changed his proposal was to win the backing of the Board of Aldermen, the majority of whom were against the right-of-way fee. According to John Franco, the proposed excavation fee would raise slightly less than half a million dollars per year.[69]

Shortly after Sanders announced his new plan, Richard Saudek, former head of Vermont's Public Service Department, issued an opinion on the matter. According to Saudek, "no Vermont community is allowed under state law to charge utilities taxes or fees based on the utilities' gross receipts." Saudek added that only the state legislature could grant a municipality the authority to do so.[70]

Sanders's chances with the excavation fee initially seemed good. In fall 1983, the city's Street Commission unanimously supported the mayor's excavation fee plan. The specifics of the plan called for a levy of $10.30 per square foot on the utilities for any excavation work. In response to the commission's vote, Sanders replied: "This vote of the Street Commission makes me very happy. . . . My hope and expectation is that with the support of the commission this will be passed by the Board of Aldermen."[71]

Sanders did not have long to wait before the utility companies attacked the new proposal as vigorously as they had the previous one. One utility company lawyer, Bill Gilbert, representing both Vermont Gas System and Green Mountain Cable, said: "It [the proposed excavation fee] is irrational. A court won't uphold it. . . . You won't find anywhere in the country a charge of $10.30." Gilbert added that a reasonable fee would be $1.18 a square foot of excavation, yielding the city only $41,000 for all the companies combined. According to Gilbert, the present excavation fee for utilities in Burlington was 37 cents a square foot. In addition, the editorial board of *The Burlington Free Press*, which had given a tentative endorsement to the excavation fee idea, now changed its position and came out against it.[72]

In January 1984, the city's Street Commission formally requested that the Board of Aldermen pass an excavation fee of $10.30 per square foot on the utility companies. The daily newspaper reported that "under the proposal, the utilities would have to repair streets, sidewalks or the grassy space between . . . and pay a fee on top of that." Said one progressive commissioner:

> The most progressive thing the Street Commission ha[s] done in the last three years was to vote [for] the excavation fee, and that was . . . when there was only one progressive on the commission. It was the most controversial thing . . . [it] . . . did and it took a lot of arm twisting from the Sanders administration.

In response to the commission's action, Bill Gilbert promised a court fight if the aldermen acted favorably on the measure.[73]

Sanders began negotiations with the Board of Aldermen to secure passage of the excavation fee proposal. The mayor said he would back an additional 16-cent property tax, to be designated solely for street repair work, if the board would back his excavation fee. The splinter tax, along with the excavation fee and some federal monies, would form the basis for a "permanent, ongoing solution" to the city's street decay problem, said Sanders.[74] This splinter tax was a major concession for Sanders, since he had supported a property tax hike in only a couple of instances and had campaigned against a 1983 proposed 32-cent property tax hike for the streets.

But the Board of Aldermen would not yield. The board's subcommittee studying the excavation fee proposal (the aldermanic Ordinance Committee) did not report Sanders's plan out of committee. Rather, it called for "negotiations between the utilities and the city" to solve the problem.[75]

Several weeks later, though, the Ordinance Committee reversed itself and voted unanimously to have the full board take up the measure. Still, chances for passage were bleak, and near the end of February 1984, Sanders stated that the measure was "politically dead." Said Sanders: "With the present composition of the Board of Aldermen, no Democrat or Republican has indicated to me that they are willing to support this fee."[76]

Yet, a few weeks later the Sanders administration and the Progressive Coalition gained some ground. At a Board of Aldermen's meeting, the excavation fee proposal was argued over well past midnight. While Democrats and Republicans initially appeared against the measure, some seemed willing to compromise on the issue. Also, two Republican aldermen and one Democratic alderwoman were absent from the meeting. Still, no decision was reached.[77]

The following week's board meeting proved sweet for Sanders and his allies. The daily newspaper reported: "After nearly three years of trying, Burlington Mayor Bernard Sanders and his Progressive Coalition on the Board of Aldermen . . . succeeded in enacting a means of raising money other than through the property tax." What made this remarkable event possible? First, Linda Burns, a Democratic alderwoman, had just resigned from the board. Second, the night of the vote, three board members were not present—two Republicans and one Democrat. Said one progressive alderman:

I think it [the excavation fee] had been expected to come . . . [up] within a range of time, and it was during what people humorously call Republicans' Florida vacation time, . . . [but] it was only at the last moment [that] we realized . . . [we] were going to have a majority . . . that night.

The Progressive Coalition took advantage of their effective majority on the board that night, and by a 6–3 vote, passed the excavation fee. Maurice Mahoney was the only Democrat on the board to vote in favor of the excavation fee after Progressive Coalition board members made a few concessions to him on the wording of the measure. After the vote, Sanders exclaimed: "I am beaming." He claimed the vote was of "historic importance" since it was the first real alternative to the property tax to be passed in Vermont.[78]

The legal battle over the excavation fee started almost immediately. In their first legal maneuver, attorneys for the utility companies claimed that the Board of Aldermen's action the night it passed the measure "was illegal and unjust." The utility companies' lawyers requested that the board vote again on the measure. Furthermore, the city's cable company requested that the Public Service Board permit Green Mountain Cable "to charge new customers . . . the cost of Burlington's new excavation fee."[79]

For the next year and a half, the city and the utility companies jockeyed back and forth in the courts over the case. First, there was a fight concerning the utility companies' need to "continue paying Burlington's new excavation fee" into an escrow account. Eventually, the utilities did so, at least for a while. Then there was a tussle between the city's lawyers and the utility companies' lawyers over which court—federal or state—would hear the case. The utility companies wanted the case to be in state court, which eventually happened. Utility company lawyers won another legal round when they successfully convinced the court to stop the city from "collecting its new $10.30-per-square-foot street excavation fee while the issue is being disputed in court." By this time, Burlington had already collected about $85,000.[80]

The utility companies' major argument against the excavation fee was that it really was not a fee but rather was an "excessive" tax on their business. Since it was a tax, said utility company lawyers, "the city exceeded its authority," since most taxing powers lie with the state. The city's position, on the other hand, was that the city charter granted the Board of Aldermen the ability to control the use of its streets, including the right to levy fees on them.[81]

When the judge hearing the case called a hearing "to set the amount of the city's controversial excavation fee," it appeared as if the city was in trouble. The judge called the hearing because there was another provision in Burlington's charter granting the courts the power to set the fee if the utility companies disputed the city's fee. This was clearly a blow to the city's position, since Burlington argued that it had the sole power to establish the fee under the city charter.[82]

But when the judge finally issued his decision in January 1985, the city prevailed. According to the daily newspaper, "a Superior Court judge has ruled that Burlington has the right to collect an excavation fee from utilities to recoup 'all costs attributable to maintenance, repair and deterioration' caused to streets by excavation." While the court still had to set the amount, John Franco called the decision a "major victory for the city of Burlington." Bill Gilbert simply said: "The ruling was not a win for the city."[83]

About a year elapsed between the judge's decision and the next major event in the excavation fee case. During this period of time, many Progressive Coalition members expressed frustration with the legal system and how long it was taking to get any action on the fee. Said one administration insider: "It took them less time to defeat Hitler than it does to get that thing passed!" But there was behind-the-scenes maneuvering between the parties to the case, and this eventually produced results. In December 1985, the daily newspaper reported that "the city of Burlington has agreed to a $1.76 million out of court settlement with two utility companies." The settlement, which would be spread out over thirty years, would have Vermont Gas Systems "pay the city $45,000 a year for the next 10 years. After that, the amount will increase by $5,000 every five years until the agreement runs out." Because it does not do as much digging as the gas company, New England Telephone got off easier. The phone company was required to pay the city only 10 percent of what Vermont Gas Systems had to pay out over the same period of time.[84] (Green Mountain Cable had already come to an agreement with the city over the excavation fee in its $1 million cash settlement earlier that year.) An administration insider commented that one incentive for the city to reach this agreement with the utility companies was that they (the utilities) agreed to allow the city to keep the $100,000 that had already been collected in the escrow account.

Sanders stated that the settlement with the utility companies would bring in roughly half as much as the city initially hoped to collect from the utilities with the proposed $10.30 excavation fee. The mayor also reported that "more than half of the expected excavation fees had been projected to come from the city's water and sewer departments," which would most likely pay the $10.30 fee, too.[85]

Both the city and the utility companies were happy with the out-of-court settlement. In assessing the agreement, Sanders said: "We did not get everything we wanted . . . but I think this is a reasonable settlement for the city of Burlington." He also felt an important precedent was set for other Vermont towns and cities regarding the excavation fee.[86]

The right-of-way or excavation fee is an important issue to examine. Although many would agree that it was a major accomplishment of the Sanders administration, a number of people across the political spectrum expressed the feeling that it was not really a nonreformist reform or a socialist proposal. While the settlement garnered $1.76 million from the utilities to the city, the payments were spread out over thirty years. Furthermore, several city departments ended up paying the bulk of the excavation fee, meaning that the city's residents would ultimately pay for about half of the $1.76 million through a sewer bond issue covering the city's share of the fee.

Several of Sanders's critics have legitimately claimed that the excavation fee is a form of indirect taxation on Burlingtonians. For example, one Democratic alderman said: "The ratepayers are going to end up paying most of the excavation fee and the big utilities are going to slide." Another Democratic alderman commented:

> It wasn't a big socialistic fight against private enterprise and private utilities; more than half of the excavations in the city of Burlington were done by Burlington . . . and we were taxing ourselves. So what we had was a lot of back-door taxation for people who could very little afford it. . . .
>
> So in a sort of quiet, back-door way, you end up shafting the low-income people while you get out in front and shake the sword and say you're fighting the utilities, . . . those big, bad utilities.

One Republican offered a detailed analysis of the excavation fee. He thought the whole idea of an excavation fee was wrong: "People who are poor have to pay the excavation fee when they need water." He added that "the only entity paying the excavation fee on a . . . full-ticket basis" is the city itself, through its various municipal departments. These city departments, he said, were paying more than half of the excavation fee from funds that were included in the sewer bond issue. While the utilities have to pay some "upfront money," in the long run they're getting off pretty easy through the settlement. "Analytically, from a financial point of view, he [Sanders] lost badly, but it was in his interest to play them as big wins. . . . [Before, there was a] different kind of fee structure, and what they're [the utilities] paying is comparable, but it was front-ended a little bit, so it looked good," he said. This Republican added that although Sanders knew the city departments would be the big spenders, "it was OK with him, cause he got the headline: 'Hey, big settlement.'"

This analysis was partially corroborated by *The Burlington Free Press.* In a story in summer 1986, the daily paper said: "The city's Water, Wastewater and Electric Departments may wind up paying about half the fees expected to be collected during the fiscal year starting July 1." According to the story, these city departments would end up paying $250,000 for the excavation fee. Most, if not all of this money would come from the "$22 million bond issue to repair the sewer system." Over the long haul, $4 million of that bond issue would be put aside to cover excavation fee payments. On the other hand, the utilities companies, specifically Vermont Gas Systems and New England Telephone, would only pay $48,000 in fiscal year 1986. In response to criticisms that the excavation fee would raise residents' utility rates, the city treasurer, Jonathan Leopold, Jr., "denied that the excavation fee is a way for Sanders . . . to avoid raising property taxes at the expense of higher utility costs."[87]

Communities across the country have excavation fees. The fee was labeled radical in Burlington only because few, if any, Vermont towns have such a fee and because it was the Sanders administration that proposed it. (This is true of other Sanders initiatives as well.) The excavation fee established the precedent of having businesses take more financial responsibility for their street diggings, but the measure in its final form was not anti-business in nature. Although the excavation fee was progressive in that Burlington taxpayers did not have to pay for the utility companies' digging up the city streets through the regressive property tax, it does seem that ultimately city residents will have to pay for the fee through higher city sewer and water rates and possible increases in their utility bills. At the very most, then, we could call the excavation fee a compromise proposal, as many Progressive Coalition members realized. And as one prominent businessperson said: "The excavation fee . . . looks good, but either the user will ultimately pay for it or you scare people [that is, businesses] away."

CONCLUSION

What can we conclude about Sanders's alternative tax initiatives? Clearly, on the local level, and less so on the state level, the mayor has changed the nature of the tax debate. He implemented alternative tax policies on the municipal level, as well as raised issues concerning statewide taxation, that are sure to be on the Vermont agenda for the foreseeable future. As an example, local option taxation for cities (that is, home rule) is now seriously being discussed.

Sanders moved the taxation issue in a progressive direction in Burlington as well as in the state, despite local and state constraints.

Although the long-term impact of his tax reform efforts on Vermont probably will not be known for some time, there seems to be a somewhat fairer distribution of the tax burden in Burlington than before he took office.

The mayor summed up the accomplishment of his administration concerning taxation on the local level in this way: "I think it would be fair to say that in five years we have pretty much revolutionized—that's too strong a statement—we've gone a long way toward making fundamental changes in the way the city raises revenue." Regarding the statewide implications, Sanders said: "I think there's no question that . . . the feeling of the legislature and the people has changed a good deal in understanding the regressivity of the property tax and I think that can be attributed to some degree to what we have done in Burlington." Sanders concluded: "At the heart of all these [tax] issues, is the relationship between the state and the cities and towns, [and] we're winning."[88]

One Progressive Coalition member had this observation:

I think what he's [Sanders] done is call attention . . . to the inequity of the property tax and the need to find alternative taxes. . . . I think what he's done is provide a blueprint for how municipalities . . . can and will have to deal with the revenue shortfalls that are going to come in because of Reagan's budget and Gramm-Rudman . . . and I think that's important.

Support for Sanders's tax initiatives was not limited to his circle of advisors and supporters on the Board of Aldermen and in the Progressive Coalition. For example, one businessperson said in this surprising confession:

I guess I've had the bias that businesses are not paying their fair share in Burlington—like us. People that own and run businesses like this or own real estate in Burlington generally don't live in the city. People work in the city, frequent restaurants and bars, and enjoy cultural events, and don't pay anything for it, for all practical purposes, except what taxes their buildings pay, which, in general, in my judgment are fairly low.

Progressive critics of the administration were generally supportive of Sanders's alternative tax initiatives, but raised some questions as well. For example, one commented: "What kind of tax reform is he [Sanders] for? Is he just getting money for Burlington or is he for redistributing taxes?"

One academician familiar with many of the alternative tax reform proposals felt generally positive about the initiatives, but added: "I worry about the mentality of: 'We can just continue to accelerate our demands on business indefinitely.'" Her assessment was that Sanders had accomplished quite a bit in the area of alternative taxation through negotiations and "compromise[s] with the business community." However, she was unclear whether Sanders's alternative tax ideas really would help redistribute wealth between classes in Burlington because the "business community [may] pass [it] on to consumers." The "local tax structure," she commented, was a "poor way to redistribute wealth." That included both the property tax and reclassification. The ideal solution, she said, would be a city income tax, but the city charter does not permit it.

Are nonreformist reform or socialistic tax policies more likely now in Burlington? Not really. Even if Sanders had pushed for a progressive city income tax, this would not have brought the city of Burlington closer to socialism. After all, Sanders's initiatives are only addressing the unequal income distributional effects of the capitalist system we live in. They do not address the causes of these income inequalities; for that, our economic system would have to be fundamentally altered. Through his speeches, though, Sanders has addressed the systemic causes of the inequities in wealth in this society. In terms of actual tax reform, Sanders probably has done all that is possible given the systemic constraints. Thus, we again see the limits of municipal socialism in a capitalist society.

Quality-of-Life Issues and the Sanders Administration

During his tenure as mayor of Burlington, Bernard Sanders left an indelible mark on the city's quality of life. From art to youth to baseball, Sanders took initiatives that have changed the atmosphere in Burlington.

In this chapter, we will explore the mayor's initiatives in several diverse areas. By examining the work of the Mayor's Council on the Arts, the Mayor's Youth Office, the Burlington Women's Council (formerly known as the Mayor's Council on Women), and the Mayor's Task Force on the Elderly, as well as the administration's track record on the issue of gay and lesbian rights, we will have an opportunity to see how Sanders fared on quality-of-life issues. We will conclude this chapter by taking a brief glance at one of Sanders's more passionate concerns—the bringing of a minor league baseball team to Burlington.

MAYOR'S COUNCIL ON THE ARTS

Sanders has played a pivotal role in supporting the arts in Burlington. He set up a task force on the arts soon after he was elected mayor in 1981, which was to inform him about the arts situation in Burlington. According to Doreen Kraft,[1] executive director of the Mayor's Council on the Arts from 1981 to 1985, Sanders reportedly said after seeing their report:

> Yes, there's a lack of access for artists in the community, there's no performance space, there are beautiful outdoor spaces that are never used, there [is] Battery Park that [is] [a] park of great beauty

and it has a bandshell and it's underused, and there's no . . . access for low-income people to art events because the only art events are the Lane Series and the Mozart Festival, and they're expensive. . . . Well, what are we going to do?

At a subsequent task force meeting, members decided to "first put on a Battery Park concert series," said Kraft. Sanders was enthralled with the idea. According to Kraft, he exclaimed: "A fabulous idea! You're going to do it? Go ahead. Let's go out and raise the money, and I'll help you write some letters." This initiative marked the birth of the Mayor's Council on the Arts.

The first year Sanders was in office, Kraft went before the Board of Aldermen several times to try to get some start-up money for the Arts Council. The board, however, was not sympathetic. "We didn't really prepare ourselves well for that fight; I guess I sensed there wasn't going to be support there. We had to go out and really prove ourselves first," said Kraft.

With the help of Sanders, Kraft raised some money from the business community. The Arts Council collected $10,000 from the businesspeople with whom Sanders had begun to butt heads—from "the Pomerleaus to Pizzagelli to IBM to the banks," said Kraft.

Kraft believed that the business community responded to the council's fundraising appeal "because they felt bad on one level. I mean they were being such bastards to him on the political level that the arts could . . . step outside of that political realm." Furthermore, she said, it was "real good PR for them" to support free concerts in the parks.

Kraft described the first event done by the Arts Council and explained why she thought the Burlington business community supported it:

The first thing we developed [was] the Battery Park concert series—the free concerts in the park. In a sense, it was more than just developing a concert series; it was an area that was the center of a lot of trouble between the police and teenagers and it was not a family park at all. . . . People were afraid to go there and believed that that was where the criminal element lived. So doing the concert there was also an attempt to take back that neighborhood park and [was supported by] the business community.

According to Kraft, eight free concerts were given during the summer evenings of 1981, including country music, jazz, dance, puppetry, and storytelling.

The next step for the Arts Council was to get an office at city hall. Once that was done, said Kraft, "the phone started ringing." Because artists and the community at large expressed a great deal of enthusiasm, things began to snowball.

In 1982, Kraft once again went before the Board of Aldermen to ask for funding. She described what happened:

> [We] brought forth a proposal to the Board of Aldermen—the record of the amount that had been raised the year before, the success of the programming. . . .
>
> I remember [Republican] Diane Gallagher was on the board. [She made] all these sort of insinuations, like: "Doreen, do you really need the money? Should you really be paid a salary? Shouldn't you want to do these things free for the city? Aren't you just a political hack?"—real nasty stuff through[out] that budget hearing.
>
> They [members of the board] basically tabled me and tabled me and [would not] deal with it and then at the last minute when they had to make certain cuts they cut me out and refused to pay my salary again.

But she was not to be deterred. The 1982 season proved to be a very productive one for the Mayor's Council on the Arts. It produced the second annual Battery Park concert series, a Waterfront Festival (which had "movies on floating boats"), concerts, exhibitions, and neighborhood festivals in the North and South Ends of town. The Arts Council also set up a "municipal art gallery" in city hall. The first show was a "very controversial" one by the Artists for Nuclear Disarmament. Commented Kraft: "That got a lot of mixed reviews, stirred a lot of people up [about] politics and the Arts Council." Another show hung in city hall was an exhibition of women's suffrage movement posters. The Arts Council also experimented with "programming at City Hall," said Kraft. The council arranged for performances by "touring artists" in "city departments, all of the work places in the city, [and] factories," which were well received.[2]

The Mayor's Council on the Arts had a watershed year during 1983. Once again, Kraft went before the Board of Aldermen, only this time the results were different:

> We were asking . . . for $12,000 . . . and again they tried [to block it], only this time . . . [there] was just too much public support. I mean I had packed the audience and I think a number of aldermen were convinced that what I was doing was really good for the community, they had too many of their constituents who really liked the Arts Council, and they could not vote against me.

On a 9–2 vote, said Kraft, the board approved funding the Mayor's Council on the Arts.

Kraft said that the "Arts Council just kept growing and growing in terms of the number of people who were coming in." One of the first things the council did that season was a Hiroshima show several weeks before the mayoral elections. Said Kraft:

> I thought he [Sanders] was going to kill me when he found out that two weeks before [the] election I was putting up a show with portraits of burnt bodies . . . . Bernie's [response was]: "Everyone is waiting for the one thing that they can nail a person onto . . . and you've given it to them." He calmed down and realized we could weather this one.

Besides the third annual Battery Park concert series, the Arts Council once again sponsored a series of neighborhood festivals, "which dr[e]w the local community together in a day of music, dance, food, and children's activities right in their own neighborhood[s]." The Community Arts Program, which was initiated in 1983, was an attempt to assist "low-income or underemployed artists whose projects reach out at the community level." The $7,500 program, funded with Community Development Block Grant money, gave small grants to local artists. The Arts Council saw the program "as something like the WPA [Work Progress Administration] by Franklin Delano Roosevelt . . . in which unemployed artists were paid to create."3

The 1983–1984 Arts Council season was led off by the Burlington Winter Waterfront Festival, complete with a "ski hill" on the waterfront. Kraft explained that while the city contributed a few thousand dollars to the event, the council raised about $32,000 from local businesses in a little over a month. The Discover Jazz Festival was another addition to the Arts Council repertoire that season. According to the annual report, "this City-wide festival reaches into outlying areas of Burlington with jazz musicians playing in unexpected places: buses, ferries, restaurants, on the streets, at the airport, and in the parks." Still other new ideas for 1984 were the Nashfull Bash Country Music Festival, which saw various country artists play at Oakledge Park, and the Senior Citizens Arts Program, which brought arts events to various senior centers. Also throughout the year were shows at the auditorium in city hall (such as the Bread and Puppet Theater), exhibits at the art gallery in city hall, and, of course, the summer Battery Park concert series.4

In 1985, Kraft began working for the council only on a part-time basis, phasing out of the day-to-day work. Despite the change, the 1984–1985 season again proved to be a very productive year for the

Arts Council. All of the standards from previous years were carried over, including the Battery Park concert series, the neighborhood festivals, the Burlington Winter Festival, the Discover Jazz Festival, and the Nashfull Bash Country Music Festival. In addition to these events, the Senior Citizens Arts Program, the Community Arts Grants Program, and the municipal art gallery also were continued. According to the city's 1985 annual report, the Mayor's Council on the Arts put on a total of 213 events, of which about one-quarter were free; about 39,000 people attended these arts events; about $75,000 was spent on the arts program, not including administrative costs; and over 300 people were involved in presenting the events. In recognition of its work, the Mayor's Council on the Arts got a "livability award" from the U.S. Conference of Mayors in 1985.[5]

During its 1985–1986 season, under the direction of co-directors Susan Green and Lou Andrews, the council put on 132 different events (of which 25 were free), drawing about 65,000 people. The Arts Council received over $100,000 to put on these events and counted on over 300 volunteers to help out. Regarding events that season, the Mayor's Council on the Arts repeated some past favorites, such as the Battery Park concert series, the Discover Jazz Festival, and the neighborhood festivals. Other continuing programs included the municipal art gallery, the Community Arts Grants, and the arts program for the elderly. There also were some new events, such as the Vermont Blues Festival, the San Francisco Mime Troupe's production of "Steeltown," and the Burlington Film Society's showing of art and foreign films.[6]

Despite some changes at the council during the 1986–1987 season (Susan Green became the sole director), it continued to provide a great range of cultural events for the city. Again, over 200 events were produced, with an estimated 75,000 city residents taking advantage of them. In addition to the Battery Park concert series, the Discover Jazz Festival, the neighborhood festivals, and the Burlington Film Society's showing of classic U.S. and foreign features, the Arts Council sponsored some special events, such as a performance by the Celtic band Silly Wizard.[7]

The 1987–1988 Arts Council season saw the sponsorship of over 200 events (100 of them free) reaching an estimated 80,000 people at a cost of about $100,000. With over 500 volunteers helping out, the council clearly matched, if not exceeded, previous years' activities. Some notable events included the annual Battery Park summer concert series, the annual Discover Jazz Festival, and a new addition—the cosponsorship of the Vermont Reggae Festival. The annual Burlington Film Society series also were successful. The Community Arts Grants program gave money to twelve poor or working-class artists and for the first time handed out the Mayor's Peace Prize. The newest addition to the council's repertoire was The Deep Focus Broadcasting series, which engaged in alternative programming such as "films from Cuba, daily television fare from Nicaragua, . . . and American documentaries on various topics relating to peace and nuclear war." Most impressive, though, was the council's role in getting Burlington designated as the Most Livable City in America (tied with one other city in the under-100,000 population category) by the U.S. Conference of Mayors.[8]

The Arts Council's final year under the Sanders administration, 1988–1989, was another stellar one. The level of programming activity, the number of people attending events, the amount of money raised, and the degree of volunteerism were all very similar to the previous year. The council's standard fare included the eighth annual Metropolitan Art Gallery exhibits, the eighth annual Battery Park summer concert series, the sixth annual Discover Jazz Festival, the sixth annual Community Arts Grants program, the fourth annual Burlington Film Society series, and cosponsorship of the second annual Vermont Reggae Festival. New this year was the Great Swamp Cafe—a "weekly folk music coffeehouse at the Burlington Community Boathouse."[9] Without a doubt, the Mayor's Council on the Arts has developed a very successful repertoire of events for Burlington, and is constantly coming up with new programming ideas.

Kraft discussed the arts and their relationship to radical change in a city like Burlington, Vermont:

> I knew it wasn't a matter of doing what's possible in Nicaragua or Cuba or in other countries where the whole state and priorities are turned around so that they're giving major support and every arm of government is involved in that cultural change. But I think the Arts Council and the Youth Office especially were able to plant the seeds for people to see that there [exists] an equality between people in this society. The whole class question . . . was demonstrated most visually and most dramatically by the issues raised with the Arts Council (and the Youth Office) in terms of the haves and the have-nots. . . .
>
> Although I don't think there's been a "radical" transformation of local culture, it certainly has come a long way from where we began, whe[n] the only thing that was available in town was $18–$20 . . . tickets, and artists paying enormous fees for buildings, . . . always losing money and no money being given to low-income artists.

Kraft said there had been a "redefining [of] where art takes place, . . . who art should be made for, and [who art] should be given to."

Regarding future changes, Kraft envisioned a charter change whereby businesses would be required to pay a 1 percent tax to aid the arts, as they do in Chicago. But she conceded that this would be difficult to get passed in Burlington.

By most accounts, the Mayor's Council on the Arts has been a huge success. It received praise from most quarters, including those that were often critical of the administration. One Progressive Coalition alderman summed up the sentiments of many when he said: "We've made the city a more livable city and we've made it a lot more interesting."

Perhaps the most important accomplishment of the Arts Council has been to make art and culture accessible to people of all incomes. Clearly, the extent and diversity of the arts program in the city also has had some impact on the general consciousness of the population. Shows like the one on Hiroshima in city hall, for instance, have raised people's awareness of the effects of nuclear war. The Arts Council has done little, if anything, that can be directly labeled a nonreformist reform, but it has unquestionably furthered efforts toward a new, more egalitarian society. By making the arts part of the public domain and no longer the exclusive privilege of the middle and upper classes in the city, the arts become less of a commodity and more something to be created and enjoyed by everyone.

MAYOR'S YOUTH OFFICE

Sanders is not unusual in citing the disaffection of youth as a problem, but his unwavering commitment to programs designed by and for youth stands out. Jane Driscoll,[10] formerly on the staff of the King Street Youth Center, explained how the Youth Office got started:

> In 1981, when Bernie campaigned for office the first time, he said that he felt that the youth were disenfranchised, that they weren't represented, that not enough was being done by the city of Burlington for the young people in our city. And he felt that that was a responsibility of city government.
> The absolute first thing he did when he was mayor-elect . . . [was] within two days [to] call a meeting of people . . . to have a task force on youth established. . . . He wanted a report within nine weeks saying what the city government should be doing. What are the needs of people in Burlington? What should we be doing about it?

According to Driscoll, the task force report said the establishment of a Youth Office should be the first priority. Sanders supported the report's recommendations and urged Driscoll to approach the Board of Aldermen. The board was receptive to the proposal and authorized "an office, a desk, and a telephone. No money, we didn't ask for money," she said.

The office opened with Jane Driscoll as Youth Coordinator, appointed by the Youth Council, a twelve-member council appointed by the mayor and charged with overseeing the Youth Office. Two businessmen in particular—Ernie Pomerleau and Nick Wylie, the manager for FM Burlington—helped generate business support and money for the idea, said Driscoll.

During 1981, Driscoll said the Youth Office engaged in a lot of recreational activities "that didn't cost anything" to show it could be done and that the programs could be self-sufficient. She explained that the guiding philosophy that first year was to be a "credible and visible" force in the community. But the modest beginnings of the Youth Office should not be mistaken for a lack of vision, which Driscoll described in the city's 1983 annual report:

The theory which guides the Youth Office is simple. We believe that in these difficult times, young people need help in developing a sense of belonging and a sense of involvement in their community. It is our view that kids turn to drugs, alcohol and other self-destructive behavior only to fill a void in their lives which occurs when they are unable to express their energies in creative and fulfilling ways. We are attempting to provide our young people with affordable, accessible opportunities which develop competence, usefulness and a sense of commitment. We are working to prevent delinquency by building neighborhoods and involving residents of all ages with each other in their community.[11]

First-year activities of the Youth Office (1981–1982) included an after-school program for aspiring young actors and actresses. "We had ninety kids every day during the week in Memorial Auditorium and just me," said Driscoll. That first year, the performing arts group, better known as Burlington Broadway, put on a production called "Annie's Christmas Surprise." The Youth Office also helped get a few teenage bands started, employed youth from the Comprehensive Employment and Training Act program and college interns to work in city hall, and began the Building Understanding between Seniors and Youth (B.U.S.Y.) program, whereby youth helped out older people in various ways, such as shoveling snow through Operation Snowshovel.[12]

Fostering the development of teenage bands was especially important. Former Mayor Paquette had banned rock music in Memorial Auditorium. According to Driscoll, the Youth Office brought teenagers "before the Finance Board to convince them to drop the ban." The board agreed and let them have a battle of the bands at the auditorium. There were three bands the first year, and the idea was later expanded to "a summer concert series in the park where it's all teenage performances."

The start-up of Little League baseball in the Old North End, in Driscoll's estimation, was "a major accomplishment" of her office. She said that although there had been Little Leagues in other parts of the city, there had never been one in the poorer Old North End. Sanders pushed hard for it, and it turned out to be a huge success. In 1981, she lined up "coaches and umpires" from the area, and there was such enthusiasm for the program that the following year parents constructed dugouts in the park. The Old North End baseball league has now become the biggest league of them all. "We really empowered the people—the people were in charge of the whole thing," said Driscoll.

In its second year (1982–1983), the Youth Office received $9,800 from the city through the Community Development Block Grant (CDBG) program. The Youth Office's after-school program continued to be successful. It put on another original production called "Fame Fever," which the young people wrote, choreographed, and produced. "It was a great show. We put it on at the Flynn [Theater], and we had 1,000 people" show up, said Driscoll. The Youth Office again sponsored summer teenage band concerts in Battery Park, and the second annual "Battle of the Bands" occurred in Memorial Auditorium. Over 1,000 youths came to hear and judge Burlington's best teen bands during the City Halloween Party.[13]

A joint initiative sponsored by the Youth Office and the Burlington Peace Coalition in summer 1982 was an International Peace Workcamp. Aimed "to foster an enduring peace through mutual understanding, . . . fourteen young people from nine different countries [came] to live and work in . . . [Burlington] for three weeks." The project was enormously successful. The other major program that year was through the Youth Employment Service program, which placed teenagers in "part-time or temporary jobs" either in the public or private sector. To address teen employment on a more comprehensive basis, the city, working with the state, started the Burlington Youth Employment Program. In its short existence, the program has placed about a hundred teenagers "on agricultural, recycling, and weatherization projects" and expects to branch out to housing rehabilitation work.[14]

To start the 1983–1984 season, the Youth Office got about $30,000 in Community Development Block Grant money to fund their work, which included the popular teenage band concerts in Battery Park, the Battle of the Bands, the City Halloween Party for about 800 youngsters, the International Peace Workcamp and a foreign student exchange program, and the B.U.S.Y. program, especially Operation Snowshovel. The ongoing Performing Arts Program put on a production of "Grease."[15]

One new program for the office that season was the tree-planting project. Driscoll went to the city's Finance Board to ask for $1,000 to plant new trees in an area of the city that had been devastated by Dutch Elm disease a number of years ago. The board was reluctant and, instead, gave the Parks Department the money to plant trees in Battery Park.

About half of those trees died, according to Driscoll. However, trees that the Youth Office received free from a local dealer and then planted, all did well. As a result, Driscoll approached various businesses in town to see if they would support a tree-planting program. FM Burlington's Nick Wylie convinced the retailers in the mall to give the Youth Office $5,000 for one year plus $1,000 each consecutive year for five years to plant trees. This was "great PR" for the mall, explained Driscoll. With pledges for $10,000 in hand, Driscoll then got the Merchants Bank to pledge the same amount.

Armed with $20,000 in pledges, Driscoll then went back to the Finance Board. This time, she said, the board could not refuse her, since there was a matching stipulation attached to the business pledges. Thus, if the city did not meet the conditions, the private donations would have to be forfeited. The Finance Board decided to go along with the program, and a new tree-planting program was initiated, despite the objection of the city's Parks and Recreation Department. Driscoll explained:

We said that . . . we didn't want the Parks Department to decide where they [the funds] go, that we wanted the people to come together. We had a big Neighborhood Planning Assembly meeting, and we had all the people decide which streets . . . needed the trees . . . and all those streets have gotten trees.

The tree-planting program put in about 700 trees the first year. The Parks Department helped out by picking the type of trees to plant in a particular area and by providing directions to volunteer tree planters who turned out by the hundreds over the course of the year to plant the trees. This program proved to be tremendously successful— by spring 1987, over 2,000 trees had been put into the ground. The project continued to generate funding from the private sector. The Howard Bank gave $18,000 of a needed $23,000 in 1987. Sanders labeled it the "most far-reaching beautification effort undertaken, which earned the city national recognition—the New England Chapter of the International Arborists Association's "Golden Leaf Award." The award acknowledged the special volunteer program. "It's a way of bringing people to participate in their city, and taking pride in the planting of a tree and maintaining that tree. And we can do a lot more work for a lot less money," Sanders said.[16]

Another major activity that preoccupied the Youth Office during 1983–1984 was the opening of a child-care center in Memorial Auditorium. Driscoll said the Youth Office played an instrumental role in setting up this private, nonprofit organization. She battled with the Board of Aldermen for six months before they consented to it. Even the daily newspaper editorialized against it, said Driscoll.

But her persistence paid off and the Burlington Children's Space was opened in short order. Driscoll said the day-care center deals with people from all class backgrounds, but especially low- to moderate-income people. There is space for sixty children, and a long waiting list. She described the importance of the center:

[It has the] highest-paid quality staff . . . [the] best facility . . . [and the] lowest child-care rates. We have a sliding fee scale . . . according to the ability to pay. That's the only socialist thing we've been able to really get through. . . . [We also have] infant care, [which] most . . . [other centers] don't have in the city, part-time care, which nobody else has in the city, [and we're] one of the two places that has care for kids with special needs.

Is the provision of child care a nonreformist reform? One Progressive Coalition member had this to say on the issue:

I think if we're talking about socialism . . . day-care programs are a whole lot more important and closer to what socialism is about and how it might come about than land trusts because they speak to the relation between government and society's obligations in general and the needs of individuals and the way in which society has to help people work and raise their children. . . . Working *and* raising children is too much [for any one person] to do and it is also very sexist.

But one Republican real estate developer was wary of such interpretations:

You can make it [day care] a socialist issue if you choose to call that socialist, but the fact is it's cheaper to get our kids into day care and get single parents out working than it is to run around and put . . . those mothers or fathers on a welfare roll. . . . So it's a good commitment for the city to make.

The appearance of the *Queen City Special*, "a youth-written and -produced newspaper," rounded out new activities for the 1983–1984 season. Published monthly, it has a circulation of about 7,000 through the public schools and the weekly *Vanguard Press* distribution points. Driscoll said that some youngsters began working on the paper while in the seventh or eighth grade and continued to work on it for several years. Most of the young people on the staff are between the ages of fourteen and sixteen, and monthly production of the paper brings together about forty people to work on it.[17]

During its 1984–1985 season, the Youth Office had a banner year. The office was able to get $40,000 from the city general fund in addition to CDBG monies to support its work, said Driscoll. Ongoing events included the fourth annual teenage band concerts, the fourth annual Battle of the Bands, the third International Peace Workcamp, the Performing Arts Program, the B.U.S.Y. program, the Burlington Children's Space, and Little League baseball in the Old North End. There were several new initiatives, too. One was the First Night Teen Event, in which over 8,000 people came to events produced and performed by area teenagers.[18]

The Youth Office also continued its ongoing and innovative work that season. A long-wished-for project, a teen center, was launched. Getting it was no easy matter. The Neighborhood Planning Assembly representatives were not in favor of a teen center, Driscoll said, and they decided CDBG funding priorities. However, the NPAs were generally in favor of youth programs, and Driscoll knew the youth in the city wanted it. A *Queen City Special* survey confirmed it. Driscoll explained how she eventually got it with Sanders's help:

Bernie . . . basically said: "If you can show me the kids are for it, I'm for it. If it's your idea, I'm sorry, I'm not going to go against all the [NPA] recommendations given to me."

We got kids out to the meetings, and we got the kids in to see Bernie, and Bernie went for it. He went against everyone else's recommendation . . . and said: "I'm going to fund the teen center."

With Sanders's support, the teen center got CDBG funding in 1985. It was a tough battle at the Board of Aldermen level, but, according to

Driscoll, two of the Republicans—Ted Riehle and Fred Bailey—voted for it in a last-minute change of heart. Both of them, reported Driscoll, received a hard time from their colleagues for that vote.

Driscoll is excited about the teen center. Teenagers planned and constructed it, she said. They also serve on many of the center's committees, where the real power lies. She described what the center provides teenagers:

> It's . . . open every day after school (2 to 9 during the week, 2 to 12 on weekends). We . . . have a full-service snack bar . . . pool table, shuffleboard, juke box and stage, and an office. One night [is] video night. . . . On Sunday morning we . . . have a brunch discussion group . . . [with] a coffeehouse in the afternoon. . . . Friday and Saturday night [there are] . . . bands and performances . . . and from 6 to 8 . . . a restaurant kids chef and run.

The new teen center is a place where youth can socialize, put on events, engage in recreational activities, get counseling, partake in educational discussions on a variety of issues, and explore job training options.[19]

Another new initiative that year was the youth dance troupes. One group, the Breakers, was formed with the help of the Youth Office, and performed breakdancing all over town. Also, a modern dance group called the Contrasts was formed. The Youth Office also started a Summer City Campus program for youths, where they could take various art-related courses with area professionals for a two-week period of time. There was a Summer Festival of Art, too,[20] which had "every kind of art imaginable on the marketplace. . . . We had paintings, sculpture, drawings; we had kids playing craft ensembles, we had young pianists, choruses, . . . plays written by . . . and performed by kids," explained Driscoll.

Several new programs were added during the 1985–1986 season. In response to a newly created mayoral task force on child care, an after-school program was initiated during the 1985–1986 school year, serving about fifteen young people on a daily basis. An expanded program, called City Kids Child Care/Enrichment Program, was expected for the 1986–1987 school year. The goal was to serve upwards of fifty children daily. Lobbying for protective legislation for youngsters and families, including laws to allow videotapes as evidence in child sexual abuse cases, expanding the protection of youngsters in the area of sexual abuse and rape, and more stringent application of the state's DWI laws, became a serious priority, too. Of course, many other programs continued into the 1986 season, such as the Burlington Children's Space, Operation Snowshovel, the International Peace

Workcamp, the *Queen City Special* newspaper, the Performing Arts Program—which included such regular events as the Battle of the Bands—and the teen center, now called 242 MAIN.[21]

The 1986–1987 season saw several new initiatives. One was the first annual Kid's Day, in which Burlington and other cities in the United States recognized "the value and importance of children in our community" through activities designed for them. An alternative education program for chronically truant children also was devised by the Youth Office. The teen center, 242 MAIN, continued to flourish, and now had its own program on public-access cable television. City Kids also was successfully launched, offering "quality, affordable child care as well as interesting enrichment activities to elementary school age children."[22]

During the 1987–1988 Youth Office season, all of the standard activities continued in full bloom. The Performing Arts Program for youth was expanded, 242 MAIN had an active year of teen events, the second annual Kid's Day fair was a success, the annual Halloween and Holiday parties (the latter sponsored by developer Tony Pomerleau and family) were as popular as ever, and the annual Battle of the Bands contest was again a big hit with Burlington's young people.[23]

During Sanders's last year in office, 1988–1989, the Youth Office continued its successful programs from previous years. In summing up its activities over the years, the council began the 1989 Annual Report in this way:

> Since the Youth Office began in 1981, it has identified the gaps in youth services and has acted as a catalyst to precipitate an effective response. Whether it was establishing the Burlington Youth Employment Program, founding the Children's Space, building the teen center or starting the City Kids program, the Youth Office has spearheaded programs to address the needs of young people in this community. This is not to say that the Youth Office has been primarily a direct service provider. In fact, the primary strength and intent of the Youth Office is to act as an advocate for youth, to effect changes in our society that benefit young people.[24]

The Mayor's Youth Office has not been without controversy over the years. During Sanders's second term, he was accused of "cronyism" by some on the Board of Aldermen, who attacked the mayor for providing his friend (and now his wife), Jane Driscoll, with a $21,000 salary. A number of aldermen also were upset because the "youth office job was not advertised to allow people to compete for it." One newspaper editor thought that Sanders was wrong for appointing his "girlfriend" to the position. There was an ironic twist to the charge. When Sanders first ran for mayor, he attacked Paquette for cronyism at city hall. However, Sanders defended the move, noting that Driscoll was appointed because of her qualifications, not because she was his friend. Since she had done such a good job in the eyes of many, including Sanders's critics, the charge simply did not stick.[25]

Driscoll looks back at the accomplishments of the Youth Office and believes the effects will be long-lasting:

> The thing that I'm most proud of is that most of the things we've done are permanent. If we [the Sanders administration] were removed . . . the child-care center would continue, the trees would still be there, all the youth-run businesses and all the youth bands would continue to go on, and they would continue to flourish because the schools now use them. Everything we [have done] cannot be undone when we're gone, and that's exciting.

If there was one regret Driscoll had, it was that the Youth Office could not do more for youths who were in high-risk categories.

The Mayor's Youth Office has provided an opportunity for young people to have a stronger voice in their community in such diverse ways as producing their own newspaper and designing and constructing their own teen center. The ability of the Youth Office to engage the talents and aspirations of a segment of the city's youth has made a real difference in the quality of life for these young people and the city as a whole. Although the Youth Office programs, like those of its counterpart the Arts Council, are not nonreformist reforms, they certainly address the problems faced by youth from low- and moderate-income families. Its leadership has been important on the issue of day care, which has socialist implications for the way society deals with its children. The efforts of the Youth Office are a fine example of how to build toward a more productive society that utilizes the capacities, skills, and talents of all its members.

Driscoll pointed out that the Arts Council and the Youth Council were two of the major accomplishments of the Sanders administration. Because they were, in her words, "highly visible, highly effective, and uncontroversial," they helped contribute to Sanders's reelections. These two councils not only accomplished a lot, but through their "Mom and Apple Pie" activities, they proved that the administration did things—good things—for the city. The biggest drawback to the Arts Council and the Youth Office is that they lack independent status from city hall. Their long-term survival may depend on the development of identities apart from Mayor Sanders, his administration, and the Progressive Coalition, though this will most likely depoliticize them.

MAYOR'S COUNCIL ON WOMEN/BURLINGTON WOMEN'S COUNCIL

The Mayor's Council on Women, which changed its name to the Burlington Women's Council in 1985, began as a task force shortly after Sanders was elected mayor in 1981. Peggy Luhrs,[26] who was hired in August 1985 to coordinate the council's activities, provided an overall perspective on the dilemmas faced by the council and why it did not experience the same kind of early success as its counterparts in the arts and with youth. Concerning her first interaction with the council, Luhrs said: "I belonged to it—attempted to belong to it early on—but it didn't [look] like the right organization for me at that time because of how it was structured." She explained her disenchantment with the early council:

> I think it [the council] must have first started with a lot of women who were very involved with the Sanders campaign. . . . The very first meeting I went to . . . [the] women had come in and set themselves up at the aldermen's table and Bernie came in and said he didn't like that; he wanted us all to sit at this long table, which we did, and [he] set himself up at the head.
> He later went into how . . . this was his council, and he didn't want independent stuff coming from it, it would all have to reflect his policies. It was the Mayor's Council . . . and so at that point, I felt . . . this wasn't a place that I was going to want to work because I would want to have independent ideas.

During its first two years the council had no official leader or coordinator. Instead, it ran more like a cooperative. Perhaps because of this structure, the number of activities was limited. In 1981, the council held a Women's Health Day in addition to sponsoring "free health clinics at the Community Health Center." The council sponsored a seven-day event in 1982 called "The Balancing Act: Women and Their Work," which featured films, speakers, and workshops on many areas of interest to women. That same year, the council brought the Rhode Island Feminist Theatre to Burlington.[27]

The Mayor's Council on Women was restructured in 1983. An important step in the council's development, it brought in an entirely new group of people, based on the decision that the council should represent the diversity of women's groups. Said Luhrs:

> What we have now . . . [is] a council that has representatives from
> about twenty different women's groups attending fairly regular-
> ly, plus anyone can come and be an at-large member. I think it's
> been really rather amazing that we've got this range from radical
> lesbians to business and professional women and we work on a
> consensus model.

A number of new initiatives were undertaken during the 1982–1983
season. One of these was the Whistlestop Program, which provided
women throughout Burlington with whistles to establish "safe houses
in neighborhoods." That year, said Luhrs, Sanders encouraged the
Women's Council to put "more women on the [city] commissions." To
do so, a Commission Appointment Information Night was held. As a
result, a record sixty-eight women sought commission positions and
twelve of them were appointed. The Women's Council also sponsored
self-defense classes for women. Luhrs estimated that over 150 women,
including twenty-five who had some physical difficulties, attended
them. A Women and the Law Conference was sponsored by the
Women's Council that year "to address the severe needs of low-income women and their inaccessibility to the legal system." The council
also sponsored a Job Fair Day, which helped women become aware of
jobs available throughout the city, and endorsed the Lesbian and Gay
Pride March.[28]

Quite a few projects were extended into the 1983–1984 season. The
Whistlestop Program distributed "over 1,000 whistles . . . to residents
of Burlington's Old North End through door-to-door canvasses." The
Women's Self-Defense Project also was carried over. A new project for
the council, cosponsored with the Women's International League for
Peace and Freedom (WILPF), was a War and Militarism Conference on
Mother's Day. The goal of the day was "to examine militarism and
women's involvement in war—both women's experiences and roles
in resisting war. . . . The weekend was a celebration of peace and
women's contributions to creating peace."[29]

Since one of the goals of the Women's Council was "to work for
equal status for Burlington women," the Women for Economic Justice
Committee was set up. The new committee was "committed to the
long-term goals of economic equity and equal job opportunities, along
with child care and training opportunities." A major impetus for the
committee's formation was Ginny Winn's study, "Burlington's Boom
Pie: What's in It for Women?" The study indicated "that while Burlington's economy grew, women's earnings shrank." Also contributing to
the committee's formation was a CEDO study entitled *Jobs and People:
A Strategic Analysis of the Greater Burlington Economy*, which indicated
that over half of Burlington's single female-head-of-household fami-

lies were below the poverty line. These two reports provided "a big boost" to the Women's Council and its activities, according to Luhrs. The other major accomplishment of the Women's Council in that season was the creation of a Media Watch Committee, whose goal was "to monitor reporting of news and other items in the media and to respond to those issues from a woman's perspective."[30]

The 1984–1985 season was a landmark year for the council. One major change was the transformation of the Mayor's Council on Women into the Burlington Women's Council. Regarding the name change, the 1985 Annual Report stated: "While the Council is grateful for and wished to acknowledge the support it has received from the present administration, members felt the new name was reflective of our desire to be an independent advocacy organization for women."[31]

The second major change was city funding for a coordinator position and the provision of office space in city hall for the council. According to Luhrs, they sought a Community Development Block Grant to set up the office and were given $15,000 despite competition from the CEDO, which was asking for $75,000 to start up a women's economic opportunity project. While the CEDO did not get the money for their project, it still was not easy for the council to get funded. The women who worked on securing CDBG money for the council "felt they had an educating process to go through" with CEDO director Peter Clavelle and Sanders to get the administration's support, said Luhrs. Although Luhrs would have been pleased to see both the council and the CEDO project funded, she stressed the importance of funding the council: "It's important that the council had an office— that programs for women were really overseen by women who were advocates for women more than just as part of some other office. . . . In my work here, I've found that indeed they've needed . . . women who are real focused" [on women].

In addition to the $15,000 grant, there was $5,000 in the CEDO's budget for the Women's Economic Opportunity Program. This money was used to add a part-time staff person, Martha Whitney, who helped Luhrs "develop a program to do nontraditional job training for women."

A number of previous council projects continued during that season, such as the Women's Self-Defense Project and the War and Militarism Conference. Regarding the former, the council created a "striking poster" against rape in conjunction with the Women's Rape Crisis Center, and produced a video demonstration tape about self-defense.[32] Concerning the latter, the theme of "pornography and militarism" was addressed. The first day featured a program of speakers, and the next day there was a rally. After the rally, there were "some demonstrations in front of some of the worst [bookstore] offenders . . . [and] two bookstores in town voluntarily stopped stocking pornography," said Luhrs.

The Women and Economic Justice Committee continued its work in 1984–1985, too. Luhrs explained that "the major focus of that committee has been working on an ordinance . . . [that] will have hiring goals for women in the construction trades—in all the trades." Luhrs also was "trying to get together a job bank in the trades." A final carry-over project was the attempt to increase the number of women on the city commissions. This effort had met with initial success, with women on all but two of the city commissions that year. New initiatives included several women's legal clinics—"Sexual Harassment in the Workplace," "Understanding the Court System," and "Divorce, Child Custody, and Adoption." In late 1985, the Women's Council sponsored a successful conference called "Women Speak Out Against Violence Against Women."[33]

In 1985–1986, the most important accomplishment of the council was the passage of an affirmative-action ordinance requiring a certain percentage of women to be hired for trade jobs that were federally funded. The ordinance, sponsored by Alderwoman Zoe Breiner, would force contractors with more than sixteen employees to give 10 percent of the available jobs in areas "like carpentry, painting and plumbing," to women. It was designed to counteract sex discrimination in trade jobs, since over 6 percent of the employed men in Burlington had jobs in this field while less than 1 percent of the women did. The ordinance was modeled after a similar one in Seattle, Washington. For businesses with six to fifteen employees, at least one woman would have to be hired; if there were less than five employees, there would be no hiring quotas. Over the protests of contractors, the ordinance finally passed the board in a 12–1 vote in March 1986, with only Republican Fred Bailey voting against it. The Women's Economic Opportunity Program also developed a project called Step-Up for Women, "aimed at training low-income and underemployed women and single mothers in the skilled trades." The National League of Cities and Towns gave the Women's Economic Opportunity Program a second-place City Innovations Award in 1988.[34]

In light of the new ordinance, the Women's Council and the Women's Economic Opportunity Program hosted a forum "for women interested in work in the skilled trades." The forum included women already working in construction and potential employers. However, a year after the ordinance was adopted, contractors complained that they were unable to find enough qualified women for the jobs. In fact, they said, it was not possible to even find enough men to fill the jobs. Despite these difficulties, women comprised 15 percent of the forty-person work force on Kessel-Duff Construction's South

Meadow Project. While the number of women doing construction jobs in the city had more than doubled in the year since the ordinance was implemented (from 3 percent to 7.5 percent), many firms could not yet meet the 10 percent goal. Consequently, the city considered them within the boundaries of the law if women made up 10 percent of their entire labor force.[35]

A new project to prevent sexual assault against women—the Burlington Sexual Assault Prevention Project—was initiated by the council during its 1986–1987 season. Luhrs, noting the staggering increase in violence against women and young people in recent years, asked the city's Finance Board for $1,500 to set it up. Less than a week later, the Women's Council had its money. Besides "free self-defense classes for women, girls, and seniors," the project planned to set up a Burlington-wide prevention program. Other new projects included The Women's Consortium for the Construction of Housing, which would provide emergency family shelters for homeless women and their children as well as try and arrange for "more permanent housing, perhaps by forming cooperatives or land trusts." Other council activities included the cosponsorship of International Women's Week, involvement in "hiring an enforcement officer for the Women in the Trades Ordinance, and the production of a video entitled 'Women at Work: Local Tradeswomen.'"[36]

During the 1987–1988 season, the Burlington Women's Council expanded its programming activities. The office in city hall continued its advocacy and referral role, handling over 1,500 calls and many hundreds of visits over the year. The council published the results of its Sexual Assault Prevention report and helped secure overwhelming passage of a March 1988 town meeting resolution urging the Board of Aldermen to support and fund programs in this area. The largest Take Back the Night march ever held in Burlington (over 500 people attended) was cosponsored by the council. Free self-defense classes for women, girls, the elderly, and people with disabilities were offered by the council and funded by the Burlington Police Department. The Women's Consortium for the Construction of Housing played a key role in the opening of the Emergency Family Shelter in Burlington. Many cultural events were sponsored or cosponsored by the council, including the annual International Women's Week event. Finally, the council produced a newsletter called *Network News* for the first time.[37]

The Women's Council's last season under the Sanders administration saw more advocacy and referral services for women (over 150 requests per month), the continuation of the Sexual Assault Prevention Project, the offering of women's self-defense classes (reaching 400 people per year), the cosponsorship of the annual Take Back the Night march, the production of a "Taking Charge of Our Neighborhood" conference, and the sponsorship of numerous cultural events.[38]

Luhrs perceived her role on the Women's Council in the following way: "My priorities are really women and generally progressive politics, but from a pretty feminist point of view. I don't trust capitalism or socialism to take care of women." Luhrs felt the relationship between Sanders and the women's community in Burlington was initially difficult for Sanders because

> it was ... a matter of [his] attitude; a matter of making this connection between socialism and workers and women—that they [women] were included. ... I think Bernie's always been really good about issues of child care ... but separate issues around women, I think he used to be a lot more suspicious of what it was about.

Moreover, said Luhrs, it didn't seem that Sanders really understood the feminization of poverty issue, that is, "that the poor are women and children."

Things began to shift in the relationship between Sanders and the council in 1983, according to Luhrs:

> [There was a] problem ... when we reorganized the council because then it wasn't a lot of these women that he knew and had worked for him. It was a whole other set of women who were saying: "We have an agenda of our own, and we're going to take some power and we would like your support—we are basically supportive of this administration."

As a result there was a transformation on Mayor Sanders's part, from his having been "somewhat threatened" to his being more open to women's initiatives. Luhrs felt generally positive about the role Sanders played in helping the council obtain funding from the city, at least in recent years. However, the lack of funding in the early years was a reflection of the administration's priorities, according to Luhrs. "The council wasn't one of the major priorities in terms of Bernie's personal interest. I think he was more interested in the Arts Council and the Youth Council happening."

Asked if there were any real points of conflict between the Sanders administration and the women's community in Burlington, Luhrs responded that there have been no big political differences and that the administration has proved generally supportive. But what conflict exists is of a more vague nature:

The kinds of things I would hear in the women's community have to do more with style—have to do with the feeling of rather unilateral decision-making style and that women's issues aren't going to be the first thing to come up in the administration.... There's just a perception ... "Yeah, socialism, but it seems to be the same sort of hierarchy with a man at the head."

The Sanders administration was involved in other women's issues that are not officially part of the Burlington Women's Council, namely pay equity for women, or comparable worth, and the funding of a battered women's shelter and rape crisis center.

As early as winter 1983, during a mayoral forum, Sanders said he had "started a reclassification of city jobs to ensure that women get paid the same as men for the same work" to rectify the terrible working conditions of women in city hall. Right after Sanders's reelection in 1983, the Board of Aldermen, with no dissenting votes, endorsed the concept of comparable worth for women city workers. At that time, women city workers were making an average of about $50 less per week than male city workers. Also, at the urging of Progressive Coalition Alderwoman Zoe Breiner, the board agreed to check into "sex discrimination and work to eliminate it in hiring new employees," since over three-quarters of city jobs were held by men.[39]

An administration official explained that a "reclassification plan" was put into effect by the city in the summer of 1983, but that for the most part it "was a disaster." The reason, he said, is that reclassification studies "inherently are terribly destructive things to get involved in and ours proved no different." The problem lies in analyzing a job and assigning worth, to "get someone to understand it's not you personally ... [but rather] a particular job you are in. And there is no way you can separate that out."

The original plan was not very sophisticated, according to this official, and the city's first plan "wasn't a true comparable worth study." The reasons are technical, relating to arriving at equal pay for comparable work across the various work categories set up by the study. In "phase two" of the implementation of comparable worth, the equalization of various work categories so that everyone rated with x number of points receives the same amount of pay will be achieved. The city has informed its workers that no one would lose pay due to reclassification.

In summer 1988, the city and the union representing city workers (the American Federation of State, County and Municipal Employees, or AFSCME), came to an understanding on the comparable worth issue. Using a "classification system" devised by an independent consultant in 1987, "pay inequities among workers who make less money than other employees with equally demanding jobs would be eliminated over a three-year period." While no one would experience pay cuts due to the implementation of this agreement, over half of the city's work force would see pay increases ranging from several dollars to $80 per week.[40]

In another area, two CDBG-funded projects in Burlington were also aimed toward women. In summer 1982, the Board of Aldermen's allocation of block grant funds included $85,000 for a battered women's shelter and $1,000 for the Rape Crisis Center. Through fiscal year 1987, block grant funds consistently funded the Women Helping Battered Women Shelter and the Rape Crisis Center.[41]

The comments concerning Sanders and his administration's relationship to women and their issues ran the gamut from accusations of a "macho" style and tokenism to praise for his accomplishments. One administration insider noted that Bonnie Vander Tuin, Personnel Department director after Jim Dunn, was the only woman appointed by Sanders to head a department, and she didn't stay long. Sanders, however, appointed women to head the Mayor's Council on the Arts and the Mayor's Youth Office, and also appointed women to the positions of assistant city attorney, assistant city clerk, assistant city treasurer, city constable, and the newly created position of personnel manager. (The Personnel Department was consolidated under the City Treasurer's Office during the 1987–1988 fiscal year.)[42] In another administration insider's estimation, "the tension comes with the women's groups because they don't see Bernie as a feminist—and he's not—and partly that's his age, and he tries hard. I think he relies on men primarily." Still another administration insider thought Sanders "has a lot of respect for individual women," but that he does not seem to get enough "input" from women and that "women would like to have more influence" regarding the administration's decision-making process. Two men in the administration praised the mayor's accomplishments on women's issues, the former citing the comparable worth "victory," the latter touting block grant funding for the battered women's shelter and day-care programs.

One progressive activist had heard from others that Sanders "is not a reliable feminist." However, this activist reported, "it has not been my experience at all." She elaborated: "In situations I've been in, he's been very respectable. It doesn't seem like he's a feminist from his agenda, I mean that's not on the top of his list of issues, though he and his administration ha[ve] pushed for pay equity." She also pointed to Sanders's support of day care and after-school programs as being important issues for women.

Progressive critics of the Sanders administration were generally harsh on Sanders's record with women. For example, one said:

I guess he's finally agreed to set up a women's committee [that is, Women's Council] that has some teeth to it, but for years women were trying to get him to take their concerns seriously . . . and it was the same thing—he just wasn't listening.

There's a quote in the paper—people raised the issue about women in responsible positions in city hall, and he came out with this classic reactionary statement about how he's not going to single out women because he doesn't believe in tokenism.

Another progressive critic explained her view of the situation of women at city hall: The "lack of women around him and his seeming inability to have women in any leadership positions in city hall [is a problem]. He has some strong women there and I give them credit for being able to stay there and contribute; I think his inner circle's . . . all men."

Still another progressive critic had this to say about Sanders's relation to women:

If you look at all . . . the big jobs, very few [go] to women. Only through great pushing was there finally a Women's Council . . . in the city . . . after four years in office. . . . He hasn't done anything affirmative, he hasn't done anything necessarily too bad, but he's done nothing that would make any great changes for women at all.

One academician felt Sanders has no special focus on feminist concerns because of his class analysis. Thus, for him to separately put attention on women's issues would "detract from [his] ultimate concern [with the] working-class struggle," she said. However, she added, Sanders has improved on his handling of women's concerns.

Sanders defended his position on women's issues in this way:

[People say]: "I'm in the women's movement. I'm in the environmental movement. I'm in this movement and I'm in that movement"—and Ronald Reagan is President of the United States.

Should we vote for Madeline Kunin [governor of Vermont] because Madeline Kunin is a woman? To the degree people think that that's true, I would regard that as a sexist position. I get distressed when somebody looks at things from a single point of view. I think we need to develop a movement. And the movement has got to be based on a class analysis. The class issue [is the most important].

The reason women are excluded ... [and] working for miserable wages (are treated like shit, to my mind), or the reason that companies destroy the environment, has to do with a class analysis of America—who owns the country and the political life. ... A woman is making minimum wage or an inadequate wage [and] that has got to be dealt with not just because she is a woman but because she is a worker. The goal of democratic socialism is that women should have as much representation as they are [a percentage of] the population.[43]

Asked specifically about the situation of women in city hall, the mayor replied:

There are more men department heads than there are women [department heads]. We have done more than any other administration—local administration—in Vermont history to bring women into the process. There are a whole lot of women involved in the process. ... It's not an intentional effort, needless to say, to exclude women, and I think our record on the whole issue of women's rights is a very good record.

The bottom line for me—and I have a strong criticism for those who think otherwise—the issue to me [is] the quality of the individual and if the administration were to end up with all women and no men, I wouldn't blink an eye. The people that we have are the best people that I could find for the particular job.[44]

While the Arts Council and the Youth Council are clear success stories, the Burlington Women's Council is another matter. For a variety of reasons, it got off to a slow start and is only now building some momentum. Ironically, by distancing itself from the administration on some level, the Women's Council may have a better chance for long-term survival than do the Arts and Youth Councils.

Sanders appears to have made progress on women's issues. While few, if any, would consider him a feminist, it is clear that he has a greater appreciation of women's issues than when he first took office. Furthermore, it seems he now makes links between economic issues and women's concerns. By letting go of the Women's Council and no longer feeling a need to control it, as well as giving support to its concerns through city hall when appropriate, Sanders showed an ability to grow in an important area for democratic socialism.

Despite progress, women's issues were not one of Sanders's top priorities. Many women interviewed, both inside and outside the administration, raised concerns around the mayor's style and process. There was also an interesting difference between administration respondents based on gender: The women generally spoke of his "male style" of doing things and his not being a feminist, while men spoke of his accomplishments for women. This is reflective of gender differences; women tend to be more in touch with issues of process while men tend to be more concerned with accomplishments.

These gender differences were less pronounced for Progressive Coalition members outside the administration, probably because they did not have day-to-day contact with Sanders. The mayor was given credit by both those inside and outside his administration for dealing with the issue of day care. This is an important issue, since the care of children has profound implications for a society and must be addressed by democratic socialism.

The mayor's support for a number of women's issues outside the purview of the Women's Council, such as comparable worth, the Battered Women's Shelter, and the Rape Crisis Center, is noteworthy. These are important accomplishments, and the fact that Sanders supported them must be acknowledged.

Sanders's leftist critics were harsh in their assessment of the mayor's interactions with women, though they seemed somewhat fixated on what I perceive to be his earlier attitudes and/or actions. However, people from various groups raised the issue of Sanders's inner circle of all male advisors. The mayor's inner circle, while changing somewhat over the years, included David Clavelle, Peter Clavelle, Jonathan Leopold, Jr., John Franco, Jim Schumacher, and George Thabault. Some women expressed feelings of having been "overlooked" or "cut out of the decision-making process" at various points. Sanders's statement that "if the administration were to end up with all women and no men, I wouldn't blink an eye," seems a bit gratuitous, given the situation.

In conclusion, the academician's comments seem to hit the mark. She pointed to Sanders's primary focus on class analysis as being an impediment to his taking women's issues as seriously as he should, since this orthodox Marxist position sees the struggles of women (and others) as secondary to the class struggle. However, she said, Sanders has moved forward in his dealings with women and their issues, and this may ultimately influence his analysis.

MAYOR'S TASK FORCE ON THE ELDERLY

In setting up his original task forces, Sanders had included a Mayor's Task Force on the Elderly to look into "transportation, housing, employment, health and nutrition" for the elderly.[45]

The Mayor's Council on the Elderly was officially convened in 1981. Although short-lived, the council accomplished a number of things. In the area of housing, a standardized application was created for the elderly wanting subsidized housing, so that individual applications for each housing complex did not need to be filed. Limited progress was made to enlarge the subsidized elderly housing stock in the city. In the area of health care for the elderly, the council fought against a Blue Cross/Blue Shield rate increase, raising a number of important issues. The council also got doctors in the Burlington area to make their elderly clients more aware of the methods for contesting high doctor fees and their ability to use Medicare in certain situations. Regarding transportation, the council made the local transportation agency "much more receptive" to their elderly clientele. Finally, the council was able to solicit input from the elderly in all the housing projects concerning their needs. The major issue was "snow and ice on sidewalks." A Senior Citizens Day also was sponsored by the council.[46]

The 1982 Burlington Annual Report was the last time the Mayor's Council on the Elderly was mentioned. Asked what had happened to the council, the mayor responded: "We put together some good people, and in fact it just faded out." According to Sanders, it flopped because no one really wanted to take primary responsibility for it. The person who was the most likely candidate refused after the daily newspaper attacked Doreen Kraft, who was taking responsibility for the Arts Council, commented Sanders.[47]

Another reason the Mayor's Council on the Elderly did not work, said Sanders, was that "you already have a lot of entrenched[elderly] groups ... people have their own turf ... [and they were] not all that sympathetic [to] working together." Sanders felt the idea of the council was important, but admitted failure. Said Sanders: "That's an area I can take responsibility for; we kinda gave up." However, the mayor pointed out, programs were still being carried out for the elderly. "We have a very fine program where we are bringing live entertainment—as well as film and video stuff—to the senior citizen housing places," said Sanders.[48]

This task force, although accomplishing some minor things, never got off the ground. Again, the task force was not high on the mayor's list of priorities. However, without a key person to take responsibility for the task force, and with competing organizations already existing in the city, it proved to be a difficult endeavor. The failure of the Mayor's Council on the Elderly is unfortunate, as it could have played an important role in Burlington.

BURLINGTON DISABILITY COUNCIL

In 1987, the Burlington Disability Council was formed to help the city "in increasing access for people with disabilities in employment, recreation, business and housing opportunities." By lobbying for disability rights and promoting access throughout Burlington, the council is moving toward its goal of a "barrier-free city." Its first projects have sought to achieve access for people with disabilities to public facilities, events, and services.[49]

In 1987–1988, the council published a guide on accessibility, helped the Department of Public Works "bring curb ramp specifications into compliance with federal standards," began work on the passage of an affirmative-action policy in city hall specifically for people with disabilities, and surveyed public buildings in the city that need to be architecturally redesigned in order to make them accessible. Money from Burlington's Capital Improvements Bond has been set aside for this purpose.[50]

GAY AND LESBIAN ISSUES

The first time Sanders issued a public statement on the issue of gay men and lesbian women's rights came during a mayoral candidates' forum in February 1983. At that time, in response to a question from the audience, Sanders and the other mayoral candidates came out in "support [of] equal rights for homosexuals."[51]

However, one of Sanders's harshest progressive critics had this to say about the forum:

Take his [Sanders's] position on gays—it was unbelievable. [At] a huge meeting . . . at the Flynn Theater [a] question was asked: "How does everyone . . . stand on . . . [the issue of] gay discrimination?" [Judith] Stephany came out immediately and said she opposed any discrimination against gays. Sanders came next and got up there and said he was for human rights. So the guy who asked the question said: "Say gay, Bernie" . . . and he flustered and said: "G-g-gay." But before he did that, [Jim] Gilson, the Republican, jumped up and said: "I'm for gay rights," and then Bernie came up and said: "I'm for gay rights."

When the first Gay Pride march took place, he was absent. He sent a telegram. This is a socialist?

In summer 1983, an issue related to gay and lesbian rights was presented at a Board of Aldermen meeting. The board was asked to support the annual Gay Pride march and to endorse a resolution favoring city support for a Lesbian and Gay Pride Day. When it came to a vote, the city endorsed both the march and the day by a 6–5 vote. Democratic alderman Maurice Mahoney voted with the Progressive Coalition board members and a Republican and Democrat were absent from the meeting, making passage of the measure possible. After it passed, Sanders reiterated his support for gay and lesbian rights, commenting: "In the city of Burlington and the state of Vermont people have a right to exercise their lifestyles. . . . This is a civil liberties issue."[52]

The next year the board took a step backward. In 1984 the progressives were outvoted at the meeting, and consequently a watered-downed version of the prior year's proclamation was endorsed, which "affirm[ed] the rights of homosexual men and women, including the right of assembly, but deleted a section that would have proclaimed June 15 Lesbian and Gay Pride Day in Burlington."[53]

A new resolution was passed in 1985 which went further than the 1984 one but fell short of the 1983 wording. This time, with the support of progressives and Democrats, the resolution endorsed "the civil rights of homosexuals, specifically with respect to employment, housing, child custody and public services," but deleted "any reference to gay pride or a special day."[54]

In summer 1986, gubernatorial candidates Madeline Kunin and Bernard Sanders gave speeches at the annual Gay Pride march. During his speech, Sanders stated that "it was time to judge human beings on the quality of their lives and not their sexual preferences." In 1988, Sanders urged the Board of Aldermen to support a bill in the state legislature to ban discrimination against gay men and lesbians, and the Progressive Coalition successfully introduced and passed a resolution against "queer-bashing" in the city.[55]

Burlington's role in promoting gay rights has been acknowledged. In an article about life as a gay or lesbian in Vermont, the *Rutland Herald/Times-Argus*'s Sunday magazine reported that "the city of Burlington has taken the largest step toward acceptance of gay people of any community in the state, and many communities in the country." The article cited Burlington's "fair housing ordinance" which does not permit landlords to deny housing to people due to their sexual preference.56

The record seems to speak in Sanders's favor on this issue. His statements and actions consistently supported gay and lesbian rights (though he often couched his support in the language of civil rights), and Burlington made real progress during the Sanders years in the area of gay and lesbian rights. The most forceful statement to this effect occurred during Sanders's first term, when the city went on record in support of Lesbian and Gay Pride Day. Despite some backpedaling, in subsequent years the board agreed to a resolution supporting gay and lesbian civil rights and backed that up by approving housing legislation that prohibited discrimination against people based on their sexual preference.

Overall, Sanders and the Progressive Coalition have played a very positive role on this important issue, especially in light of their lack of a majority on the board. The city is certainly far ahead of other Vermont towns and cities, and nationally has done better than most.

VERMONT REDS BASEBALL TEAM

Early into his second term, Sanders—a baseball aficionado—and one businessperson in Burlington attempted to bring a Pittsburgh Pirates AA farm team to Burlington. The talks were unsuccessful, but the mayor and the businessperson persisted, and in 1983 were finally successful in attracting the Cincinnati Reds AA to Burlington. Getting the Board of Aldermen's approval was easy, particularly because the $30,000 needed to upgrade the University of Vermont's Centennial Field to meet the Eastern League's requirements would be raised by one businessperson's "Friends of Baseball" group.[57]

This businessperson explained how he helped in getting the team to Burlington:

I worked hard with him [Sanders] to get a professional baseball team here. He got them here, [but] had it not been for the business community—raising money to do the things that were promised to get the team here—it wouldn't have happened, and he knows that.

I was criticized for it by some businesspeople. They didn't want to support anything that would make him look good and that was pretty sad. . . . I was turned down for contributions by some businesses that were very generous. There are people now who won't give Bernie credit for bringing that baseball team here.

The Vermont Reds played the 1984 to 1987 seasons and were a very successful team. In each of its first three seasons, the Reds captured the Eastern League title.[58] According to one Progressive Coalition member who also helped get the Reds to Burlington, many thousands of people have enjoyed Reds games—with as many as 5,000 people turning out for some games. He assessed the political impact of having the Reds in Burlington this way:

It creates a sense of local pride and [it is a] regular attraction. It's good for business in town. You talk to the mayor of Indianapolis—if you ask him the best thing he did, it was get[ting] the Colts [a football team]. It gives them a sense of excitement and being in the [big] time, and I think that's not such a small accomplishment.

However, the Reds were not destined to stay in Burlington. For the second time, the Reds parent club, the Cincinnati Reds, threatened to move their farm team to a warmer climate. This time, they carried it out. The 1988 baseball season saw a new team, the Vermont Mariners (a farm club for the Seattle Mariners), playing in Burlington. The Mariners, however, lasted only one season.[59]

There were intense negotiations between the Sanders administration and the owner of a minor league team in Pittsfield, Massachusetts, to relocate the club to Burlington. Despite the best efforts of Sanders, a segment of the business community, and Lt. Gov. Howard Dean (who got the state to commit up to $1 million for improvements to the ball field), there wasn't enough time to meet the owner's precondition—$225,000 in season ticket sales. In 1989, Burlington was without a minor league team for the first time in four years, and it was unlikely that another one would locate in the city in the foreseeable future.[60]

CONCLUSION

There is little doubt that Sanders did much to improve the quality of life for Burlingtonians during his tenure as mayor. From the arts to youth to baseball, the mayor championed issues that have enriched all residents' lives. The fact that Sanders had some extremely competent people to help him accomplish this does not diminish the contribution he personally made in this area.

Other efforts met with more limited success or failure. In the area of women's issues, Sanders's record is mixed. He seems to have heightened his consciousness around women's concerns, although there was little, if any, change when it came to process and decision-making issues. And although Sanders strongly supported the concerns of the elderly, they do not have the institutionalized voice at city hall that other groups have.

Quality-of-life concerns are very important when we consider nonreformist reforms toward a socialist society. While none of these accomplishments by the Sanders administration, in their own right, can be considered nonreformist reforms (with the possible exception of child care), cumulatively they at least begin to challenge traditional cultural hegemony. Too often, socialist concerns have been framed as only economic and political questions, and consequently, interpersonal relationships and cultural issues are often short-shrifted. The fact that the Sanders administration addressed many of these quality-of-life concerns is encouraging, for they must be on a democratic-socialist agenda if positive change in society is to be accomplished.

Central America: Sanders and the Peace Movement

Mayoral administrations in the United States, as a rule, do not get involved in foreign policy matters. The reason, it seems, is two-fold: First, most mayors do not see foreign policy as being under their purview, since these issues supposedly don't affect localities and they have little, if any, jurisdiction over these matters, and second, they are too busy with the everyday tasks of running municipalities to get involved in such issues.

Not true for Sanders. A significant amount of his time and energy was devoted to national and international issues, and during his tenure as mayor, he addressed such issues as Reagan's social welfare budget cuts and increased U.S. militarization, wealth disparity in America, world hunger, nuclear disarmament, U.S.-Soviet relations (Sanders set up a sister city relationship between Burlington and the Soviet city of Yaroslavl in summer 1988, which led to a visit from a Soviet delegation in fall 1988), the invasion of Grenada, the situation in South Africa, and U.S. policy in Central America, in particular, Nicaragua. The mayor made it very clear that he sees a connection between local concerns and national/international issues. At one point, Sanders remarked: "Military spending becomes a local issue because those billions of dollars are not available for schools, housing, medical services, street repairs and other services."[1]

The theme of this chapter will be Sanders, Central America, and the peace movement. Our goal will be to see how a socialist mayor grapples with U.S. foreign policy on the local level, and the contradictions it raises and opportunities it provides for peace activists in the community.

GENERAL ELECTRIC (GE) ACTIONS

During Sanders's first term, Burlington's peace community was active in protesting U.S. involvement in Central America, although the mayor was not speaking out on this issue at the time. In August 1982, a group of activists targeted the General Electric (GE) plant in Burlington because it "is the only significant producer anywhere of the high speed, multi-barrel machine guns that are a basic component of virtually all the fighter aircraft in the Western world"—the Gatling gun, which is used extensively in Central America.[2]

Peace activists in Burlington also put an initiative measure on the ballot in fall 1982 that asked for termination of all U.S. aid to El Salvador—both military and economic—as well as the removal of all U.S. advisors from that country. The nonbinding proposal won by an almost 3 to 1 margin.[3]

In summer 1983, the Burlington peace community planned another demonstration. This time protesters planned to engage in civil disobedience (CD) actions at the plant, which drew criticism from both the GE union (International Union of Electrical Workers) and Sanders. In fact, after discussing the matter with union officials, Sanders publicly stated that

he hopes the protesters will abandon plans to try to stop trucks from entering or leaving the armaments manufacturing plant. . . . The result of what they are doing is to point the finger of guilt at working people. . . . Not everybody has the luxury of choosing where they are going to work . . . or [has] the money not to work.[4]

Likewise, GE union president Frank Moisan was displeased with the impending demonstration. He was disappointed that "peace activists" were planning the protest since "he and other members of his union have supported past peace marches and protests over the Reagan administration's defense buildup in the past." Robin Lloyd, affiliated with the Burlington Peace Coalition, responded by saying: "We are blocking the product and don't intend that to be seen as a threat to the workers or the plant."[5]

Sanders was being pulled in opposite directions by two of his constituency groups—workers and peace activists—and chose to side with the former. He urged peace activists not to create a "potential confrontation" with workers, but instead to direct such actions against the decision makers, that is, "the U.S. Congress and the president, not the guys at GE." This made sense, said the mayor, because "the answer is not to blame the workers who are trying to make a living, but to change the government."[6]

During an interview, Sanders elaborated on his position concerning the peace activists' protest and its effect on the GE workers:

> Their [the peace activists'] position is: "GE is manufacturing Gatling machine guns. Gatling machine guns are killing people in Central America. That is immoral. [Therefore] GE should be closed down tomorrow. . . ."
> I see that as a short-sighted position in two senses: 1) As mayor of the city of Burlington, I'm not going to throw 3,000 people out of their jobs at union wages and create a depression. . . . 2) The issue of machine guns and . . . how those machine guns are utilized is an issue of federal policy.[7]

About a week later, according to the daily newspaper, Sanders helped negotiate a compromise between the workers and the peace activists, with the protesters agreeing to curtail the demonstration by doing civil disobedience at the back gate rather than at the front gate where the workers entered. However, one of the peace activists involved in the planning of the demonstration said:

> We had made a decision very early on that we weren't going to block the front gate where people come into work, that we were going to focus it on the shipping gate, out back, where the trucks carrying the guns to be tested at [the] Underhill [testing range] came in and out. All that was clear despite what it said in some of the articles, which makes it look like we compromised with the city.

Just before the planned action was to take place, one of the members of the Burlington Peace Coalition commented to the daily newspaper: "At this point there is an understanding on all sides that we are all going to do our best to keep it calm and collected. The demonstration is not directed at the workers but at the products going to El Salvador. . . . After it's all over, the workers will be able to understand the protest." On the day of the protest, eighty-eight people engaged in a peaceful civil disobedience action. Sanders watched the action from a distance and said afterwards that "he was satisfied with the action of the police and the protesters."[8]

In assessing the GE action and articulating what he thought would be an appropriate way to influence U.S. foreign policy in Central America, Sanders said:

> I'd rather see protests against Senator Stafford, protests against Reagan, turning around federal policy rather than dividing the

workers of Burlington from the peace movement. In terms of the political struggle, which clearly is going to have to be led by labor and working people, that [the GE demonstration] goes exactly the wrong way. That drives people into the hands of Ronald Reagan, into the hands of reactionaries.[9]

The following year, in March 1984, a group of fifty protesters took up Sanders's suggestion to target the federal officials who make foreign policy decisions, engaging in a civil disobedience action at U.S. Senator Robert Stafford's Winooski office "to express their disapproval of Stafford's record on U.S. intervention in Central America." This group, which became known as the "Winooski 44," did much to influence Stafford's voting record on military aid to the Nicaraguan rebels, or Contras, in subsequent years.[10]

The tension that existed between the peace community and Sanders early in his administration came to a head over the GE demonstration. One of Sanders's progressive critics offered this perspective on the differences between the peace movement and the mayor:

It goes back to '83, when we decided to sit in at GE and Bernie opposed that. On the record, his opposition was that you're going to make the workers feel guilty . . . but I think there was something else going on there. Partially it was that, and he [also] just doesn't feel it [demonstrations] should be focused on the workplace, which I think sort of shows where he's coming from ideologically. . . .

Sure, the [U.S.] senators vote, but the point is it's the nature of the local economy and the nature of corporate capitalism that requires this war-time economy. You have to point a finger at the corporations . . . and you can do that without blaming the workers.

One peace activist commented on the tensions in this way:

He [Sanders] expected us to consult him before we did it [the GE action]. One of the reasons we did it without consulting him is because we wanted to show . . . everybody that the peace movement wasn't in Bernie Sanders's pocket, that if the peace movement wanted to do something, we were going to do it because it was right, and we didn't have to tell him nothing.

One of the peace activists who actively helped organize the GE demonstration had cultivated union ties at the plant. She was particularly upset about the alienation between the peace movement and the union at GE, a rift she said still has not healed. This peace activist blamed Sanders for the split between the two groups, although she acknowledged that peace activists share part of the blame. She explained:

> It was largely affinity groups from out of city that wanted to do this [civil disobedience action at GE], and those of us in the city said: "Well, OK, you should go talk to the unions," but they didn't—they didn't know who to talk to. And we should have immediately got going and talked to Bernie and talked to the unions.
>
> I mentioned it to him [Sanders] at a spaghetti dinner and he sort of said, "Oh," [to the fact] that this demonstration was going to come up. . . . Two or three weeks before the time, . . . [when] the news was coming out about it, he was very angry that he hadn't been notified and the unions were angry, too.

She and others then met with the union "and it was a complete bust—lots of shouting and insults thrown right and left." It was after this meeting that Sanders met with official representatives from the union and the peace movement.

Still another peace activist who also participated in the demonstration had a somewhat different take on the situation. It was true, he said, that a lot of the sentiment for the GE action "came from people outside of Burlington [be]cause people in the Burlington Peace Coalition were more hesitant to confront GE because they felt closer to the jobs issue," but these groups were based in Vermont. Regarding planning for the action, he related:

> The point is that we were really careful from the beginning, and had for a whole year, been trying to be real upfront with the issue of workers and trying to talk to workers there directly. We set up a meeting . . . to try to talk to some of the people in the union and make it clear that the action wasn't directed against them.

This activist blamed Sanders for the resulting strain between the peace movement and the union at GE:

> I think it was the day after that meeting with the union people [that] Sanders came out with a statement to the press saying that this action shouldn't happen, we were holding workers in Burlington responsible for the arms race, we were victimizing the workers and it was a mistake. . . .
>
> The main effect that it had, besides getting a lot of people in the peace movement pissed at Bernie, including a lot of people who had been close supporters of his, . . . [was to convey the impres-

sion] that we don't care about workers—[that] he's [Sanders] the only one who cares about workers.

Finally, this peace activist felt that Sanders's statement "made it impossible for the discussion with the union to continue and it really polarized things a lot." Moreover, it became very difficult "politically" for the union to continue discussions with the peace movement. The consequence, he said, is that all talks between the peace movement and GE union have ceased.

The tensions between Mayor Sanders and the peace movement were confirmed by many, both inside and outside of the administration. There was a surprising amount of agreement as to why Sanders was so often at odds with the peace movement. According to one administration official, Sanders "is really an old-time socialist, that is, the revolution comes from the working class and class oppression is the paramount problem." Consequently, she explained, "Bernie will criticize demonstrations that take place at GE because people who work there are working class [and it is] wrong to protest about products they're making." Sanders's motto, she added, is "don't attack the working class." One peace activist said that Sanders's approach to it was "another classic example of what happens when the . . . old line, pre-60s, strictly economistic thinking is in control of the way a person sees the world."

One Progressive Coalition alderman explained that some members of the progressive movement in Burlington—especially those in the peace movement—have felt estranged from the Progressive Coalition and Sanders:

Sometimes the peace movement groups have felt that we have been standoffish as a city council [sic] in terms of supporting affinity group activism, for example, some of us have chosen not to actively demonstrate at certain kinds of things because we felt that it could be politically difficult for us to be in that position in terms of our abilities to work in the city towards other goals.

Another Progressive Coalition alderman, however, claimed that there were no major splits between the mayor and the peace movement.

Regarding the use of civil disobedience, a number of observers felt that Sanders did not support this form of direct action. For example, one administration official said that "Bernie was not attuned to or terribly sympathetic to CD." Another voiced similar sentiments. And one Progressive Coalition alderman felt that Sanders did not oppose civil disobedience per se, but that the mayor did not think it was the best tactic to use regarding GE.

One progressive critic often at odds with the mayor gave a perspective radically opposed to Sanders's on who "the people" are and the role of direct action (civil disobedience):

On peace issues, it's mostly rhetoric [on Sanders's part]. . . . On the Sanders administration side, they were opposed to any form of direct action. There's nothing more pathetic than to see what happened at the GE plant. . . . All my friends were being arrested [and] Sanders was on the other side of the fence. The drama of seeing Sanders—the people's mayor—on the other side of the fence was very compelling, and a lot of people haven't forgiven him for that. . . . He's [Sanders] been unusually insensitive to popular movements like the peace movement.

Another progressive critic offered his analysis of why Sanders opposed a civil disobedience action at GE:

I think the main reason is that he really didn't have any control over it; it's something that happened independently of him. The peace movement was—for the first two years he was in office—running a kind of parallel or independent course from Bernie and then the GE thing brought that out, that he was out of touch. He didn't know what was going on. And even when someone tried to tell him, he couldn't take it.

Regarding the overall impact of the GE action, one peace activist reflected:

Before that [action], it was really clear that if you asked the average person on the street what GE makes in Burlington, they probably would have guessed toasters. After that demonstration, I don't think that plant ever got mentioned in the papers, even in *The Burlington Free Press*, without it being mentioned that, by the way, this is where the Gatling guns are made.

Sanders summed up his attitude toward the GE action:

Am I happy that the GE plant is producing Gatling machine guns which are destroying people in El Salvador? The answer is, needless to say, no. . . .
   How do you deal with American imperialism? And the whole Central America question? People are very upset about it. So am I. We all have reason to be upset about it. . . .

Change will come when working people begin to fight for their rights, and you cannot split the movement and push workers to one side and have peace activists on the other side. In the long run, that is going to be destructive.[11]

According to one progressive critic, Sanders's attitude has definitely changed since the 1983 GE action. He has taken peace concerns, especially the situation in Nicaragua, much more seriously. The mayor, for his part, succeeded in getting peace activists to target the policy makers such as U.S. Senator Stafford. However, there were other tension points with the peace movement, too.

PEACE CONVERSION

At the 1983 GE action, protesters also raised the issue of "peace conversion," that is, converting the GE plant from the production of war goods to the production of civilian goods. During the meeting between peace activists and GE union officials, Sanders agreed to set up a peace conversion task force. Said one of the peace activists:

During that meeting, we all remember some kind of pledge that Bernie was going to initiate a peace conversion committee or some kind of group that would bring together the unions, the peace movement, the church people ... to at least discuss the situation. ... And nothing has ever happened, not a word has been breathed about that.

One of the peace activists present at that meeting commented: "Bernie Sanders made a commitment to work closer with the peace movement in dealing with the union and the workers ... facilitating dialogue and discussion around issues of militarism, GE and the peace movement" and this has not happened. One administration official who was also actively involved in the peace movement stated that Sanders "made a pledge" to facilitate a "dialogue" between the two groups. She reminded him of it a year later, and though he admitted making such a statement, the mayor backed off saying he did not like the idea of peace activists "go[ing] to GE and tell[ing] the workers what to do."

Sanders, when asked about it, said he did not recall formally agreeing to setting up a peace conversion task force, but expressed strong support for the idea:

We did talk to the union a little bit about it [and] there's not a whole lot of interest on the part of the union and for the obvious reason that what the union in Burlington, Vermont, feels . . . about the issue of conversion is totally irrelevant to what GE is going to do.

The discussion of conversion is in fact a very, very important discussion because clearly all over the country there are workers who are frightened about . . . losing their jobs. And in order to develop a successful peace movement, you're going to have to tell millions of workers that they're not going to lose their jobs [if] peace comes to the United States.[12]

POLICE SURVEILLANCE OF THE PEACE MOVEMENT

Police surveillance of the peace movement in Burlington became an issue after a demonstration held in spring 1985 against the war in Nicaragua. A newspaper reporter covering the event discovered that one of the demonstrators "was an undercover policeman." One peace activist explained how it came to light:

There was a police informer . . . who had actually gone to the [CD] trainings. . . . You see, he [the informer] was in line there, holding arms with all the activists, so Don Melvin [of *The Burlington Free Press*] asked him questions, and then he [Melvin] said: "Haven't I seen you before? Aren't you a member of the Police Department?" And the guy just got up and ran away.

Sanders took action by asking Antonio Pomerleau, then head of the Police Commission, to create "a policy . . . to prevent infiltration of political demonstrations by undercover police officers." However, Pomerleau believed that the police chief, William Burke, should be the one to make those decisions, and Burke responded by saying that infiltration was "a sound police tactic." Because of the police chief's stand, Sanders and Burke fought over the police surveillance issue. Several months later, the Police Commission, by a 3–1 vote, adopted guidelines around "the use of undercover police officers."[13] One Progressive Coalition police commissioner explained that even though the police chief had given "his word" that further undercover police activities would not happen without the Police Commission's approval, "members of the Commission did not feel that strongly about trusting his word." Said this commissioner: "The first amendment issues are so important that we need to have some kind of civilian group looking at it."

According to the adopted guidelines, undercover police officers could not be used unless there was good cause to suspect a felony might occur; civil disobedience actions were not included under sanctioned undercover actions. Furthermore, if undercover officers were used, the police chief, except in dangerous cases, must first have the commission's sign-off. In dangerous situations where undercover agents are used, the police chief needed to tell "the commission as soon as possible."[14]

One progressive critic felt that while the policy guidelines adopted by the Police Commission were good, there was nothing to prevent the Burlington Police Department from breaking the guidelines, since there were no penalties for violating them. Furthermore, the guidelines addressed only one way that demonstrators' civil liberties were being violated. The police could still take photographs and keep records on them.[15]

Just days before the Police Commission implemented their guidelines, this progressive critic commented on Sanders's response to civil liberty concerns: "He says there should be no taping of lawful demonstrations. On the other hand, that's as far as he goes. He won't even press the issue of files. . . . He's just totally silent on civil liberties questions beyond the most blatant things."

One peace activist elaborated:

In 1983, Bernie was the one to uncover that there was a city policeman filming a peace demonstration . . . in an undercover fashion. And he [Sanders] told him to get rid of the tape, but we wanted to find out whether there was undercover surveillance of the peace movement, whether there were policies, where that information went, whether it went to the FBI and any national and state agencies, and whether the city of Burlington was going to develop a policy that protected the democratic rights of its citizens. And Bernie Sanders . . . [was] nowhere to be found after that [uncovering]. No one in the administration, including Bernie, would go to bat.

And nothing happened until two years later when it was discovered that there was continuing undercover surveillance by the Burlington Police Department of political demonstrations . . . and Bernie Sanders did not take a strong stand until really confronted with that.

And in fact, there were almost no regulations passed until there was some sort of political heat put on a Progressive Coalition police commissioner from outside of the Police Commission. . . . Here's a person appointed to the Police Commission by the Progressive Coalition . . . and he's not sure whether the police should be allowed to spy on the peace movement?

One Progressive Coalition member said he wholeheartedly supported the guidelines regulating the Police Department's use of undercover police. But he was quick to point out the need for undercover operations in some situations:

> There are some abuses that have taken place, and yet we must prevent terrorism. . . . So there's a two-edged sword . . . in my view to how much we can restrict what our police department does. They have no business collecting files, . . . wire tapping, [and] . . . snooping into private affairs of individuals who disagree, but they must absolutely prevent someone getting hurt.

In his own defense, Sanders offered this account of the matter:

> My role has been to strongly oppose the use of undercover agents, and after enormous amounts of lobbying, [we] did get three [votes]. It was not quite so easy as it looked . . . [but we] got three members of the Police Commission to say that there would be no undercover agents used for any . . . political activities.
>
> It [the guidelines] really means . . . that there's not going to be undercover agents in any way. That I think is reprehensible. I think if one gets a call about an extreme case, it would not be inappropriate under some circumstances, . . . but I think basically it's not going to happen.[16]

Sanders found himself in a difficult position on this one, due in part to his strong support from the policemen's union, and in part to the commission form of government. Although he maneuvered around the police chief by appealing to his supporters on the Police Commission, the fact that he did not move more quickly on the issue or take a strong stand left many to wonder if police surveillance was really a pressing concern to the mayor.

SISTER CITY PROJECT

Sanders began to openly align himself with the Sandinista government in Nicaragua during his second term. In summer 1984, he issued a statement saying that "the Reagan administration is working to overthrow one of the few Central America governments actively trying to address the region's problems." A few weeks later, Sanders spoke at a rally and march of about 250 people "celebrating the fifth anniversary of the Nicaraguan revolution and protesting U.S. policies in Central America."[17]

In an effort to express solidarity with the Nicaraguan people and to provide material aid, the city of Burlington, with the backing of Sanders and his Progressive Coalition, initiated a sister city project.[18] Pat Peterson, former special assistant to the mayor and Sister City Project coordinator at the time, explained that in early 1984

> the mayor began to talk about the possibility of a sister city relationship with a city in Nicaragua and began to explore that possibility with the Nicaraguan government . . . and also talk[ed] to a lot of people in Burlington to see what the willingness would be to support such a program.[19]

In late July, Sanders said he would go before the Board of Aldermen and request that it "approve a resolution making Burlington a twin city with Puerto Cabezas, a town in northeastern Nicaragua." Two months later, the Board of Aldermen voted to support the resolution. It passed without amendment, despite the best efforts of several Democrats and Republicans. Consequently, Burlington became one of about thirty cities in the United States at the time that had sister city relationships with Nicaraguan cities.[20]

It took a while for the sister city program to get off the ground. As late as spring 1985, there had been virtually no contact with Puerto Cabezas. One complicating factor was that Burlington's sister city had a large Miskito Indian population, which was unhappy with the Sandinista government. Things began to change when the Haymarket People's Fund in Boston gave Burlington $2,500 to foster its relationship with Puerto Cabezas. Several months later, several people from Vermont visited Puerto Cabezas—"the first official delegation from the city of Burlington to the people of Puerto Cabezas," according to Peterson. When the delegation returned, they reported that the city was in "desperate need of supplies Burlingtonians can provide." This provided the motivation to organize a material aids campaign.[21]

In fall 1985, a drive to collect needed items for Puerto Cabezas began. What followed was impressive. Peterson said they "went about the task of organizing a major community-wide drive to raise material aid for the Puerto Cabezas region and the costs of financing the shipment to go down there." Within a year a massive shipment was put together. Explained Peterson:

> Once word got out that we had found this route [to the Atlantic Coast] which had eluded other people, we were contacted by eight other groups throughout the U.S., including major humanitarian groups like Oxfam, Catholic Relief Services, and

Church World Services, who had been wanting to send aid to the Atlantic Coast.[22]

The response to the material aid drive was enormous. In Peterson's words:

> For a variety of different reasons, it seems that the sister city program provided a vehicle for people to help in a very grass roots, very direct way, and it's been a[n] extraordinary effort. The kind of support that we've had [has been] from churches, labor unions, individuals, big donors, small donors, small businesses, and then of course the Medical Center [Hospital] of Vermont, with its major contributions . . . which was very, very significant in terms of our effort.[23]

In addition to the supplies, over $15,000 was raised to help defray shipping and other expenses associated with the drive, said Peterson.[24]

That winter a ship "with more than $100,000 worth of humanitarian supplies" from the Burlington area sailed from New Brunswick, Canada, carrying a 20-ton shipment of "equipment, drugs, clothing and educational supplies" to Burlington's sister city. The supplies from Burlington were part of a 600-ton shipment, "the largest ever to the Atlantic Coast of Nicaragua."[25]

Since the first material aid drive, Burlington's sister city program has been involved in a number of activities. In fall 1986, it participated in a nationwide effort to gather "material aid for the Atlantic Coast of Nicaragua." Then in February 1987, eleven people associated with the sister city program headed for Puerto Cabezas "to install medical equipment in a new hospital and to build the city's first playground."[26]

Peterson explained that "people who were very pro-Sandinista . . . and people primarily interested in the Miskitos" worked together on the project. The relationship with the people in another country provided the glue that kept the project going. Peterson said that raising material aid has not been the only focus. "We have been outspoken [against] Contra aid because we feel we must be. . . . We're seeing very directly the damage [from] our national government's policies . . . and we must have a voice in trying to stop that."[27]

Burlington's sister city program with Puerto Cabezas has been a remarkable success with few critics. And it has added a personal dimension to a conflict that has been so charged with political rhetoric.

SANCTUARY/ TRADE EMBARGO

There were other components of the Sanders administration's Nicaraguan policy. For example, in spring 1985, Sanders and the Progressive Coalition attempted to get Burlington designated a sanctuary city for Central American refugees. The first draft of the resolution, proposed by a Progressive Coalition alderman, would have had the city serve as a sanctuary and "barred city employees—including police— from assisting in federal investigations or arrests of refugees living in sanctuary." When it became clear the measure lacked the necessary votes (the opposition questioned the legality of the proposed resolution), members of the Progressive Coalition supported a watered-downed amendment by a Democratic alderman. The new resolution backed "the principle of sanctuary as well as the Presbyterian church that is harboring a five-member family from Guatemala." With the support of the other Democrat on the board, the resolution passed over the objections of the Republicans.[28]

In light of much stronger sanctuary measures that have passed in other cities across the country (Cambridge, Massachusetts, and Berkeley, Los Angeles, and San Francisco), one administration official felt the sanctuary issue was a significant loss for the Sanders administration. Pat Peterson explained the Burlington outcome in this way:

The decision here in Burlington was to not have sanctuary as it is defined in those terms . . . [but rather] supporting the existing organizations in Burlington and Vermont that support and work for sanctuary but falling short of making governmental officials obligated on the part of the city to serve as a sanctuary city.[29]

One month later, the issue of the Reagan trade embargo on goods to Nicaragua came before the board. The daily newspaper reported that "Burlington aldermen, in a special meeting Tuesday, voted to encourage trade between the people of Nicaragua and the people of Burlington, trade which would have to take place in defiance of a trade embargo declared by President Reagan." Again, members of the Progressive Coalition and the two Democrats on the board voted yes while the Republicans present voted no on this issue.[30]

SANDERS'S TRIP TO NICARAGUA

At the request of the Nicaraguan government, Sanders attended the celebration of that country's sixth anniversary of the overthrow of U.S.-backed dictator Anastasio Somoza. Sanders, part of a 300-person

U.S. delegation, was the only U.S. elected official to attend. Speaking about his trip, Sanders said his "political goal is to convey to the Nicaraguan people that, in my view, a majority of Americans do not believe it is appropriate for the United States to unilaterally overthrow governments which it dislikes." While in Nicaragua, Sanders visited Burlington's sister city, Puerto Cabezas. Sanders began to use his trip to Nicaragua to condemn U.S. news coverage of events in Nicaragua and to attack the Reagan administration's policies toward the country.[31]

After Sanders's participation in the 1985 anniversary celebrations, he was able to arrange a meeting with the president of Nicaragua, Daniel Ortega. Ortega told Sanders "that his country is not a center of terrorism and wants to normalize relations with the U.S." After their meeting, Sanders issued a public statement stating that Nicaragua was not a menace either to the United States or to other countries. When Sanders returned to Burlington from Nicaragua, he spoke out strongly for peace talks between the United States and Nicaragua.[32]

Sanders's trip to Nicaragua was a very bold move. Mainstream Vermont politicians did not quite know what to make of it or how to respond to it. The governor and Vermont's congressional delegation responded cautiously to it. Some Burlington aldermen thought the trip would hurt the mayor politically, while others felt it would not have much of an effect.[33]

None of the speculation, however, seemed to faze Sanders. Later that summer, he gave a talk "extoll[ing] the virtues of Nicaragua's leftist government," and several months later spoke at a forum in New York with Nicaraguan President Ortega. Finally, in spring 1986, the governor from the territory in which Puerto Cabezas was located visited Burlington to warn against further U.S. funding of the Nicaraguan Contras.[34]

Progressives were impressed with Sanders's trip and his outspoken support of the Sandinistas. It showed his deep commitment to the larger issues and his belief that U.S. international actions should concern all its citizens. In fact, one Progressive Coalition alderman thought that Sanders's raising the big issues, such as Nicaragua, helped to "neutralize" the opinion of administration opponents who believed international issues were not important to discuss locally.

To those critics that claimed the Sandinista government was undemocratic and repressive toward the country's Miskito Indians, Sanders had a strong response:

That's the kind of criticism that disturbs me because it's irresponsible in the sense of not understanding the reality in which you're living. . . . Many of [these people] are very anti-Sandinista, saying many of the same things Ronald Reagan says, [such as]: "The Sandinista government is massacring the Miskito Indians. Therefore we are not going to support the Sandinista government."

The Sandinista government is forced to deal with an enormously complex problem, which they are now trying to deal with in as good a way as they can. But it's not good enough for some of our critics. So [they say]: "We should allow the U.S. government to destroy the government of Nicaragua . . . because it doesn't quite meet the high standards of making a revolution, in the midst of a war with the most powerful nation on Earth [and because the revolution] hasn't gone perfectly."[35]

Sanders did not deny that the Sandinista government had made some mistakes in their dealings with the Miskito Indians. But the "real world" was not always perfect, he said, and "under the circumstances that you exist in . . . [you do] the very, very best you can."[36]

CONTRA FUNDING

Even before the 1986 Contra aid package for $100 million was approved by Congress, the Burlington Board of Aldermen had voted 8-5 for "a resolution urging national legislators to not give more military aid to rebels fighting the Nicaraguan government and urged U.S. Senator Patrick Leahy . . . to hold congressional hearings on Contra atrocities."[37]

After the congressional vote in favor of Contra funding, Sanders came out strongly against it and even recommended massive protests in Burlington and around the country to dramatize public opposition. GE corporate and labor officials were concerned about Sanders's statements calling for protests, obviously worried that his stance would encourage renewed protests at the plant. They asked Sanders for "an apology." Sanders refused and issued a rebuttal to GE, "denounc[ing] what he described as an effort by the management of Burlington's General Electric Company plant to manipulate local politics and cause division between union workers and peace activists." The editors of *The Burlington Free Press* came to Sanders's defense, saying that the mayor was not encouraging demonstrations at the GE plant. GE officials really had little to worry about, as the mayor had already publicly stated that he was against a proposed initiative to close GE. Said Sanders: "If GE in Burlington were to close tomorrow, it would re-open in Alabama or California a few months later making exactly the same product."[38]

An aldermanic public hearing was held during this brouhaha (with only six of the thirteen aldermen present) at which most of the 125 people in attendance expressed outrage over Contra funding. With the exception of Republican Fred Bailey, all the Democrats and Republicans refused to attend because of their opposition to engaging in aldermanic foreign policy debates. Due to lack of an aldermanic quorum, no resolutions could be passed. To build on the momentum of these events, anti-interventionist activists decided to place a nonbinding initiative on the November 1986 ballot that would express city voters' support or opposition to the administration's unofficial war against Nicaragua. The final vote showed a majority of voters rejected Contra aid, but the measure did not win overwhelming approval.[39]

CONCLUSION

Since 1985, Sanders has consistently spoken out against U.S. involvement in Central America, particularly Nicaragua. Some of his boldest initiatives have come in this area, and they have served, by accident or design, to mend fences with Burlington's peace community. But some disagreements and bad feeling persist, stemming, at least in part, from differences in analysis and tactics. In analyzing the problems that face the progressive movement in the United States, Sanders has consistently used the lens of class struggle to inform him. He also has shown an aversion to breaking that movement down by issues. His clash with the peace movement, then, was probably inevitable given that the mayor, on the one hand, sees the issue of war and peace through the workers' struggles, while the peace movement, on the other hand, focuses on the military-industrial complex and sees the workers as part of that machinery.

But where the mayor's and the peace movement's paths crossed was in a mutual perception that the policy makers in the United States, whether the federal government or large corporations, must be held accountable for the human cost of their respective actions. And while Sanders and the peace movement are in complete agreement when it comes to foreign policy issues, there are tensions when the issues take on a local dimension. Strains were evident over the issues of civil disobedience as a tactic and the seriousness of police surveillance of the peace movement. These differences reflect disagreements over the question of how radical change can happen in this country, who is responsible for bringing about this change, and how to confront government resistance to such changes.

Sanders probably has done more than any other elected politician in the country to actively support the Sandinistas and their revolution, and this is no small accomplishment. The mayor, by challenging the ideological hegemony and cold war mentality put forth by the Reagan administration, helped dispel the myth of a Russian threat at our doorstep. His constant articulation of important national and international issues and his ability to link them to events on the local level proved very significant, both in real and symbolic terms. The educational, nonreformist reform impact cannot be underestimated because only when people fully comprehend the extent to which they and their local governments are affected by decisions made at the federal level, be they cuts in social services while the military budget expands or the funding of the Contras which violates national and international law as well as perpetuating the regional conflict, will they become receptive to the notion of radical change in a democratic-socialist direction.

Conclusion

There is no viable U.S. Socialist Party today as there was in the early 1900s. The late-twentieth-century Socialist Party—the one that comes out of the Eugene Debs and Norman Thomas tradition—is so small as to be almost negligible on the U.S. political scene. Other leftist parties in the United States—many in the Marxist-Leninist or Maoist tradition—are even more fragmented and isolated from mainstream U.S. politics. Two somewhat more viable progressive-leftist electoral formations today—the Democratic Socialists of America (which is an offshoot of the U.S. Socialist Party and was created through the merger of the Democratic-Socialist Organizing Committee and the New American Movement in 1982) and the Rainbow Coalition (the electoral base for Jesse Jackson's 1984 and 1988 Democratic presidential campaigns, which has organizations in a number of states, including Vermont)—both are still pre-party formations and are very small in comparison to the early-twentieth-century Socialist Party.

If there were still a viable Socialist Party today, Bernard Sanders probably would belong to it. Given how strongly Sanders identified with Debs, it is ironic that he falls within the moderate/right-wing tendency (that is, the Hillquit and Berger tradition) of the old Socialist Party rather than the syndicalist/left-wing tendency (that is, the Debs-Hayward tradition). Sanders definitely sees elections as a viable and important means for moving toward socialism, while Debs and others saw elections more as an educational vehicle of the masses. Sanders puts a lot more faith in electoral politics and its potential accomplishments than Debs ever did. Thus, if there were a viable Socialist Party today with the same tendencies that existed in the early twentieth century, Sanders probably would receive a lot of criticism for practicing "sewer socialism." One of Sanders's progressive critics commented that he is a socialist, but "his idea of development is to make the most out of our city and then maybe translate that into goods and services for the poor—a real sewer socialism idea."

We must keep in mind, though, that after his almost miraculous election as mayor of Burlington in 1981 (which was chronicled in Chapter 2), Sanders had to overcome great obstacles to govern the city effectively. As we saw in Chapter 3, once Sanders was able to make his initial appointments to city government, his administration began to do good things for Burlington. With competent people in several city posts, Sanders was able to steer some city funds and services in the direction of his low- and moderate-income constituency.

Throughout Sanders's tenure as mayor, there was a curious mix of his sticking steadfastly to certain principles in some instances while almost giving away the store in other cases. Regarding the issues of development and growth explored in Chapter 4, Sanders fought for public access with waterfront development and for a scaled-down highway project. But we also saw the socialist mayor co-opted by the powers of capitalism. Said another progressive critic:

> The socialists, when they come in [to office], bring in very centralist ideas. They are rationalists. It is my contention that socialism, in its traditional forms, and to a great extent even to this day, is not quite as radical as many people think it is—it just sounds so.
>
> They're [the socialists] . . . growth [oriented] . . . [and] believe in sound economic development. For all the claptrap that you hear about proletarians, this plays directly into the hands of the business interests, who also want rational development . . . [and] planned growth, otherwise it won't be profitable. . . .
>
> In the cities, the socialists often prove to be the most efficient capitalists when they come into power in the name of socialism because the two ideologies can sometimes become painfully compatible with each other—the needs of capitalism and the ideology of socialism. It also gives capitalism some kind of color; it slaps its face and gives it a little complexion . . . [from] a gray, purely egotistical [one] to high-minded and socially oriented [one].

Chapter 5 discussed the Sanders administration's attempts to increase citizen involvement and participation in local government, from exciting low- and moderate-income voters to setting up Neighborhood Planning Assemblies. But along with this trend, there was the unfortunate tendency within the administration to confine important decision making to a small inner circle of men and increase the centralization of various governmental functions. Sanders's personality plays a role here, but the more important point is that the U.S. political system sets up a pattern whereby individualism is favored over collectivism. As a result, the electorate looks for dynamic and strong individual leaders, which tends to reinforce individualistic behavior within the political system.[1]

Chapter 6 pointed out some of the more radical initiatives of the Sanders administration in the area of land trusts, tenants' self-management and ownership, and worker-owned businesses. However, the unsuccessful fight for municipal cable television and the mayor's $1 million settlement from the cable company reinforces the lure of the almighty dollar, even for a socialist. The contradiction between his need to appear successful and the educational principles of socialism are most starkly evident in this case.

Chapter 7 indicates that Sanders could tenaciously pursue an idea like tax reform and eventually succeed in getting it, though in a watered-down form. This issue, more than any other, shows Sanders's persuasive powers; he was able to ultimately convince the business community that a new, progressive tax was necessary for Burlington. His ability to approach the business community in a way that engendered support rather than opposition indicated a "mellowing" on the mayor's part; gone was his strident rhetoric blaming the business community for the city's financial problems. Yet at the same time, Sanders had to compromise on some of his principles and negotiate a truce with the "big, bad capitalists."

In Chapter 8, Sanders's work toward the improvement of the quality of life in Burlington was most evident, especially in the area of the arts and youth. But the pernicious effect of institutionalized sexism has not been eliminated by the Sanders administration. How else can one explain Sanders's early struggles with the Mayor's Council on Women, the lack of women as department heads, and ongoing process concerns at city hall?

The ways in which a mayor can take bold stands on international issues and make important connections between events on the local and global level was explored in Chapter 9. However, we also saw that Sanders does not support all the tactics of leftist movements today, such as the use of civil disobedience to bring about social change.

Some say politics is the art of compromise: If you are elected to political office and expect to accomplish anything, you must be willing to negotiate and get half a loaf rather than no loaf at all. It is certainly true that Sanders compromised in a number of instances, sometimes successfully (for example, cable television, the excavation fee, the gross receipts tax, and the Southern Connector) and in other cases unsuccessfully (for example, the waterfront). On the whole, it is possible to say that the Sanders administration was more successful than not. However, there is an irony here. For a socialist administration to become successful, many actions must be taken that are clearly not socialistic in nature. How successful a socialist administration is, then, has little to do with socialism. In fact, it may be true that there is an inverse correlation—the more socialistic a socialist administration is, the less successful it might be from the public's point of view, since many of the attempts to implement its goals would be thwarted.

In their analyses of early-twentieth-century socialist municipal administrations (see Chapter 1), Bruce Stave and Sally Miller in particular appear to blame elected socialists at the local level for not being able to do the impossible, rather than explicitly acknowledging and recognizing the inherent limitations of the system, which prevents municipal socialism from becoming a reality. On the other hand, James Weinstein's analysis of what early municipal socialists were able to accomplish in light of systematic constraints is similar to my analysis of what Sanders has been able to achieve in Burlington.

The Sanders administration provides an excellent case study of the possibilities and limitations on municipal socialists. Various structural constraints on the local, state, and federal levels, as well as contextual, legal, and capitalist limits, shape what is and is not possible concerning municipal socialism. The rubric of reformist reforms versus nonreformist or radical reforms will allow us to judge the overall successes and failures of the Sanders administration.

Local structural constraints that limit radical change by a socialist mayor on the city level include the city charter, the separation of the executive and legislative branches of local government, city commissions, and the local power structure. We have seen how these various local constraints operated to hinder Sanders's attempts to implement his socialistically oriented agenda. Many of the mayor's struggles have been to maneuver around these obstacles. On many issues, the mayor had to contend with unified Democratic and Republican opposition to his initiatives. And on many occasions, the local business community and the city's daily newspaper fought tooth and nail to stop various Sanders proposals. Yet, even those in the business community recognized the limitations within which the mayor operated. Upon Sanders's election in 1981, Herluf Olson, president of the Medical Center of Vermont, commented that Sanders would not be able to implement radical changes "because of the constraints of city government."[2]

Turning to the state level, there were also many constraints impeding the Sanders administration. One of the most important was the lack of home rule for towns and cities in Vermont. Vermont is not a home rule state, that is, cities or towns are unable to change their city charters without approval from the state legislature. As the daily newspaper pointed out: "In Vermont, communities are considered 'creatures of the state.' That designation means, quite simply, that the state, via the Legislature, can dissolve a town, create it or alter its charter at will."[3] Since charter changes have to be approved by the state legislature, most nonreformist or radical reforms could easily be contained at this level of government. The clearest example of this was the area of taxation. The city of Burlington was severely limited in what it could do to ease the tax burden on low- and middle-income residents. More than once, the legislature put up a road block to prevent the city from implementing tax reform.

Sanders felt strongly about the need to shift power away from the state: "I think within the state of Vermont, what we can say is that local government is pretty powerless. One of our important fights is to give local government far more power."[4] He also stated:

> There are tremendous limitations to what local government can do, . . . and that's especially true in the state of Vermont. There are some states where you have far more flexibility in developing, for example, progressive tax laws [on the local level]. The state of Vermont, despite all the myth, gives very, very, very little power to local government. . . . It would be fair to say that [the] . . . legislature would override many of the efforts of the most progressive [local] governments.[5]

Even Republicans acknowledged the limitations the state places on the city. Said one Republican alderman:

> Because of the relationship between the city and the state, we can't do things here in the city unless the state gives us the charter power to do it, which has been a frustration of his [Sanders] and mine and everybody's . . . trying to do things here in Burlington. I support home rule for Burlington.

Besides the legislature, the city also had to deal with such regulatory bodies as the Public Service Board. In the area of utility issues, it constantly stymied Burlington's reform attempts, most notably in the municipal cable television battle. Much of Burlington's legal resources have been used in trying to fight various Public Service Board rulings. One activist commented:

> It really does appear as if a huge amount of the problem [of passing initiatives] is not from the city council [sic] or votes taken on the city council [sic], but is from outside sources of authority that are just extraordinarily powerful and hard to beat, including

the PSB [Public Service Board], the [Vermont] Supreme Court, the legislature, and probably also the state administration, . . . [and] the banks . . . [in conjunction with] . . . with the local developers . . . . My impression has been that's a lot of why things don't get done.

Regarding the federal government, there were not many examples of federal interference with the city, partially because this level of government, in some ways, is far removed from the day-to-day decisions of local government. The federal government, however, directly interfered with Burlington's affairs concerning the Southern Connector and indirectly interfered regarding federal cutbacks in revenue sharing money and housing subsidies. Said Mayor Sanders: "[I]f every time you go forward you get your wrists chopped off by the state or the federal government, it is an example of [the] limitation of power local government has to do what's right."[6]

Reflecting on the overall impact of the constraints on city government by other levels of government, one academician commented:

One of the facts of life in American politics is the interconnectedness of the various levels of government and it's very difficult to change one without changing the other. And if one changes dramatically, the . . . temptation to contain that change . . . is very great, to isolate it and to prevent it from spilling over and impacting other levels of government.

Another constraint on Burlington's attempt to implement radical policies was the legal system. One way the legal system interfered was to constrain certain actions by the city. For example, in the initial gross receipts tax fight, when the city tried to force the tax through the Board of Aldermen, one reason for switching strategies and trying to get a rooms and meals tax through the legislature was the city's fear of litigation by members of the business community. Also, the legal battles around the excavation fee pointed out how the business community could tie up issues in the courts for years. The legal system, however, also provided opportunities for the Sanders administration, such as in their fight around the cable television issue. The main conclusion, though, stands; the legal system most often protected the vested interests and property rights of wealthy individuals and corporations.

Regarding the legal system, Sanders commented that "almost any bold act we would come up with would be declared invalid by courts."[7] One administration insider believed "the historic function [of the legal system] is to drag down and slow down change, . . . a mechanism to thwart popular initiative and popular insurrection . . . of a local nature." And one Progressive Coalition alderman said that even if they had broken through what he called the "first line of defense" (that is, the opposition on the Board of Aldermen), the Progressive Coalition would still have had to face the "second line of defense" (that is, the courts). There were many ways, said this alderman, for the power structure to obstruct "radical change."

Still another constraint was a contextual one based on the socio-political-cultural milieu. The environment in which a particular town or city—in this case Burlington—is located has an enormous impact on what is perceived as radical for that particular area. For example, the issue of property tax classification was perceived by the business community and others in Burlington as a radical idea. However, in a place like Boston, such an idea was seen by the business community as a liberal reform. One Republican alderman put the issue succinctly:

> He's [Sanders] talking about [a] 120% . . . tax classification scheme [on business]. It's 2–1 in Boston. A socialist should be going for 4–1. [In] Boston, some of the properties [are] on rent control, developers' fees that developers have to pay makes some of the things that Sanders has proposed look very mild in comparison, but for Vermont, in Burlington, [they're radical].

The political climate, then, in Burlington in particular and Vermont in general is clearly more conservative and less cosmopolitan than in some other parts of the country. Thus, the general context of various proposed changes must be kept in mind when judging how radical or reformist they might be. One administration official lamented:

> A real lesson about what happens to people's frame of reference on the political spectrum is what goes down as being avant garde in a particular area because something hasn't been tried before; . . . it's viewed as being radical. . . .
> It's bizarre, but it takes [those] who are called radicals to put forth what's essentially a reformist program because the Democrats [in Burlington] are so pathetic. Oh God, a radical program—we don't have a radical program. A rooms and meals tax is considered radical.

Finally, the most important constraint of them all—the capitalist system itself—must not be overlooked. The capitalist economic system was particularly important when speaking about the possibilities and limitations of socialism at the local level. While the word socialism is often associated with state ownership of the means of production, this was not a realistic possibility on the local level, since the lack of public capital, among other things, prevented the municipal owner-ship of factories and services. One administration official spoke of the economic restrictions on the city:

> You certainly are constrained, particularly in the area of housing and economic development, as to what you can do at the local level.... [The] primary constraint, probably, is one of resour-ces—at [a] time of dwindling federal resources, it's been par-ticularly difficult to achieve our objectives.

The constraints mentioned above—local, state, federal, legal, con-textual, and capitalist—are not unique to Burlington or its socialist administration. Any mayor in any town or city across the United States has to deal with these limitations on the exercise of municipal power, though with variations. What makes the Burlington situation unique is how these constraints were used to limit the kinds of re-forms, radical or otherwise, that the Sanders administration at-tempted during its tenure.

In Burlington, a socialist grabbed the reigns of power in the execu-tive branch of government. Later, he got a plurality of supporters on the Board of Aldermen, thereby winning the power of sustaining a mayoral veto. The mayor and his Progressive Coalition supporters were then in a position to win control of several important city commissions. But the limit of the socialist administration's and Pro-gressive Coalition's powers became quite evident once these incre-ments of power were attained. Despite domination of the executive branch and a strong position in the legislative branch of local govern-ment, the Sanders administration had to fight for, and often lost, the reforms that they initiated.

The reason, clearly, had to do with successive lines of defense. The "first line of defense," as one Progressive Coalition alderman pointed out, was the Board of Aldermen. If the Progressive Coalition, for one reason or another, was successful in breaking through this line, then the next line of defense awaited them, be it the courts (in the case of the excavation fee), the Public Service Board (in the case of the attempt to municipalize the cable television station), state governmental agen-cies (in the case of the Southern Connector), or the state legislature (in the case of progressive taxation issues).

Even if by some miracle the socialists were able to take over the reigns of state government, we would see a similar phenomenon—only this time in relation to the federal government. The different branches of the federal government—the executive, legislative, and judiciary—would act as the "third line of defense" to maintain the status quo. Herein lies the story of the U.S. federalist system of government.[8]

Unless there is a challenge to the status quo, there is no need for the various checks and balances of radical change to show themselves. For the most part, the people of the United States feel that there is nothing fundamentally wrong with our economic, political, and social system. Consequently, it isn't until someone, at some governmental level, attempts to do something out of the ordinary that underlying conflicts within the system emerge. Sanders, by constantly testing and pushing the limits of what is defined as acceptable, often brought down the full wrath of the protective mechanisms of the federalist system. The latent functions only became manifest when there was a challenge to the existing power arrangements.

This is where Gorz's[9] and Gowan et al's[10] earlier distinctions between reformist reforms and nonreformist or radical reforms becomes useful (see Chapter 1). For the most part, serious challenges to the status quo will result in reformist reforms. The overwhelming nature of the forces that maintain the current economic, political, and social system in this country make it very difficult to do more. However, in certain limited cases, nonreformist reforms are possible.

In Burlington the "logic of capitalist accumulation" has been challenged in several places. The Burlington Community Land Trust is a radical reform with revolutionary possibilities. By challenging the dominant mode of private land ownership, the land trust makes the possibility of home ownership available to many more people and interferes with the "logic of capitalist accumulation." Also, the city's experiment in setting up a limited equity co-op at the South Meadow Project and its support for Northgate Non-Profit Housing have radical implications in the area of housing. They challenge the predominant mode of operation in the area of rental housing, allowing people over a period of time to cooperatively purchase their own dwelling. And although the Sanders administration could not really foster city ownership of firms, it did promote worker-owned businesses. This step can be viewed as a radical reform, too. Worker ownership clearly challenges the prevailing method of operating businesses and organizing work in this country, and combined with democratic worker self-management, also has revolutionary potential. In the areas of land trusts, tenant self-management and ownership, and worker-owned businesses, then, the Sanders administration has pursued cutting-edge reforms. Although mostly symbolic in their impact at this point in time, in the long run these initiatives may do more to challenge capitalism than any other legacy of the Sanders years.

The Sanders administration also made progress in challenging the ideological hegemony of the current economic, political, and social system, though nonreformist reforms in this area are harder to judge. It has promoted the involvement of the Burlington citizenry, especially low- and moderate-income people, in the decision-making processes of the city—both nonelectoral and electoral. Many more people vote now and are actually involved in running for local office. While the democratization of the decision-making process may not extend all the way to the top of the political structure in Burlington, what has happened is a step in the right direction. More people also attend a wide range of neighborhood and city meetings to voice their opinions. Despite their shortcomings, the Neighborhood Planning Assemblies provide a forum for increased citizen participation on the neighborhood level. While an imperfect vehicle, they nonetheless allow a diversity of opinions to be heard.

The Sanders administration challenged traditional cultural hegemony through the work of its Arts Council, which made art more affordable for low- and moderate-income people. Similarly, the Youth Office tackled the issue of child care on a citywide basis. The Women's Council worked hard to raise feminist concerns in city hall and educate the public about women's issues.

Citizen education on the larger issues has also occurred in Burlington. Sanders and other Progressive Coalition members have related local concerns to domestic and international issues. The citizenry is probably more aware today about the connection between the decrease in federal funding for social programs and the increase in U.S. military spending. As Sanders is fond of saying, the repaving of city streets would be moot if Burlington was destroyed in a nuclear attack.

The administration took steps, too, in raising the consciousness of its citizenry. Sanders's clear and unequivocal stand against U.S intervention in Nicaragua (which is the clearest example of a nonreformist reform in the ideological sphere) and the various displays by the Mayor's Council on the Arts, such as the Hiroshima exhibit, did much to increase people's level of awareness concerning the situation in Central America and the devastation of nuclear weapons.

While not a radical reform, the Sanders administration also made a concrete effort to bring about the redistribution of wealth on the local and state levels—within the given constraints. Certainly, the equalization of wealth, even if desirable, cannot be implemented by one municipality in Vermont. Locally, the Sanders administration looked to shift the burden of taxation from poor and working-class people to the more wealthy, at least in some respects. The long moratorium on any increase in property taxes (apart from reappraisal) certainly benefited low- and moderate-income homeowners, as well as the well-to-do. Almost all of the alternative taxes proposed by the administration, such as the gross receipts tax and property tax reclassification, were aimed at those who could afford to pay them. Sanders also concentrated his efforts on the working class, both in rhetoric and in action. The Sanders administration tried to provide city services with a working-class focus. Some examples of this are the redirection of federal Community Development Block Grant monies and the replanting of trees in low- and moderate-income neighborhoods.

However, there are cases where the Sanders administration did not go far enough in pushing for radical reforms, for example, municipal cable television and the waterfront. In the first case, the administration could have pushed harder for municipalization and perhaps achieved it in the long run. The probability of proving victorious was low, but if the principles of socialism rather than the expediency of winning a large cash settlement is the key criterion, then pushing all the way for municipalization, with its potential long-term benefits for the city and its residents, was worth the possibility of losing a million dollars. After all, the principle of municipalization is one of the most cherished by socialism at the local level.

Regarding the issue of the waterfront, the Sanders administration initially failed to pursue a true socialist strategy by pushing for public ownership of the waterfront land. The Sanders administration should have pursued the "public trust" doctrine in the courts much earlier. While it is true that the administration eventually sought, to a limited degree, public ownership of parts of the waterfront through bond issues, and finally won a court victory in the "public trust" doctrine case, it was too little, too late to affect the Sanders administration's overall record on this issue (though it may bode well for the newly elected Clavelle administration).

Because of the various structural constraints discussed earlier, the Sanders administration was unable to bring about radical social change in most instances. It must be remembered that the capitalist state takes on a life of its own, supporting the "logic of capitalist accumulation" and making it virtually impossible for socialists in office to interfere with its internal dynamics. The state, by helping to reproduce capitalist relations, forces those holding local office, regardless of their politics, to do the same. This also helps maintain capitalism's "ideological hegemony." To seriously challenge these mechanisms, a socialist politician faces almost certain defeat. Consequently, socialists elected to local office (and for that matter, state or national office), are forced to accommodate to the logic of capitalism if they desire to be reelected. Members of the "power elite" in a particular city could help assure compliance by threatening to have key industries leave town and relocate elsewhere, thereby creating the potential of a local economic crisis, or by having the city default on its loans, as the banks did to Dennis Kucinich (a populist, not a socialist) in Cleveland in 1979.[11] Given these factors, it is not at all surprising that Bernard Sanders, not to mention all the other socialist mayors ever to serve in office, has not been able to usher in the new socialist order. Socialism simply is not possible in one city.

One progressive critic offered a somewhat different analysis on the "failure" of the Sanders "revolution":

> Theoretically, it should be possible to develop a direction toward socialism at the local level and have a series of examples, but I don't think you can do it and have things run as they always have.
>
> I think we'd be closer if the establishment would really worry here—and they're not. They're pretty happy . . . Fidelity Mutual (owner of Burlington Square Mall) is not unhappy—especially. The insurance companies, although some policies changed, are not unhappy. The banks are not unhappy. The major financial interests in the city and the state don't feel deeply threatened. . . . If they were really worried, they would really be trying to destabilize the administration and they're not. And they're not, because what's happening doesn't threaten them.

And why did this critic feel that to be the case?

> We [the Sanders administration and the Progressive Coalition] have adopted a process of accommodation and so we won't have a movement toward socialism. And that's . . . a tactical choice—it has to do with wanting to stay in power. . . . [Instead], Bernie and the progressives [could have] said: "We're going to have a good time for two or four years, we're really going to push the system to the limit, then they'll organize [against] us, probably overthrow us, but in the meantime we will have demonstrated the bankruptcy of the system."

One peace activist disagreed with the above analysis:

> I think it [socialism on the local level] is very hard. Critiques have been made on Bernie where he could have been and where people feel he should have been more radical, and yet I think that in a lot of cases there wasn't any viable superstructure to give him an alternative. . . .

I mean he [Sanders] could say no, he doesn't want that kind of development, but then there's no way to really be able to push through the kind of socialist development he would want.

Others misinterpreted or underestimated the structural limitations faced by Sanders and his administration, claiming that he was little more than a liberal Democrat. Some in the media liked to refer to him as a "self-described" or "self-proclaimed" socialist, as if to say that his actions indicated otherwise. However, these charges seem patently false, failing to take into account the enormous obstacles a socialist in local office has to face.

Municipal socialism is clearly a step in the right direction, but it is fraught with inherent limitations and various political traps. While Sanders accomplished quite a lot and implemented some radical reforms in certain areas, his administration appeared to move away from the ideal vision of democratic socialism. This, however, is inevitable; perfection is not possible in the material world.

The important question to ask is whether it makes any difference having a socialist administration on the local level. The answer clearly is yes. On one level, the difference was expressed well by one administration insider, who said that "the real difference . . . of a socialist administration is not that objectively you're able to accomplish [the] proletarian revolution, it's that you're a fucking pain in the ass." In a more serious vein, he added: "It's real hard. There's nothing we've done that a good liberal Democrat couldn't and hasn't run on. Most of the ideas that we've presented to the city are ideas that have been tested and tried in other municipalities in this country." One academician put it this way:

A socialist elected to local office can make a difference. . . . Can you more equitably distribute the goods and services that the city has available? You can do that. You can make sure that the first streets to be plowed are not the ones in the richest wards of the city but are equally distributed . . . ward to ward. You can make sure that poor people have as much right to get into the city meetings to speak and see the mayor as the better-offs do. . . . But the city does not have the kind of independent taxing authority to involve itself in a unilateral redistributional policy because the state has to have final authority on that kind of stuff.

While there are few accomplishments of the Sanders administration that can be considered nonreformist reforms or socialistic in nature, the administration did have a significant impact. Local government is run better and more efficiently than previous Democratic and Republican administrations in the city, there is a somewhat fairer distribution of wealth and services and a more equalized tax burden, citizens are more aware of and involved in local government, innovative projects in housing and business ownership have been introduced, the quality of life in the city has improved, and important domestic and international issues have been addressed.

But what is perhaps even more significant is that Sanders has used his position to speak out for the disenfranchised and to address the pressing global issues of the day. It is true that most of his socialist agenda has been frustrated, but in the process of working for fundamental changes in the economic and political arenas it becomes obvious why radical change is very difficult, if not impossible, at the local level, and the myth of an insular local government divorced from the reality of national and international concerns is exposed. Thus, the inherent connections between these issues manifest themselves, and capitalism has to show its face. The cherished U.S. political system thus functions as a vehicle for Sanders and his Progressive Coalition to articulate important issues and, simultaneously, lends credibility and popular legitimacy to a vision of a new, democratic-socialist society.

Epilogue

On November 6, 1990, Bernie Sanders made the leap from Burlington city politics to the Washington, D.C., political scene. By defeating incumbent Republican Peter Smith 56 to 40 percent, Sanders became the first independent to win election to Congress in almost forty years. Amazingly, the Democratic contender won only 3 percent of the vote. Sanders's victory was all the more remarkable because, since the Civil War, Republicans have won in sixty of the last sixty-one Congressional elections for Vermont's lone House seat. The victory has national significance, too. Prior to Sanders's election, only three politicians in this century have been elected to the House of Representatives (and none to the Senate) from leftist political parties. In the early 1900s, Meyer London, from New York City, and Victor Berger, from Milwaukee, were elected from the Socialist Party. Vito Marcantonio, also from New York City, was elected from the American Labor Party in the 1930s and served nonconsecutive terms until his defeat in 1950.[1]

Having lost a close congressional race to Smith in 1988, Sanders was determined to win this time. When he announced his bid in March 1990, he ran on familiar themes: the need for a national health-care system; a steeply progressive income tax for individuals and corporations; a 50 percent decrease in military spending by 1995, and concomitant increases in federal spending for agriculture, education, housing, and social security; environmental issues; and the need for a grass-roots "revolution" for participatory democracy in the United States.[2]

Almost from the start, political pundits expected a close contest between Sanders and Smith, despite the latter's incumbency, since Sanders lost to Smith by only a 3 percent margin in the 1988 congressional race. In a July *Burlington Free Press* poll, the two were running neck-to-neck, with Smith leading by only one percentage point, and one-third of the voters still undecided.[3]

Early in the campaign, Sanders began to mobilize what he called "the strongest grass-roots movement that Vermonters have ever seen." His goal was to have over 1,000 volunteers working on his campaign. In analyses of the potential impact of the race, national political observers were saying that Sanders's campaign could be of historic importance. If he won, they said, other politicians across the country would seek to emulate him and his class-based, poor-versus-rich politics in the 1992 elections.[4]

During summer 1990, Sanders's efforts began to pay off. He collected endorsements from many women's, peace, environmental, and labor groups, with the Vermont AFL-CIO giving their blessing to an independent candidate for the first time in its history. Smith's campaign, meanwhile, was having problems. Even though he had raised several hundred thousand dollars to date, the National Rifle Association (NRA) targeted the incumbent for defeat because Smith, who had gone to Washington as an opponent of gun control, voted to put restrictions on the purchase of semi-automatic weapons.[5]

Sanders's appeal, once again, cut across party, cultural, and generational lines. For example, one-half of those who voted for Reagan in 1984 also cast ballots for Sanders as mayor in 1985. In 1990, it was no different. After a Rotary Club meeting in South Burlington, one retired business executive commented that he was willing to vote for Sanders so that the former mayor could raise cain in Washington. All across Vermont, it was a similar story: After hearing a rousing Sanders speech, rock-ribbed Republican Vermonters were willing to consider voting for Sanders, and not necessarily because they agreed with him on all the issues. At least, people said, they knew where Sanders stood. Moreover, Vermonters seemed to respond to Sanders's pledge: "I will raise the right issues in Congress, and I will be effective. Standing up for what is right is the way to be effective. Telling it like it is is the way to be effective."[6]

Ironically, Sanders also had the public support, or at least the silence, of many of Vermont's Democratic officeholders,[7] despite his constant railing against the two-party system and his claims that there was no difference between the Republicans and the Democrats. When no credible candidate entered the Democratic Party's primary, Sanders became the *de facto* candidate of the Democrats.

The 1990 congressional campaign, unlike the previous one, was not an amicable race. Personal attacks were initiated by Smith, with Sanders occasionally responding in kind. Toward the end of the campaign, Smith seemed to panic. Caught in Washington budget negotiations until a few weeks before the election, he sensed the campaign slipping away from him. Sanders led in most, if not all, public opinion polls. Vermont's only statewide television station conducted a poll in late October which showed Sanders ahead 42 to 38 percent, despite Smith's having raised almost $500,000 compared to Sanders's slightly more than $375,000. Sanders's own polling data was even more optimistic: The challenger had a 45 to 35 percent lead. Finally, one of the major Vermont newspapers, the *Rutland-Herald*, endorsed Sanders in late October, which gave his campaign a boost, since he had lost the 1988 congressional race due to the heavy pro-Smith vote in the southern part of the state.[8]

In light of these events, in the final weeks of the campaign, Smith gambled on a strategy of hard-hitting, red-baiting ads, which backfired. In one of these ads, Smith accused Sanders of having become "physically nauseated" when he heard President John F. Kennedy's inaugural address and of supporting Fidel Castro.[9]

On election day, Sanders's various constituencies—progressives, younger people, the elderly, working class people, and well-educated middle-class professionals—plus various disaffected conservative voters, helped pave the way to the independent socialist's stunning victory.[10]

Sanders won his congressional race for several reasons. First, there was his extensive grass-roots campaign, especially in the southern part of the state. Hundreds of volunteers made an estimated 30,000 calls before the election. Sanders had obviously learned important lessons from his unsuccessful 1986 and 1988 statewide campaigns.[11]

Second, Smith was tied up in Washington until several weeks before the election. When he returned, he was attacked by Sanders for both the savings and loan bailout debacle and the stalled budget negotiations. Smith's support for the first ill-fated federal budget compromise, eventually rejected by Congress, was unpopular in Vermont.[12]

The third reason for Smith's loss, previously mentioned, was the NRA's active campaign to defeat Smith. The NRA's direct-mail campaign to its members and its political advertising against Smith in the waning days of the campaign had an impact.[13]

A fourth reason was the incumbent's negative advertising campaign. As one political commentator said about negative advertising: "The rule on negative ads is that they only work against unknown commodities. Bernie Sanders is a very well-known commodity as the mayor of Burlington. People may or may not like him, but they certainly know him." Vermonters, who often are on a first-name basis with their politicians, do not like negative campaigning, and this election was no exception.[14]

Finally, and perhaps most importantly, the nation's political climate helped set the stage for Sanders's upset victory. Not only did Sanders run a "brilliant" campaign, according to some observers, but the political timing was fortuitous. Said former Vermont Democratic Governor Thomas Salmon: "You could not have divined a more perfect script than the current national, regional and local scenario." Outgoing Vermont Democratic Governor Madeline Kunin added: "If political timing is everything in politics, this was perfect timing for his campaign." Finally, Brian Cosgrove, executive director of the Vermont Republican Party, commented: "There was a widespread dissatisfaction with Congress as an institution, and Bernie was the beneficiary. The time was right for his message."[15]

For the first time in decades, class issues were once again part of U.S. mainstream political discourse. The excesses of the Reagan years, with its huge tax breaks for the well-to-do, created the basis for a political backlash. Taxing the rich became a popular theme in Washington, pitting the party of the rich against the party of low- and moderate-income people. Kevin Phillips new book, *The Politics of Rich and Poor: Wealth and the American Electorate in the Reagan Aftermath*, helped to draw the battle lines, and also forecasts the possibility of a progressive populist electoral response to the extravagances of the Reagan-Bush years. The anti-incumbency mood among the voters also helped fuel a Sanders victory. Sanders wasn't the only one who benefited; Paul Wellstone, a political science professor at Carleton College and a left-leaning Democratic political newcomer, upset incumbent Republican Senator Rudy Boschwitz in Minnesota.[16]

In his victory speech, Sanders sounded his usual themes. But he also added: "Our small state might go down in history as the leading state in a political revolution which takes power away from the multinational corporations and the wealthy and gives it back to the people." After his election, though, Sanders was careful to distinguish between his brand of Swedish-style democratic socialism and the authoritarian communism seen in the Soviet Union and Eastern Europe until recently. Furthermore, while still blasting the two-party system, Sanders said he was willing to join the House Democratic Caucus in order to win committee assignments favorable to Vermont and his own political agenda. While the Democrats decided not to include him in their caucus, he was assured of some committee assignments. Sanders's preferences were Commerce and Energy (dealing with health-care issues); Education and Labor; and Banking, Finance, and Urban Affairs; he was assigned to Banking, Finance, and Urban Affairs, as well as Government Operations.[17]

What are Sanders's prospects as Vermont's lone congressman? As one voice among 435 others, he will be hard-pressed to find a forum

for his radical views. Yet his charisma, his fiery oratory, his unwilling-
ness to pull punches, and his outspokenness on crucial social problems should garner media attention and provide national exposure.
For example, Sanders has spoken out very strongly against the Persian
Gulf war, calling for the United States to pull out its troops and to
reinstate economic sanctions. He also was one of only six congressional representatives to vote against "a resolution praising
America's armed forces and commending the president for his efforts
and leadership . . . as a commander in chief." Sander was severely
criticized by part of his working-class constituency for this vote, but
it is too early to tell whether his unique political coalition will sustain
irreparable damage.[18]

Assuming he can retain his House seat, Sanders will be well-posi-
tioned to become Vermont's governor or U.S. senator. (Since Vermont
has only one House seat, its representative runs statewide.) From here,
who knows where Sanders will go? Only time will tell. One thing is
sure: From Burlington's city hall to the halls of Congress, Sanders will
continue to speak for ordinary working people, offer a vision of a
democratic-socialist U.S. society, and test the limits of our capitalist
economic, political, and social system.

Notes

CHAPTER 1

1. James S. Weinstein, *The Decline of Socialism in America: 1912–1925* (New Brunswick, N.J.: Rutgers University Press, 1984).

2. Ibid., p. xi.

3. Ibid., p. 93.

4. Ibid., pp. 5–6.

5. Ibid., pp. 9–10.

6. Ibid., pp. 10–12.

7. Ibid., p. 13, quoting "What Haywood Says on Political Action," *International Socialist Review* 13, no. 8 (February 1913), p. 622.

8. Ibid., p. 111.

9. Ibid., p. 108.

10. Ibid., pp. 108–9.

11. Ibid., p. 109.

12. Bruce Stave, ed., *Socialism and the Cities* (Port Washington, N.Y.: Kennikat Press, 1975).

13. The following information on Milwaukee's socialist administrations, with the exception of the Zeidler administration, is from Sally M. Miller, "Milwaukee: Of Ethnicity and Labor," in *Socialism and the Cities,* ed. Bruce Stave, pp. 41–71.

14. The information on the Zeidler administration is from a phone conversation with Frank Zeidler, 10 June 1986.

15. Bruce Stave, "The Great Depression and Urban Political Continuity: Bridgeport Chooses Socialism," in *Socialism and the Cities,* ed. Bruce Stave, pp. 157–83.

16. Ibid., p. 166.

17. Ibid., p. 167.

18. Kenneth E. Hendrickson, Jr., "Tribune of the People: George R. Lunn and the Rise and Fall of Christian Socialism in Schenectady," in *Socialism and the Cities*, ed. Bruce Stave, pp. 72–98.

19. Ibid., p. 83.

20. Ibid., p. 89.

21. Miller, "Milwaukee: Of Ethnicity and Labor"; Hendrickson, "Tribune of the People"; Walter Lippman, "On Municipal Socialism, 1913: An Analysis of Problems and Strategies," in *Socialism and the Cities*, ed. Bruce Stave, pp. 184–96.

22. Stave, *Socialism and the Cities*, pp. 5–6.

23. See Pierre Clavel, *The Progressive City: Planning and Participation, 1969–1984* (New Brunswick, N.J.: Rutgers University Press, 1986), pp. 97–138; Kevin J. Kelley, "Berkeley: A Zone of Control," *The Guardian* (New York), 2 October 1985, p. 1; "Winning Power in Berkeley, California," *National Committee for Independent Political Action (NCIPA)* Newsletter, January-February 1986, p. 5; Mark Johnson, "West Coast Mayor Tells of Successes on City Tax Issues," *Burlington Free Press*, 14 December 1985; also, speech given by Gus Newport, Unitarian Church, Montpelier, Vermont, 14 December 1985.

24. See Mark E. Kann, "Radicals in Power: Lessons From Santa Monica," *Socialist Review* 3 (May-June 1983), pp. 81–101; Clavel, *The Progressive City*, pp. 139–61; Derek Shearer, "Left in Santa Monica Loses a Battle, but Not the War," *In These Times* (Chicago), 27 April-3 May 1983, p. 11.

25. See David Moberg, "Surf City Socialism," *In These Times*, 26 January–1 February 1983, pp. 12, 22; Mike Rotkin, "Reflections of a Socialist Mayor," *Democratic Left* 3 (March 1983), p. 5.

26. Albert Szymanski, *The Capitalist State and the Politics of Class* (Cambridge, Mass.: Winthrop Publishers, 1978), p. 261.

27. Paul M. Sweezy, *The Theory of Capitalist Development: Principles of Marxian Political Economy* (New York: Monthly Review Press, 1970), p. 80; Szymanski, *The Capitalist State*, p. 262.

28. Erik Olin Wright, *Class, Crisis and the State* (London: Verso Press, 1970), pp. 230–32.

29. André Gorz, *Strategy for Labor* (Boston: Beacon Press, 1967), pp. 6–8; John Stephens, *The Transition from Capitalism to Socialism* (London: Macmillan Press, 1979), pp. 81–87; Susanne Gowan, George Lakey, William Moyer, and Richard Taylor, *Moving Toward a New Society* (Philadelphia: New Society Press, 1976), pp. 270–81.

30. Ibid.

31. Scott McKay, "Mayor to Continue in Same Vein," *Burlington Free Press*, 20 March 1983.

32. Sanders interview, 17 October 1985.

33. *Idem*, 12 December 1985.

34. *Idem*, 17 October 1985.

35. *Idem*, 12 December 1985.

36. Ibid.

37. "Magazine: Sanders One of Top 22 Mayors," *Burlington Free Press*, 21 December 1987; Enrique Corredera, "Burlington Wins National Honor," *Burlington Free Press*, 14 June 1988.

CHAPTER 2

1. City of Burlington, Vermont, *121st Annual Report for the Year Ending June 30, 1986,* front page. These are 1985 Vermont Department of Health population estimates; Vermont's ranking as of 1 July 1986.

2. Community and Economic Development Office, *Community and Economic Development Policies* (Burlington, Vt.: Community and Economic Development Office, n.d.), pp. 24–25.

3. Ibid., p. 24.

4. Ibid.

5. Ibid., p. 25.

6. Industrial Cooperative Association, *Jobs and People: A Strategic Analysis of the Greater Burlington Economy,* Commissioned by: Community and Economic Development Office (Burlington, Vt.: December 1984), pp. 54–55.

7. Ibid., p. 54.

8. One exception is the would-be developers of the Burlington waterfront, the Alden Waterfront Group, backed by the personal fortune of Paul and Elizabeth Flinn, recently listed as one of the 400 richest families in the United States and worth over $600 million (see Chapter 3). However, they also live in Shelburne, a small, wealthy community just south of the city of Burlington. Another exception is the General Electric corporation.

9. Don Melvin, "Sanders: A People-Oriented Man," *Burlington Free Press,* 10 February 1985; Alan Abbey, "Bernard Sanders: Working Class Hero?" *Burlington Free Press,* 15 March 1981.

10. Interview with Bernard Sanders, 17 October 1985.

11. Bernie Sanders: *We Shall Overcome* Cassette, Side B: "A Conversation with Bernie Sanders" (Burlingtown Recordings, 1987).

12. Melvin, "Sanders: A People-Oriented Man"; Bernie Sanders: *We Shall Overcome.*

13. Mark Johnson, "Bernie," *Times-Argus/Rutland-Herald* Vermont Sunday Magazine, 10 April 1988.

14. Bernie Sanders: *We Shall Overcome.*

15. Ibid.

16. Ibid.; Melvin, "Sanders: A People-Oriented Man."

17. Sanders interview, October 1985; Johnson, "Bernie."

18. Jonathan Evan Maslow, "The Liberty Union of Vermont," *Nation,* 18 October 1975.

19. City Clerk's Office, *City of Burlington Election Records,* 1953–1983.

20. Cheryl Benfield, "Sanders Urges Action to Avert Depression," *Burlington Free Press,* 14 December 1973; Maslow, "The Liberty Union of Vermont"; City Clerk, *Burlington Election Records.*

21. City Clerk, *Burlington Election Records.*

22. Katherine Gregg, "Sanders Gives Up Party Post," *Burlington Free Press,* 6 January 1975; Dirk Van Susteren, "Liberty Union Leaders Quit," *Burlington Free Press,* 12 October 1977.

23. Sanders interview, 17 October 1985.

24. Sanders 1981 mayoral campaign tabloid.

25. Alan Abbey, "Campaign for Mayor Lively One," *Burlington Free Press*, 28 February 1981; Alan Abbey, "Sanders Stuns Paquette in Close Mayoral Race," *Burlington Free Press*, 4 March 1981; Alan Abbey, "Recount Puts Sanders Up by 10 Votes," *Burlington Free Press*, 14 March 1981.

26. Scott McKay, "Sanders Win Stirs Major Parties Out of Lethargic State," *Burlington Free Press*, 10 March 1981.

27. City Clerk, *Burlington Election Records*.

28. Industrial Cooperative Association, *Jobs and People*, p. 4; Community and Economic Development Office, *Community and Economic Development Policies* (Burlington, Vt.: Community and Economic Development Office, 1984), p. 2.

29. Tom Rice, "Who Votes for a Socialist Mayor?: The Case of Burlington, Vermont," *Polity* 4 (Summer 1985), pp. 795–806.

30. Alan Abbey, "Mayor Elect Sanders Offers Olive Branch," *Burlington Free Press*, 5 March 1981.

31. Scott McKay, "Democrats Fight to Trim Sanders' Sails in March," *Burlington Free Press*, 1 March 1982.

32. Scott McKay, "Burns and Paterson Win Runoff Elections," *Burlington Free Press*, 21 March 1982; Scott McKay, "Democrats Swept Off City Board by Sanders Supporters, Republicans," *Burlington Free Press*, 4 March 1982.

33. Scott McKay, "Sanders Supporters Gain Three Council Seats," *Burlington Free Press*, 3 March 1982; McKay, "Democrats Swept Off."

34. Candace Page, "Students Could Make a Difference," *Burlington Free Press*, 22 February 1983; Scott McKay, "Old North End Has Been Strong Source of Sanders' Support," *Burlington Free Press*, 23 February 1983; Candace Page, "Middle Income, Middle Class Has Meant Moderate Politics," *Burlington Free Press*, 24 February 1983; Sanders interview, 17 October 1985; Don Melvin, "Democrats Have Been Strong in City's Most Diverse Ward," *Burlington Free Press*, 25 February 1983; Scott McKay, "Heavy Youth Vote Could Break Republicans Hold in Ward 6," *Burlington Free Press*, 26 February 1983.

35. Scott McKay, "Plotting Sanders' Downfall," *Burlington Free Press*, 20 June 1982.

36. Scott McKay, "Mayor Sanders Crushes 2 Challengers," *Burlington Free Press*, 2 March 1983; Candace Page, "Election Retains Deep Divisions Among Aldermen," *Burlington Free Press*, 2 March 1983.

37. Scott McKay, "Gilson Announces Mayoral Candidacy," *Burlington Free Press*, 13 November 1982; Candace Page, "James Gilson Takes a Businesslike Approach," *Burlington Free Press*, 13 February 1983; Scott McKay, "Gilson Bases Campaign on Pro-Business Issues," *Burlington Free Press*, 16 January 1983; Scott McKay, "Burlington Mayoral Campaign Enters Last Phase," *Burlington Free Press*, 27 February 1983.

38. Scott McKay, "Stephany Takes Middle Ground in 3-Way Race," *Burlington Free Press*, 30 January 1983; Scott McKay, "Three Mayoral Hopefuls Trade Political Barbs," *Burlington Free Press*, 11 February 1983.

39. Scott McKay, "Democrats Labor to Find a Mayoral Candidate," *Burlington Free Press*, 9 January 1983.

40. Scott McKay, "Bernard Sanders Reminds Voters of His Record," *Burlington Free Press*, 13 February 1983.

41. Scott McKay, "Voters to Stick with Bernie for Burlington," *Burlington Free Press*, 2 March 1983.

42. Tom Rice, "Research Note: Who Votes for a Socialist Mayor."

43. "Sanders Group Plans Rally Tonight," *Burlington Free Press*, 20 January 1984; Don Melvin, "Organizational Edge Is Held by Progressives," *Burlington Free Press*, 13 February 1984; Sanders Stamps Approval on 3rd Party Candidates," *Burlington Free Press*, 2 March 1984.

44. Don Melvin, "Sound, Fury of City Campaign Coming to End," *Burlington Free Press*, 4 March 1984.

45. Don Melvin, "Sanders Fails to Get Control," *Burlington Free Press*, 7 March 1984.

46. Sanders interview, 17 October 1985; Don Melvin, "Democratic Victory Leaves Mayor Short of Board Majority," *Burlington Free Press*, 16 May 1984.

47. Don Melvin, "1985 Politicos Angle Gingerly for Mayoral Race," *Burlington Free Press*, 23 July 1984.

48. Don Melvin, "Sanders Uncertain Whether He'll Run for a Third Term," *Burlington Free Press*, 14 November 1984.

49. Melvin, "Sanders Uncertain."

50. Don Melvin, "Gallagher Will Run for Mayor, Green Won't," *Burlington Free Press*, 1 December 1984; Don Melvin, "It's Official: Sanders, Gallagher Are Running," *Burlington Free Press*, 7 December 1984; Don Melvin, "Burns Kicks Off Campaign for Mayor," *Burlington Free Press*, 20 December 1984.

51. Don Melvin, "Gallagher Doffs GOP Hat, Will Run as Independent," *Burlington Free Press*, 15 January 1985; Don Melvin, "Gallagher Pressured to Drop Out of Race," *Burlington Free Press*, 21 December 1984; Melvin, "Gallagher Doffs GOP Hat."

52. Don Melvin, "Sanders Will Run for Third Term as Mayor," *Burlington Free Press*, 6 December 1984; Don Melvin, "Mayoral Candidates Will Target Sanders' Record," *Burlington Free Press*, 23 December 1984.

53. Don Melvin, "Candidates Put Last Gasp into Mayoral Race," *Burlington Free Press*, 2 March 1985; Don Melvin, "Sanders Easily Wins Re-election," *Burlington Free Press*, 6 March 1985; City Clerk, *Burlington Election Records*; Don Melvin, "Burlington Has More Voters Eligible This Year," *Burlington Free Press*, 5 March 1985.

54. Don Melvin, "Candidate Burns to Put On New Image," *Burlington Free Press*, 3 February 1985.

55. Sanders interview, 17 October 1985; Deborah Schoch, "Sanders Replies to Burns' Remarks," *Burlington Free Press*, 22 December 1984.

56. "Seven Trade Unions Stamp Approval on Sanders," *Burlington Free Press*, 18 February 1985; "UVM Faculty Endorse Sanders," *Burlington Free Press*, 26 February 1985; "2 Democrats Support Sanders," *Burlington Free Press*, 4 February 1985.

57. Don Melvin, "Financial Reports Show Burns Big Spender in Mayoral Bid," *Burlington Free Press*, 16 March 1985.

58. Tom Rice, "Why Vote for a Socialist Mayor: The Case of Burlington, Vt., 1986. (Typewritten.)

59. Don Melvin, "City Aldermen Races Begin to Shape Up," *Burlington Free Press*, 7 January 1985; Don Melvin, "Mayoral Hopefuls Rev Up for Last Campaign Push," *Burlington Free Press*, 24 February 1985.

60. "Mayoral Hopefuls Rev Up"; City Clerk, *Burlington Election Records*.

61. Mark Johnson, "2 Key Sanders Backers Rule Out Re-election Bid," *Burlington Free Press*, 4 January 1986; Mark Johnson, "Some Aldermen Finding Pace Is Too Much," *Burlington Free Press*, 15 January 1986; Mark Johnson, "Dream Eludes Burlington Progressives," *Burlington Free Press*, 19 January 1986; Mark Johnson, "March Election Puts Coalition at Crossroads," *Burlington Free Press*, 3 February 1986.

62. City Clerk, *Burlington Election Records*; Mark Johnson, "Progressives' Power Base in Question," *Burlington Free Press*, 5 March 1986; Mark Johnson, "Survey: Ward 1 Runoff Swings on Sanders," *Burlington Free Press*, 19 March 1986; Mark Johnson, "Mahnke Wins Ward 1 Seat by 31 Votes," *Burlington Free Press*, 26 March 1986.

63. In November 1986, Bernard Sanders ran for governor as a third-party candidate against incumbent Democratic Gov. Madeline Kunin and former Republican Lt. Gov. Peter Smith. On election day, Kunin received 47 percent, Smith 38 percent, and Sanders 15 percent of the vote, as reported in Don Melvin, "Kunin Falls Short of 50%," *Burlington Free Press*, 5 November 1986. For a more detailed account of the race, see Steven Soifer, "Electoral Politics and Social Change: The Case of Burlington, Vermont" (Ph.D. dissertation, Brandeis University, 1988), pp. 130–48.

64. Mark Johnson, "Early Prediction: Sanders Name Atop City Ballot," *Burlington Free Press*, 16 November 1986; Peter Freyne, "Sanders Sounds the Charge," *Vanguard Press*, 23–30 November 1986.

65. James E. Bressor, "Sanders to Seek 4th Term," *Times-Argus*, 1 December 1986; Charles Finnie, "Sanders Proclaims '87 Race Will Be His Last Mayoral Bid," *Burlington Free Press*, 7 December 1986.

66. "GOP Candidate Would Expand Mayoral Choice," *Burlington Free Press* editorial, 20 November 1986; "GOP Fails to Find Candidate," *Burlington Free Press*, 7 January 1987.

67. Debbie Bookchin, "Burlington Democrats Square Off in Primary," *Times-Argus*, 6 January 1987; Mark Johnson, "Lafayette Picked for Mayoral Run," *Burlington Free Press*, 15 January 1987; Mark Johnson, "Sanders Admits He Faces Tough Mayoral Race," *Burlington Free Press*, 16 January 1987.

68. Mark Johnson, "Sanders to Back Tax Increase," *Burlington Free Press*, 12 January 1987; "City Outlines Use of Funds from Proposed Tax," *Burlington Free Press*, 16 January 1987; Mark Johnson, "City Workers Union Backs Paul Lafayette," *Burlington Free Press*, 31 January 1987; Mark Johnson, "GE Union Supports Lafayette for Mayor," *Burlington Free Press*, 5 February 1987; Mark Johnson, "Paul Lafayette: Must Nice Guys Finish Last?," *Burlington Free Press*, 1 February 1987.

69. Debbie Bookchin, "Sanders in Rugged Race for Re-election," *Times-Argus*, 22 February 1987.

70. "Mayor Bernie Sanders . . . Working Hard to Keep Burlington a Great Place to Live," Sanders's mayoral campaign piece, 1987.

71. "Sanders Better Qualified for Mayor," *Burlington Free Press* editorial, 24 February 1987.

72. Mark Johnson, "Sanders Captures 4th Term," *Burlington Free Press*, 4 March 1987.

73. Mark Johnson, "Progressives Close to Majority," *Burlington Free Press*, 4 March 1987; "City of Burlington Election results," *Burlington Free Press*, 3 March

1987; Mark Johnson, "Chioffi Captures Aldermanic Seat," *Burlington Free Press,* 25 March 1987.

74. Enrique Corredera, "Burlington Democrats Gain Third Seat," *Burlington Free Press,* 2 March 1988.

75. In the 1988 U.S. House of Representatives race, Sanders once again astounded the political pundits by finishing a close second to former Republican Lt. Gov. Peter Smith. When the votes were tallied, Smith received 42 percent, Sanders 38 percent, and Democratic state representative Paul Poirier 19 percent. Needless to say, Sanders's strong finish shook up the state's Democratic Party. For more information, see Nancy Wright, "Smith Narrowly Defeats Sanders," *Times-Argus,* 9 November 1988; Debbie Bookchin, "How Did Sanders Make History?," *Times-Argus,* 9 November 1988; James E. Bressor, "Sanders' Strong Finish Shakes Up Democrats," *Burlington Free Press,* 10 November 1988.

76. *Progressive Coalition Newsletter,* 6 (December 1988), p. 1; Enrique Corredera, "Leopold Won't Run for Mayor," *Burlington Free Press,* 6 December 1988; Lisa Scagliotti, "Clavelle Wins Progressive Nod," *Burlington Free Press,* 9 December 1988.

77. Lisa Scagliotti, "Chioffi Captures Democratic Nod by Mere 5 Votes," *Burlington Free Press,* 12 January 1989.

78. Lisa Scagliotti, "Greens Party's Baird Announces Run for Mayor," *Burlington Free Press,* 10 January 1989; Lisa Scagliotti, "Mayoral Race Is Wide Open in Final 5 Weeks," *Burlington Free Press,* 29 January 1989.

79. Lisa Scagliotti, "Clavelle Vows to Follow Sanders' Path," *Burlington Free Press,* 11 February 1989; Scagliotti, "Mayoral Race."

80. Sam Hemingway, "Poll Shows Clavelle in Lead," *Burlington Free Press,* 26 February 1989; "Clavelle for Mayor," *Burlington Free Press* editorial, 26 February 1989.

81. Lisa Scagliotti, "Clavelle Ices Chioffi," *Burlington Free Press,* 8 March 1989; Candace Page, "Coalition Progresses without Sanders," *Burlington Free Press,* 8 March 1989.

82. Peter Freyne, "Life After Bernie: Sanderistas Put Structure Into Movement," *Vanguard Press,* 29 June–6 July 1986.

83. Tom Rice, "Identity Crisis: Liking Bernie but Ignoring His Party," *Vanguard Press,* 22–29 March 1987.

84. Steven J. Rosenstone, Roy L. Behr, and Edward H. Lazarus, *Third Parties in America: Citizen Response to Major Party Failure* (Princeton, N.J.: Princeton University Press, 1984).

85. The Vermont Rainbow Coalition is the statewide affiliate of the National Rainbow Coalition, the electoral vehicle for 1984 and 1988 Democratic presidential contender Jesse Jackson.

CHAPTER 3

1. Burlington, Vt., *Charter of the City of Burlington, Vermont* (Revised 1977), Acts of 1977, no. 298.

2. Interview with Jonathan Leopold, Jr., 26 September 1985; Joe Mahoney, "Grant Opinion Bolsters Mayor's Position," *Burlington Free Press,* 17 September 1981.

3. Scott McKay, "Board's 1st Test: Elect a President," *Burlington Free Press*, 4 April 1982.

4. Scott McKay, "No Faction Likely to Win Aldermanic Majority," *Burlington Free Press*, 20 February 1983.

5. Burlington, *1986 Annual Report*, pp. 12–14.

6. Don Melvin, "Progressives Win Seat on Electric Commission," *Burlington Free Press*, 4 December 1984; Leopold interview; Scott McKay, "Gilson Bases Campaign on Pro-Business Issues," *Burlington Free Press*, 16 January 1983; City Clerk, *Burlington Election Records*.

7. Alan Abbey, "Mayor Reflects on First 100 Days in Office," *Burlington Free Press*, 16 July 1981; Alan Abbey, "Mayor Reaches Compromise with Aldermen About Aide," *Burlington Free Press*, 15 April 1981.

8. "Aldermen Ask Sanders to Reappoint Officials," *Burlington Free Press*, 19 May 1981; Alan Abbey and Joe Mahoney, "Mayor's Appointments Spark Bickering," *Burlington Free Press*, 30 May 1981.

9. Alan Abbey, "Board Hands Mayor Stinging Defeat," *Burlington Free Press*, 2 June 1981.

10. Alan Abbey, "Sanders' Lawyers Prepare Suit Against Board," *Burlington Free Press*, 5 June 1981; Alan Abbey and Jeff Good, "Some Aldermen Served As Sanders' Suit Begins," *Burlington Free Press*, 27 June 1981; Alan Abbey, "Sanders Rallies Supporters to Bring Aldermen to Heel," *Burlington Free Press*, 9 June 1981.

11. John Reilly and Alan Abbey, "Aldermen Can't Rescind Resignation," *Burlington Free Press*, 6 June 1981.

12. William H. Braun, "Mayor Asks to Fill 2 Posts, Despite Legal Battle," *Burlington Free Press*, 26 June 1981; Alan Abbey, "Sanders Wins Board's OK to Bring on 2 Appointees," *Burlington Free Press*, 1 July 1981.

13. William H. Braun, "Sanders Suit Dismissed," *Burlington Free Press*, 1 September 1981; Joe Mahoney, "Sanders Turns to Supreme Court," *Burlington Free Press*, 4 September 1981; Alan Abbey, "Board Refuses to Pay Legal Bill," *Burlington Free Press*, 29 September 1981; Alan Abbey, "Board Votes to Pay Sanders' Legal Fees," *Burlington Free Press*, 14 October 1981.

14. Alan Abbey and Rob Eley, "Mayor Reprimands City Clerk Wagner," *Burlington Free Press*, 12 August 1981; Rob Eley, "Sanders Hands 2nd Reprimand to City Clerk," *Burlington Free Press*, 7 November 1981.

15. Scott McKay, "Will Appointments Issue Again Rock City Boat?," *Burlington Free Press*, 28 March 1982; Scott McKay, "Hearings to Set Tone for Year, Sanders Thinks," *Burlington Free Press*, 10 April 1982; Scott McKay, "Sanders Nominees Approved," *Burlington Free Press*, 13 April 1982.

16. Scott McKay and Jodie Peck, "Aldermen Approve 2 of Sanders' Appointees," *Burlington Free Press*, 8 June 1982; Scott McKay, "Assistant Treasurer Oked by Aldermen," *Burlington Free Press*, 8 July 1982.

17. Scott McKay, "Sanders Is Victor, All Top City Aides Are Reappointed," *Burlington Free Press*, 7 June 1983.

18. Interview with Doreen Kraft, 5 December 1985.

19. Alan Abbey, "Finance Board Eyeing Change in City's Insurance," *Burlington Free Press*, 20 October 1981; Don Melvin, "Board OKs Plan to Save

$200,000 on Insurance," *Burlington Free Press*, 30 June 1982; Scott McKay, "Sanders Goes on the Defense," *Burlington Free Press*, 20 May 1982.

20. Scott McKay, "Burlington Discovers Windfall—$1.9 Million Surplus," *Burlington Free Press*, 21 December 1982.

21. Leopold interview; Scott McKay, "Treasurer Outlines Savings," *Burlington Free Press*, 16 July 1982; Scott McKay, "Sanders Cites Reawakened Interest in City Government," *Burlington Free Press*, 17 February 1983; Scott McKay and Nelson Hockert-Lotz, "City Switching Cash from the Chittenden to Merchants Bank," *Burlington Free Press*, 27 August 1982.

22. Leopold interview.

23. The following discussion concerning city finances is based on the interview with Jonathan Leopold, Jr.

24. Don Melvin, "$2 Million City Surplus Now Has Disappeared," *Burlington Free Press*, 13 October 1985; Stephen Casimiro, "City of Burlington Has Surplus of More Than $1 Million," *Burlington Free Press*, 2 December 1986; Enrique Corredera, "City Finances in Good Shape, Report Shows," *Burlington Free Press*, 3 December 1987; City of Burlington, Vermont, *122nd Annual Report for the Year Ending June 30, 1987*; City of Burlington, Vermont, *123rd Annual Report for the Year Ending June 30, 1988*; City of Burlington, Vermont, *124th Annual Report for the Year Ending June 30, 1989*.

25. McKay, "Sanders Cites"; Leopold interview.

26. Debbie Bookchin, "Assessing Sanders," *Vanguard Press*, 31 December–8 January 1982.

27. Scott McKay, "City Eyes Sanders Savings Plans," *Burlington Free Press*, 7 September 1982.

28. McKay, "City Eyes"; Susan Youngwood, "Leopold Says City to Be Awash in Red Ink," *Burlington Free Press*, 8 October 1985.

29. "City Aldermen Refuse Delay, Fill 2 Vacancies," *Burlington Free Press*, 18 March 1981.

30. McKay and Peck, "Aldermen Approve 2."

31. Scott McKay, "Commissioners Don't Represent Wards Equally," *Burlington Free Press*, 3 October 1982.

32. Scott McKay, "Burlington to Keep March Election Date," *Burlington Free Press*, 3 June 1984.

33. Scott McKay, "City Council to Pick 31 New Commissioners," *Burlington Free Press*, 1 June 1983; McKay, "Sanders Is Victor."

34. Don Melvin, "Commission Posts Settled," *Burlington Free Press*, 5 June 1984; Melvin, "Progressives Win Seat."

35. Don Melvin, "City Council Takes Single Voice Vote to Fill 20 Positions," *Burlington Free Press*, 4 June 1985.

36. Don Melvin, "Sanders Influence Leaving Its Mark on Commissions," *Burlington Free Press*, 9 June 1985.

37. Mark Johnson, "Coalition Loses 2 Key Posts," *Burlington Free Press*, 3 June 1986.

38. Burlington, *1987 Annual Report*; Burlington, *1988 Annual Report*; Burlington, *1989 Annual Report*.

39. Scott McKay, "Department Heads Are Upset with Mayor," *Burlington Free Press*, 8 May 1982; Scott McKay, "10 Department Heads Will Square Off Against

Sanders," *Burlington Free Press,* 19 May 1982; Scott McKay, "Sanders, Department Heads Trade Criticisms," *Burlington Free Press,* 21 May 1982.

40. Jim Cheng, "Sanders, Paquette Show Different Government Views in Commission System Meet," *Burlington Free Press,* 8 November 1984; Sanders interview, 7 April 1987.

41. Don Melvin, "Bouricius, Mahoney Divided Over Value of Commissions," *Burlington Free Press,* 13 March 1985; Michael Powell, "Housing Program 'Too Much, Too Fast,'" *Burlington Free Press,* 16 December 1984.

42. Scott McKay, "Alderman May Back Mayor Over Panel Appointments, " *Burlington Free Press,* 5 June 1983; "Commission System Hearings Set Tonight," *Burlington Free Press,* 7 November 1984.

43. Mike Connelly, "Group Vigorously Debates Methods of Government," *Burlington Free Press,* 23 June 1983.

44. Scott McKay, "Commission Issue One of Who Should Govern," *Burlington Free Press,* 4 October 1983.

45. Ted Tedford, "Panel Urges Changes in City Government," *Burlington Free Press,* 2 November 1985.

CHAPTER 4

1. "Sanders Lauds City's Development," *Burlington Free Press,* 6 June 1985.

2. Sanders interview, 27 January 1986.

3. Scott McKay, "Sanders and Pomerleau: Burlington's Odd Couple," *Burlington Free Press,* 6 June 1982.

4. Susan Youngwood, "Developers Say Welcome Mat Not Out in City," *Burlington Free Press,* 11 June 1986.

5. "Sanders Lauds City's Development"; "Vermont Has Lowest Joblessness," *Seattle Post-Intelligencer,* 14 September 1988.

6. Sanders interview, 27 January 1986; Mark Johnson, "Dream Eludes Burlington Progressives," *Burlington Free Press,* 19 January 1986.

7. Peter Freyne, "Radical Mayor Seeks Conventional Wisdom," *Vanguard Press,* 10–17 September 1982.

8. Leopold interview.

9. Ibid.

10. Scott McKay, "New City Agency Okayed by GOP, Sanders' Backers," *Burlington Free Press,* 24 May 1983.

11. Ibid.

12. Scott McKay, "Clavelle to Get Economic Development Position," *Burlington Free Press,* 19 July 1983.

13. Center for Community Change, *UDAG "Payback" Money: A Potential Resource For Community Based Organizations* (Washington: Center for Community Change, 1983), p. 1; Debbie Bookchin, "Sanders' Pragmatism, Not Socialism, Foremost in View as He Seeks Third Term," *Times-Argus,* 3 February 1985.

14. Interview with Bruce Seifer, 30 January 1986; City of Burlington, Vermont, *119th Annual Report for the Year Ending June 30, 1984,* p. 39; City of Burlington, Vermont, *120th Annual Report for the Year Ending June 30, 1985,* p. 46; Seifer interview, 30 January 1986.

15. Jim Cheng, "Developer Unveils Plans for Lakefront," *Burlington Free Press*, 6 September 1984.

16. Rob Eley, "Preliminary Waterfront Project Plans Include 100-Slip Marina, Apartments," *Burlington Free Press*, 24 March 1978; John Letten, "City Board Approves Phase I of Lakefront Building Plan," *Burlington Free Press*, 17 August 1978; Rob Eley, "Waterfront Plan Gets Preliminary OK," *Burlington Free Press*, 18 August 1978; Gayle Gertler, "Phase I of Lakefront Plan Approved," *Burlington Free Press*, 25 August 1978; "National Life Pulls Out of Development," *Burlington Free Press*, 18 January 1979.

17. Alan Abbey, "Burlington Unveils Waterfront Park Plans," *Burlington Free Press*, 20 November 1979; Alan Abbey, "Pomerleau Wants Federal OK before Work Begins," *Burlington Free Press*, 6 February 1980; Rob Eley, "Pomerleau to Start on Lakefront Next Year," *Burlington Free Press*, 3 March 1980.

18. "It's Time for a Change, A *Real* Change," Sanders's mayoral campaign piece, 1981; "Plans for Condos on Waterfront Delayed," *Burlington Free Press*, 8 May 1981.

19. Debbie Bookchin, "Assessing Sanders," *Vanguard Press*, 31 December 1981–8 January 1982.

20. Scott McKay, "Waterfront Plan May Go Before Voters," *Burlington Free Press*, 5 February 1982.

21. Scott McKay, "Storm Clouds Move in Over City's Waterfront," *Burlington Free Press*, 12 April 1982.

22. Scott McKay, "Mayor, Aswad Clash on Plans for Waterfront," *Burlington Free Press*, 29 July 1982.

23. Scott McKay, "Pomerleau Puts Waterfront Condo Plan on Hold," *Burlington Free Press*, 9 November 1982; Scott McKay, "Waterfront Protection Plan Aired," *Burlington Free Press*, 2 December 1982; Scott McKay, "Board Rejects Interim Waterfront Zoning," *Burlington Free Press*, 11 January 1983.

24. McKay, "Waterfront Protection"; Scott McKay, "Residents Describe Waterfront Desires," *Burlington Free Press*, 16 April 1983; Scott McKay, "Mayor to Continue in Same Vein," *Burlington Free Press*, 20 March 1983; Scott McKay, "Sanders: Workers Must Stand Up and Fight," *Burlington Free Press*, 5 April 1983.

25. Scott McKay, "Aldermen Say No to Sanders on GMP Bids," *Burlington Free Press*, 14 October 1983.

26. Scott McKay, "Alden Pledges to Work with Sanders," *Burlington Free Press*, 22 October 1983; John Donnelly, "Sanders Sees City Profit in Waterfront Plan," *Burlington Free Press*, 16 January 1984; Don Melvin, "$100M Waterfront Plan Unveiled," *Burlington Free Press*, 27 January 1984.

27. Deborah Schoch, "Aldermen to Get Report on Waterfront Survey," *Burlington Free Press*, 12 March 1984; Don Melvin, "Agreement Struck on Title to Waterfront Land," *Burlington Free Press*, 17 October 1984; Don Melvin, "Waterfront Funding Plans Considered," *Burlington Free Press*, 26 August 1984; "City Files for Waterfront Grant," *Burlington Free Press*, 2 December 1984; Don Melvin, "Decision on City Waterfront Grant Put Off," *Burlington Free Press*, 29 January 1985; Don Melvin, "City Waterfront Developers Put Hopes on Federal Grant," *Burlington Free Press*, 30 January 1985; Don Melvin, "Chances Dim for Lakeside Development Grant," *Burlington Free Press*, 28 March 1985.

28. "Development Bond Plan to Be Submitted to City," *Burlington Free Press*, 14 May 1985; Don Melvin, "Committee OKs Waterfront Bond Agreement,"

Burlington Free Press, 12 September 1985; Don Melvin, "Alden Waterfront Plan Remains Just a Vision," *Burlington Free Press*, 6 October 1985.

29. Melvin, "Alden Waterfront Plan."

30. Rob Eley, "Alden Investor Dow Jones Heiress," *Burlington Free Press*, 2 March 1984.

31. "Assemblies to Hear Waterfront Plans," *Burlington Free Press*, 19 November 1985; Michael Powell, "The Battle for Burlington's Waterfront Heats Up," *Burlington Free Press*, 25 November 1985.

32. Powell, "The Battle for Burlington's Waterfront."

33. Ibid.; Mark Johnson, "Sanders Denies Sellout to Alden on Waterfront," *Burlington Free Press*, 26 November 1985.

34. Powell, "The Battle for Burlington's Waterfront"; Mark Johnson, "Waterfront Plan Goes Down to Defeat," *Burlington Free Press*, 11 December 1985.

35. Mark Johnson, "City Seeks Reasons for Waterfront Defeat," *Burlington Free Press*, 19 December 1985; Mark Johnson, "Survey: Waterfront Plan Was Judged Too Elitist," *Burlington Free Press*, 6 May 1986.

36. Mark Johnson, "Aldermen to Vote on Waterfront Improvement Bond, *Burlington Free Press*, 18 December 1986; "Burlington Election Results," *Burlington Free Press*, 4 March 1987.

37. Ross Sneyd, "Court Rules on Waterfront," *Burlington Free Press*, 25 September, 1987; Enrique Corredera, "Waterfront Dispute Goes to Court," *Burlington Free Press*, 21 November 1988.

38. Mark Johnson, "Waterfront Zoning Approved by Board," *Burlington Free Press*, 16 December 1986; Peter Freyne, *Vanguard Press* photograph caption, 21–28 December 1986.

39. Enrique Corredera, "City Will Consider Waterfront Purchase," *Burlington Free Press*, 6 November 1987; Enrique Corredera, "Sanders Prepared to Try Lakefront Condemnation," *Burlington Free Press*, 9 January 1988; "Buying the Waterfront," *Burlington Free Press* editorial, 17 November 1987.

40. Corredera, "Sanders Prepared to Try"; "Greed on the Lakefront," *Burlington Free Press* editorial, 18 January 1988; "Finally, a Lakefront Plan," *Burlington Free Press* editorial, 8 February 1988.

41. "City OKs Waterfront Buy," *Burlington Free Press*, 9 February 1988; Enrique Corredera, "City to Use Navy Building on Waterfront for Public," *Burlington Free Press*, 21 April 1988; Judith Shulevitz, "Burlington May Make a Deal to Take Over Navy Building," *Burlington Free Press*, 25 April 1988.

42. Enrique Corredera, "Just-Cause Eviction Lags in Early Returns," *Burlington Free Press*, 9 November 1988; Enrique Corredera, "City Moors Hopes on the Waterfront," *Burlington Free Press*, 30 October 1988; Enrique Corredera, "Harbor Bond Irks Aldermen," *Burlington Free Press*, 31 August 1988; Enrique Corredera, "City Officials Support Bonds on Waterfront," *Burlington Free Press*, 1 November 1988.

43. Lisa Scagliotti, "Railway to Have Its Say on Waterfront," *Burlington Free Press*, 17 January 1989; Lisa Scagliotti, "Railway Not Shocked by Criticism," *Burlington Free Press*, 19 January 1989.

44. Don Melvin, "Aldermen Clear Way for Waterfront Vote," *Burlington Free Press*, 5 November 1985.

45. Sanders interview, 12 December 1985.

46. Ted Tedford, "Southern Connector May Be Ready to Build," *Burlington Free Press*, 15 December 1984; "3 Meetings to Discuss Downtown Access Road," *Burlington Free Press*, 7 January 1974.

47. "3 Meetings to Discuss"; Russ Garland, "Highway Plans Near Construction," *Burlington Free Press*, 1 January 1977; Gayle Gertler, "West Connector Route Gets Burlington Backing," *Burlington Free Press*, 23 November 1977; Peter Freyne, "Hazardous Wastes in Connector Path," *Vanguard Press*, 21 October 1980.

48. Rob Eley, "Group Announces Its Opposition to Southern Connector," *Burlington Free Press*, 6 December 1978; Alan Abbey, "Complaints Rain on Southern Connector," *Burlington Free Press*, 30 August 1979.

49. Alan Abbey, "Pedestrian Overpass Rejected," *Burlington Free Press*, 7 August 1980; Alan Abbey, "Burlington Aldermen Return Connector Plan Unchanged," *Burlington Free Press*, 25 November 1980; Alan Abbey, "Mayor Kills Vote on Connector Delay," *Burlington Free Press*, 4 February 1981.

50. Alan Abbey, "Dear David: Cut Our Funds, Please," *Burlington Free Press*, 23 March 1981.

51. Sanders interview, 12 December 1985.

52. Alan Abbey, "Legislators Aren't Detoured from Connector Plan," *Burlington Free Press*, 6 November 1981; Scott McKay, "Sanders Delaying Connector Road, Gilson Charges," *Burlington Free Press*, 5 January 1983; Alan Abbey, "Aldermen Ignore Sanders, OK Connector Land Purchasing," *Burlington Free Press*, 20 October 1981.

53. Don Melvin, "Group Draws Up Compromise on Southern Connector," *Burlington Free Press*, 9 January 1983; Scott McKay, "Politics Could Dig Potholes in Southern Connector Plan," *Burlington Free Press*, 7 February 1983; Scott McKay, "Southern Connector Land Transfer OK'd," *Burlington Free Press*, 11 January 1983.

54. Don Melvin, "Compromise Could Put Connector on Track," *Burlington Free Press*, 3 April 1985.

55. Don Melvin, "Sanders Eyeing Two-Lane Connector Plan," *Burlington Free Press*, 16 May 1985.

56. Ibid.

57. Don Melvin, "Burns: Connector Would Aid Lakeshore Development," *Burlington Free Press*, 12 February 1985; Marsha Young, "Sanders, Planners Interpret Resolution Differently," *Burlington Free Press*, 9 November 1985.

58. Susan Youngwood, "Business, Mayor Collide on Connector," *Burlington Free Press*, 8 November 1985; Ernie Pomerleau, "It's Time for Action on the Southern Connector," *Burlington Free Press* perspective, 13 November 1985.

59. Christopher Graff, "City, State Put Pen to Accord for Connector," *Burlington Free Press*, 16 November 1985.

60. Mark Johnson, "Lawsuit, Compromise Lead to Connector Pact," *Burlington Free Press*, 18 November 1985.

61. Ibid.; Joanne Beauchemin, "Sanders Helped in Reaching Sensible Connector Compromise," *Burlington Free Press* perspective, 4 December 1985.

62. Sarah Wilson, "EPA Completes Initial Cleanup of Barge Canal," *Burlington Free Press,* 6 December 1985; Mike Donoghue, "New Barge Canal Study Will Delay Connector," *Burlington Free Press,* 9 May 1986.

63. Mark Johnson, "Connector Manager Briefs City on Canal Study," *Burlington Free Press,* 13 May 1986.

64. Enrique Corredera, "Connector Work Delayed Until '89," *Burlington Free Press,* 3 October 1987.

65. Sanders interview, 12 December 1985.

66. Ibid.

67. Ibid.

CHAPTER 5

1. City Clerk, *Burlington Election Records.*

2. Ibid.; Phone conversation with Burlington Voter Registration Board, 13 April 1988.

3. City Clerk, *Burlington Election Records.*

4. Ibid.; Phone conversation with Burlington Voter Registration Board, 13 April 1988.

5. Sanders interview, 12 December 1985.

6. Alan Abbey, "Fair Housing Proposal Won't Be on Ballot," *Burlington Free Press,* 21 January 1981.

7. Alan Abbey, "Fair Housing Proposal Goes on Ballot," *Burlington Free Press,* 17 March 1981.

8. Alan Abbey, "Housing Commission Plans Crushed," *Burlington Free Press,* 22 April 1981.

9. Ibid.; "Sanders Reiterates Support of PACT Housing Proposal," *Burlington Free Press,* 16 April 1981.

10. Sanders interview, 27 January 1986.

11. John Gittlesohn, "Housing Ordinance Debated," Burlington Free Press, 2 August 1984; Don Melvin, "Aldermen Vote Housing Ordinance, Burlington Free Press, 10 October 1984; Mark Johnson, "Rental Ordinance Gets Aldermanic Approval," Burlington Free Press, 11 March 1986.

12. Don Melvin, "Burlington Passes Watered-Downed Rent Deposit Law," *Burlington Free Press,* 10 October 1984.

13. Mark Johnson, "Aldermen Stall on Ballot Items," *Burlington Free Press,* 14 January 1986; "Tenants' Group Begins Petition Drive," *Burlington Free Press,* 17 January 1986; Mike Donoghue, "Renters' Petition Drive Is Successful," *Burlington Free Press,* 3 February 1986; City Clerk, *Burlington Election Records.*

14. Mark Johnson, "City Eyeing Tax on Real Estate Speculators," *Burlington Free Press,* 3 January 1986.

15. Ibid.; Mark Johnson, "Rental Speculation Tax Causes Heated Hearing," Burlington Free Press, 13 February 1986; Mark Johnson, "Report Criticizes Speculation Tax, Splits Aldermen," Burlington Free Press, 19 February 1986.

16. Mark Johnson, "Sanders Criticizes Study on Tax Plan," *Burlington Free Press*, 20 February 1986; Mark Johnson, "Anti-Speculation Tax Plan Divides Residents," *Burlington Free Press*, 24 February 1986.

17. Johnson, "Aldermen Stall"; "Tenants' Groups"; Donoghue, "Renters' Petition Drive"; Mark Johnson, "Suit Filed to Take Plan Off Ballot," *Burlington Free Press*, 25 February 1986; Mark Johnson, "Judge Overrules Objection to Speculation Tax Vote," *Burlington Free Press*, 28 February 1986; City Clerk, *Burlington Election Records*.

18. Mark Johnson, "Anti-Speculation Tax to Go Before Voters," *Burlington Free Press*, 17 September 1986.

19. Stephen Casimiro, "Sanders Vetoes Speculation Tax Change," *Burlington Free Press*, 8 October 1986.

20. Mark Johnson, "Anti-Speculation Tax Approved by City Voters," *Burlington Free Press*, 6 November 1986; Don Melvin, "Sanders Promotes Charter Changes," *Burlington Free Press*, 6 May 1987; Don Melvin, "House Rejects Tax City Voters OKed," *Burlington Free Press*, 7 May 1987.

21. Enrique Corredera, "Burlington Told to Decide on Eviction Ordinance," *Burlington Free Press*, 11 August 1988.

22. Lisa Scagliotti, "Aldermen to Consider Ballot Items," *Burlington Free Press*, 19 September 1988; Enrique Corredera, "Landlord's Comment Irks Progressive," *Burlington Free Press*, 21 October 1988; Ted Tedford, "Tenants' Initiative to Hurt Housing, Opponents Say," *Burlington Free Press*, 5 November 1988.

23. Corredera, "Landlord's Comments"; Ted Tedford, "Opponents of Tenant Initiative Called Liars," *Burlington Free Press*, 4 November 1988.

24. Tedford, "Tenants' Initiative to Hurt Housing"; "'Just-Cause' Tops Crowded Ballot-Items List," *Burlington Free Press*, 7 November 1988.

25. "2 Neighborhood Assemblies Schedule Meetings This Week," *Burlington Free Press*, 25 October 1982.

26. "Planning Assemblies Slated This Week," *Burlington Free Press*, 31 October 1982; "NPA in Ward 6," *Burlington Free Press*, 20 January 1983; "Ward 3 Group Slates Monday Meeting," *Burlington Free Press*, 29 January 1983; "Neighborhood Planning Assemblies to Meet," *Burlington Free Press*, 3 February 1983; Scott McKay, "Assemblies Prove Talk Is Valuable Tool," *Burlington Free Press*, 30 October 1983.

27. McKay, "Assemblies Prove Talk."

28. "Residents Air Baseball Worries," *Burlington Free Press*, 18 January 1984; "Ward 2 Neighborhood Planning Assembly to Discuss Waterfront," *Burlington Free Press*, 6 November 1985; Jim Cheng, "Ward 3 Residents, Aldermen Seek Halt to Moran Emissions," *Burlington Free Press*, 26 September 1984; Ward 3 Assembly to Meet," *Burlington Free Press*, 14 July 1986; "Neighborhood Planning Group to Discuss Housing," *Burlington Free Press*, 28 September 1987; "Neighborhood Planners Meet Today Over Bonds," *Burlington Free Press*, 1 November 1988.

29. Ian Polumbaum, "Neighborhoods Planning Ahead," *Burlington Free Press*, 8 November 1987.

30. Don Melvin, "Sanders . . .," *Burlington Free Press*, 10 February 1982; Scott McKay, "Sanders Cites Reawakened Interest in City Government," *Burlington Free Press*, 17 February 1983.

31. Sanders interview, 12 December 1985.

32. *Idem*, 27 January 1986.

CHAPTER 6

1. One of the best examples of ownership by state government is the state bank of North Dakota, started in 1919 after the Non-Partisan League gained control of the state legislature. It is still in existence today. See Martin Carnoy and Derek Shearer, *Economic Democracy: The Challenge of the 1980s* (Armonk, N.Y.: M.E. Sharpe, 1980), pp. 69–70. Regarding U.S. government partial or complete ownership of business enterprises, examples include the United States Postal Service, the Amtrak railway system, and the Tennessee Valley Authority.

2. Greg Guma, "James Burke and the Progressive Era" (Burlington, Vt.: May 1984; typewritten unpublished manuscript).

3. Mike Connelly, "Residents Frustrated by Lack of Control Over Cable Policy," *Burlington Free Press*, 29 June 1983; Scott McKay, "Cable T.V. Committee to Study Burlington Service," *Burlington Free Press*, 5 May 1983.

4. The Vermont Public Service Board is a quasi-judicial panel that regulates the state's utilities; Don Melvin, "City Will Get $1 Million in Burlington Coffers," *Burlington Free Press*, 30 March 1985; David Hench, "Aldermen Unanimously Approve Cable Television Deal," *Burlington Free Press*, 3 April 1985; Ted Tedford, "Merits of City Cable System Debated by Sanders, Hart," *Burlington Free Press*, 16 September 1983; Connelly, "Residents Frustrated."

5. Scott McKay, "Sanders Urges Burlington Utility to Study Cable T.V.," *Burlington Free Press*, 26 July 1983; Scott McKay, "Electric Commission Approves Cable Television Study," *Burlington Free Press*, 4 August 1983.

6. Scott McKay, "T.V. Panel Recommends 55 Channel City Cable," *Burlington Free Press*, 29 July 1983.

7. Don Melvin, "Study Claims Big Savings in City-Owned Cable System," *Burlington Free Press*, 6 January 1984; Jim Cheng, "Cox Spokesman Hart Disputes Cable Study," *Burlington Free Press*, 14 January 1984.

8. "Cable Television Takeover Is Preposterous Idea," *Burlington Free Press* editorial, 23 July 1983.

9. Mo Shafroth, "City to Prepare Cable T.V. Application," *Burlington Free Press*, 10 April 1984.

10. Don Melvin, "Deal Drafted Between City & Cox Cable," *Burlington Free Press*, 27 June 1984.

11. Jim Cheng, "Sanders Asks More Cable Concessions," *Burlington Free Press*, 29 June 1984; Don Melvin, "Aldermen Reject City Cable Idea," *Burlington Free Press*, 25 September 1984.

12. Jim Cheng, "PSB Sides With Cox Cable on Rates; Mayor Livid," *Burlington Free Press*, 20 October 1984.

13. Jim Cheng, "Attorneys Pore Over Cable T.V. Legislation," *Burlington Free Press*, 19 December 1984; Jim Cheng, "Cable Fight Goes to High Court," *Burlington Free Press*, 9 March 1985.

14. "Cox Cable Sells 3 Vermont Franchises," *Burlington Free Press*, 2 February 1985; Melvin, "City Will Get $1 Million."

15. Melvin, "City Will Get $1 Million"; Hench, "Aldermen Unanimously Approve."

16. Don Melvin, "T.V. Deal Puts $1 Million in Burlington Coffers," *Burlington Free Press*, 21 July 1985.

17. Sanders interview, 12 December 1985.

18. Leslie Brown, "City Can Participate in Cox T.V. Case," *Burlington Free Press*, 6 March 1984.

19. City of Burlington, Vermont, *1984 Annual Report*, p. 41.

20. Michael Powell, "South End Split Puts Housing Problems in Focus," *Burlington Free Press*, 13 August 1984; "Meadow Project Debated," *Burlington Free Press*, 16 January 1985; Mark Johnson, "Neighbors Settle With Developer," *Burlington Free Press*, 8 March 1986; Mark Johnson, "Rental Ordinance Gets Aldermanic Approval," *Burlington Free Press*, 11 March 1986.

21. Andy Potter, "City Proposes Condo-Mania Antidote," *Vanguard Press*, 8–15 January 1987; Amy Killinger, "Group Tries to Buy Northgate to Keep Low-Cost Housing," *Burlington Free Press*, 11 November 1988; Michael Allen, "Agency Puts Lid on Northgate Rents," *Burlington Free Press*, 2 February 1989.

22. Potter, "City Proposes."

23. "Burlington Results," *Burlington Free Press*, 4 March 1987; Potter, "City Proposes"; Enrique Corredera, "Conversion to Condos a Rarity," *Burlington Free Press*, 20 June 1988.

24. Stephen Casimiro, "Developers Say New Law Will Slow Pace of Investing," *Burlington Free Press*, 9 March 1987; Corredera, "Conversion to Condos."

25. Mary Ann Lickteig, "Vt. Pledges $3 Million for Northgate," *Burlington Free Press*, 4 March 1989.

26. Lickteig, "Vt. Pledges."

27. Interview with Tim McKenzie, 10 February 1986; Burlington Community Land Trust, *First Annual Report: 1984–1985*.

28. McKenzie interview, 10 February 1986.

29. Phone interview with Pat Peterson, 3 and 4 August 1989.

30. Phone interview with Tim McKenzie, 2 June 1987.

31. *Idem*, 10 February 1986.

32. Ibid.; Land Trust, *First Annual Report*.

33. McKenzie interview, 10 February 1986.

34. Ibid.

35. Michael Powell, "Mother's Dream of Home Ownership Comes True with Land Trust Funding," *Burlington Free Press*, 10 February 1985; Mathias Dubilier, "New City Land Trust to Sponsor Housing," *Burlington Free Press*, 23 April 1984.

36. McKenzie interview, 10 February 1986; Doug Wilhelm, "Vermont Programs Seek to Provide Affordable Housing," *Boston Globe*, 6 September 1987.

37. Dubilier, "New City Land Trust"; McKenzie interview, 10 February 1986.

38. McKenzie interview, 10 February 1986.

39. McKenzie interview, 2 June 1987.

40. McKenzie interview, 10 February 1986.

41. Janet Dunn, "Land Scheme of Burlington Is Dangerous," *Burlington Free Press* letter to editor, 28 May 1987.

42. Powell, "Mother's Dream"; "Land Trust to Cut Back Housing Role," *Burlington Free Press*, 29 October 1984.

43. "Residents Organize North End Project," *Burlington Free Press*, 23 October 1984; "Homeowners Protest," *Burlington Free Press* photograph, 30 October 1984; "Land Trust to Cut Back."

44. McKenzie interview, 10 February 1986.

45. Ibid.

46. Sanders interview, 12 December 1985.

47. "Community Land Trust Wins U.N. Award," *Burlington Free Press*, 11 September 1986.

48. Reported quote by Sanders in interview with Bruce Seifer, 30 January 1986.

49. Burlington, *1985 Annual Report*, p. 47.

50. Seifer interview, 30 January 1986.

51. Ibid.

52. Seifer phone interview, 19 December 1989.

53. "Equity Common Thread at Wild Oats," *Burlington Free Press*, 26 November 1986; Seifer phone interview, 4 June 1987; Seifer phone interview, 8 June 1988.

54. Seifer phone interview, 8 June 1988.

55. Seifer interview, 30 January 1986.

56. Ibid.; Seifer phone interview, 8 June 1988.

57. Sanders interview, 12 December 1985.

58. Peter Jan Honigsberg, Bernard Kamoroff, and Jim Beatty, *We Own It: Starting & Managing Coops, Collectives, and Employee-Owned Ventures* (Laytonville, Calif.: Bell Springs Publishing, 1982), p. 32.

59. Ibid., pp. 44–46.

60. "Centerpiece: Resources for a HomeGrown Economy," *Changing Work* (Spring 1986), p. C2; Seifer phone interview, 8 June 1988.

61. Seifer phone interview, 19 December 1989.

CHAPTER 7

1. Don Melvin, "Lawmakers Tell Sanders: Stir Up Public Opposition," *Burlington Free Press*, 21 December 1983.

2. Sanders interview, 12 December 1985; Scott McKay, "Attorney Says City Has Right to Levy Rooms, Meal Tax," *Burlington Free Press*, 13 January 1982.

3. Sanders interview, 12 December 1985; "Burlington Election Results," *Burlington Free Press*, 4 March 1987; phone interview with Jonathan Leopold, Jr., 9 June 1988.

4. Sanders interview, 29 December 1985.

5. Rob Eley, "Property Value Disparities Surface in Study of Sales," *Burlington Free Press*, 1 November 1981; Scott McKay, "Aldermen Accept Reappraisal Proposal," *Burlington Free Press*, 25 March 1982.

6. Scott McKay, "Reappraisal to Start Soon in Burlington," *Burlington Free Press*, 28 September 1983; Rob Eley, "Property Reappraisal to Begin," *Burlington Free Press*, 28 September 1983; William H. Braun, "Coalition to Push for Property Tax Relief," *Burlington Free Press*, 25 May 1984; Susan Youngwood, "Reappraisers Assess Home Values, Tax Importance on Low-Income Owners," *Burlington Free*

Press, 5 August 1984; Jonathan Leopold, Jr., "State's Inaction Puts Tax Burden in Wrong Place," *Burlington Free Press* perspective, 16 October 1986.

7. Don Melvin and Michael Powell, "Burlington Charter Changes Defeated," *Burlington Free Press*, 14 April 1985.

8. Michael Powell, "Reassessment Analysis Shows Three-Quarters Saw House Taxes Rise," *Burlington Free Press*, 13 May 1985; Leopold, "State Inaction Puts Tax Burden."

9. Leopold, "State Inaction Puts Tax Burden"; Don Melvin, "GE Asking Further Cut in Tax Bill," *Burlington Free Press*, 15 June 1985; Danica Kirka, "Aldermen Reject GE's Tax Assessment Appeal," *Burlington Free Press*, 20 February 1986.

10. Don Melvin, "Sanders Calls on GE to Drop Tax Appeal," *Burlington Free Press*, 18 June 1985.

11. Scott McKay, "Sanders Tax Panel to Recommend Reappraisal," *Burlington Free Press*, 9 December 1981; Scott McKay, "Political Overtones Casts Shadow on City Budget," *Burlington Free Press*, 28 April 1982.

12. McKay, "Sanders Tax Panel."

13. Scott McKay, "Attorney Says City Has Right to Levy Rooms, Meals Tax," *Burlington Free Press*, 13 January 1982.

14. Ibid.

15. Ibid.; Scott McKay, "Snelling Opposes Tax Idea," *Burlington Free Press*, 21 January 1982.

16. Deborah Sline, "Burlington's 'Tax Revolt' Could Spread Quickly," *Burlington Free Press*, 28 January 1982.

17. Ibid.; Scott McKay, "Sanders Property Taxes Up 34 Cents or Down 3," *Burlington Free Press*, 19 January 1982.

18. Don Melvin, "Restauranteurs to Train Artillery on Rooms, Meal Tax Proposal," *Burlington Free Press*, 22 January 1982; "Restaurant Owners Solidify Group," *Burlington Free Press*, 17 February 1982.

19. Sline, "Burlington's 'Tax Revolt'"; Bernard Sanders, "New Ways Have Been Found to Swell Coffers," *Burlington Free Press* perspective, 4 June 1982; Melvin Hill, Jr., *State Laws Governing Local Government Structure and Administration (Athens: University of Georgia, Institute of Government, 1978), pp.* 15, 22, 29, 36.

20. Laura King, "Mayor Wins Support for Tax Plan," *Burlington Free Press*, 24 February 1982.

21. Deborah Sline, "Burlington Wins Its Battle Over Taxation Rights," *Burlington Free Press*, 26 February 1982.

22. Ibid.

23. Scott McKay, "Meals Tax Victory Advances Sanders," *Burlington Free Press*, 27 February 1982.

24. Scott McKay, "Petition Drive Starting for Rooms-Meal Tax," 15 May 1982; Scott McKay, "Rooms and Meals Tax Gains Place on Ballot," *Burlington Free Press*, 25 May 1982.

25. John Reilly, "Chamber Hits Out at Rooms-Meals Tax," 11 May 1982; "Restaurant Owners Gird for Meals Tax Battle," *Burlington Free Press*, 3 June 1982; Scott McKay, "Restaurant Owner Bove Endorses Gross Receipts Tax," *Burlington Free Press*, 5 June 1982.

26. Jodie Peck, "Tax Opponents Using Misleading Tactics, Proponents Claiming," *Burlington Free Press*, 6 June 1982.

27. Scott McKay, "Burlington Voters Say No to All Three Tax Proposals," *Burlington Free Press*, 9 June 1982.

28. Ibid.; Scott McKay, "Sanders to Do Battle for His Tax Plan," *Burlington Free Press*, 10 June 1982.

29. Rob Eley, "Tax Idea Rejected by Panel," *Burlington Free Press*, 4 August 1982; Nelson Hockert-Lotz, "Board Rejects City Food Tax Idea," *Burlington Free Press*, 28 September 1982.

30. Susan Youngwood, "School Panel Recommends Substitute Tax," *Burlington Free Press*, 7 January 1985.

31. Susan Youngwood, "City Rooms, Meals Tax Passes First Hurdle," *Burlington Free Press*, 8 January 1985.

32. Jim Cheng, "Restauranteurs Divided Over City Tax Proposal," *Burlington Free Press*, 18 January 1985; Leslie Brown, "State Officials Frowning on City's Tax Plan," *Burlington Free Press*, 22 January 1985.

33. Jim Cheng, "Board Will Ask Rooms, Meals Tax," *Burlington Free Press*, 30 January 1985; Don Melvin, "Aldermen Put Room, Meals Tax on Ballot," *Burlington Free Press*, 5 February 1985; Ted Tedford, "Restauranteurs Waiting for State to Kill Meals Tax," *Burlington Free Press*, 2 February 1985; Michael Powell, "City, Schools Pushing Hard for Tax Plan," *Burlington Free Press*, 25 February 1985; Michael Powell, "Rooms and Meals Tax Approved by Majority," *Burlington Free Press*, 6 March 1985; City Clerk, *Burlington Election Records*.

34. Steve Rosenfield, "Compromise Suggested: Forfeit Some Aid for Extra City Taxes," *Burlington Free Press*, 12 March 1985; Don Melvin, "Officials Lobby for New Taxes," *Burlington Free Press*, 15 March 1985; Steve Rosenfield, "Ristau Warns Against City's Tax Initiatives," *Burlington Free Press*, 16 March 1985.

35. Sarah Wilson, "House Panel Hears Burlington Merchants," *Burlington Free Press*, 29 March 1985; Sarah Wilson, "House Committee Rejects New Burlington Taxes," *Burlington Free Press*, 30 March 1985.

36. Peggy Grodinsky, "Parents to Lobby Lawmakers for Full Debate on Charter Changes," *Burlington Free Press*, 5 April 1985; Sarah Wilson, "Students Plead for Revisions in City Charter," *Burlington Free Press*, 12 April 1985; Sarah Wilson, "Second Panel Frowns on Charter Changes," *Burlington Free Press*, 13 April 1985; Sarah Wilson, "House Won't Yield State Tax Revenues," *Burlington Free Press*, 17 April 1985.

37. Wilson, "House Won't Yield."

38. Mark Johnson, "Gross Receipts Tax to Be Considered for Burlington," *Burlington Free Press*, 7 January 1986; Susan Youngwood, "Sanders Urges Joint Revenue Effort between City and Business Leaders," *Burlington Free Press*, 7 November 1985; "Business, Mayor Collide on Connector," *Burlington Free Press*, 8 November 1985.

39. Mark Johnson, "Sanders Panel Unveils Revenue Raising Plan," *Burlington Free Press*, 11 January 1986.

40. Ibid.; Johnson, "Gross Receipts Tax"; Johnson, "Sanders Panel Unveils."

41. Mark Johnson, "Aldermen Approve Gross Receipts Tax," *Burlington Free Press*, 31 January 1986.

42. Mark Johnson, "Four Years Later Sanders Puts Pen to New Tax Plan," *Burlington Free Press*, 1 February 1986.

43. Mark Johnson, "City's Gross Receipts Tax Now in Effect," *Burlington Free Press*, 4 March 1986.

44. Mark Johnson, "Colleges' Food Service Has to Pay New City Tax," *Burlington Free Press*, 6 February 1986; Mark Johnson, "Saga Food Service Challenges Tax," *Burlington Free Press*, 1 May 1986; Mark Johnson, "Colleges to Sue Over Receipts Tax," *Burlington Free Press*, 23 July 1986; Ted Tedford, "Food Tax Countersuit Thrown Out," *Burlington Free Press*, 24 December 1986.

45. Lisa Scagliotti, "Sanders Defends Power to Tax," *Burlington Free Press*, 21 February 1989; Lisa Scagliotti, "Hearings Continue on Taxes," *Burlington Free Press*, 22 February 1989; Lisa Scagliotti, "Taxing Bill's Danger Warned," *Burlington Free Press*, 23 February 1989.

46. Sanders interview, 27 January 1986.

47. *Idem*, 7 April 1986.

48. Mary Ann Lickteig, "Burlington Rejects School, 'Sin' Taxes," *Burlington Free Press*, 8 March 1989; "Day Care: What Now"?, *Burlington Free Press* editorial, 4 March 1988; Enrique Corredera, "Argument Heats Up Over Tax for Child Care," *Burlington Free Press*, 26 February 1988; "Day Care: What Now?"; Judith Shulevitz, "Aldermen Set to Vote on New Child-Care Proposal," *Burlington Free Press*, 21 March 1988; Enrique Corredera, "Progressives Object to Make-up of City Child-Care Study Panel," *Burlington Free Press*, 10 May 1988; Enrique Corredera, "Child-Care Panel Eyes $2 Million," *Burlington Free Press*, 14 August 1988; Enrique Corredera, "$1.2 Million Fund Advised for Child-Care," *Burlington Free Press*, 8 October 1988.

49. "Attention Burlington Voters: Keep Shoppers in Burlington," *Burlington Free Press* advertisement, 6 March 1989; Lisa Scagliotti, "Grocers Oppose 'Sin Tax' to Fund Child Care," *Burlington Free Press*, 9 February 1989; "Burlington Rejects School."

50. Ellen Neuborne, "Grocers Oppose 'Sin' Tax," *Burlington Free Press*, 22 February 1989; Sam Hemingway, "Poll Shows Voters Split on 'Sin' Tax," *Burlington Free Press*, 27 February 1989; "Burlington Rejects School."

51. Powell, "Rooms and Meals Tax Approved"; City Clerk, *Burlington Election Records*; Wilson, "House Won't Yield"; City Clerk, *Burlington Election Records*.

52. "Push on for Tax Classification Bill," *Burlington Free Press*, 23 April 1986; Mark Johnson, "Cities' Tax Plan Gets House OK," *Burlington Free Press*, 24 April 1986; Don Melvin, "Burlington, Winooski Tax Changes Approved," *Burlington Free Press*, 29 April 1986.

53. Candace Page, "A Taxing Problem for City Businesses," *Burlington Free Press*, 2 March 1987; Mark Johnson, "Building Owners Challenge State's Tax Code," *Burlington Free Press*, 26 March 1987; Danica Kirka, "Firm Challenges City Tax System," *Burlington Free Press*, 16 May 1987.

54. Candace Page, "Stephany, Gilson Take Pro-Business Stand," *Burlington Free Press*, 25 February 1983; John Gittlesohn, "Commission Goes in Reverse on Charter Change," *Burlington Free Press*, 14 February 1985.

55. Mark Johnson, "Aldermen Say UVM, Hospital Should Pay to Get Fire Protection," *Burlington Free Press*, 17 January 1986.

56. Michael Powell, "Coor to Sanders: Prove UVM Is a Burden on City," *Burlington Free Press*, 18 January 1986.

57. Mark Johnson, "Alternative Tax Plans to Appear on March Ballot," *Burlington Free Press*, 21 January 1986; Mark Johnson, "Burlington Endorses

Plan to End Tax-Exempt Status," *Burlington Free Press*, 5 March 1986; City Clerk, *Burlington Election Records*; Mark Johnson, "Sanders Cheers Tax Vote," *Burlington Free Press*, 6 March 1986; Mark Johnson, "Mayor Pushes Panel for Charter Changes," *Burlington Free Press*, 10 April 1986; Johnson, "Cities' Tax Plan."

58. Sarah Wilson, "City and UVM to Negotiate Tax Issue," *Burlington Free Press*, 11 April 1986; Mark Johnson, "UVM Proposes Paying Per Fire," *Burlington Free Press*, 29 May 1986.

59. Mark Johnson, "Medical Center May Be City's Next Target," *Burlington Free Press*, 13 August 1986; Mark Johnson, "Hospital Invites Sanders to Talk," *Burlington Free Press*, 18 June 1987; Mark Johnson, "City Sends Hospital $2.83 Million Tax Bill," *Burlington Free Press*, 25 June 1987; Mark Johnson, "MCHV Calls City Bill 'Unlawful,' Files Suit," *Burlington Free Press*, 30 June 1987; Enrique Corredera, "Hospital Bid Fails," *Burlington Free Press*, 2 July 1987.

60. Mark Johnson, "200-Year Tradition at Stake in Sanders-Hospital Court Fight," *Burlington Free Press*, 9 August 1987.

61. Mark Johnson, "MCHV Testifies It's Charitable," *Burlington Free Press*, 11 August 1987; Mark Johnson, "City Witnesses Dispute Hospital's Charity Claim," *Burlington Free Press*, 13 August 1987.

62. Enrique Corredera, "Medical Center KO's City in Tax Bout," *Burlington Free Press*, 23 September 1987; Enrique Corredera, "Sanders Blasts Tax Case Ruling," *Burlington Free Press*, 24 September 1987; Burlington, *1989 Annual Report*.

63. Candace Page, "Sanders Insists Fee Proposal Nothing New," *Burlington Free Press*, 18 November 1982.

64. Ibid.

65. Scott McKay, "Sanders Wants to Institute New Tax on Utilities," *Burlington Free Press*, 11 November 1982.

66. Scott McKay, "Right of Way Fees Face Legal Battles," *Burlington Free Press*, 16 March 1983.

67. Scott McKay, "City Won't Charge Utility Fees for Cost of Street Repairs," *Burlington Free Press*, 3 May 1983.

68. Scott McKay, "NET Says Business Will Bear Sanders' Fee," *Burlington Free Press*, 1 June 1983; Scott McKay, "Utilities Argue against Street Rents," *Burlington Free Press*, 2 June 1983; "Fee on Utilities Would Be Paid by Consumer," *Burlington Free Press*, 12 June 1983.

69. Scott McKay, "Sanders Proposes Fee for Excavation," *Burlington Free Press*, 10 August 1983.

70. Scott McKay, "Saudek Says Local Cable Fees Illegal," *Burlington Free Press*, 23 August 1983.

71. Scott McKay, "Commission Backs Mayor's Proposal on Excavation Fees," *Burlington Free Press*, 3 November 1983.

72. Scott McKay, "Utilities Aim Gun at Excavation Fee," *Burlington Free Press*, 4 November 1983; "Street Rental Fees Unfeasible," *Burlington Free Press* editorial, 11 August 1983; "Aldermen Should Reject Proposed Street Repair Fees," *Burlington Free Press* editorial, 21 October 1983.

73. Don Melvin, "Street Commission to Ask for $10.30 Excavation Fee," *Burlington Free Press*, 4 January 1984.

74. Don Melvin, "Sanders Links Tax Support to Excavation Fee Proposal," *Burlington Free Press*, 6 January 1984.

75. Don Melvin, "Council Panel Buries Excavation Fee Proposal," *Burlington Free Press*, 10 January 1984.

76. Don Melvin, "Aldermen to Review Utility Fee Proposal," *Burlington Free Press*, 25 January 1984; Don Melvin, "Mayor Reluctantly Backs Street Tax," *Burlington Free Press*, 29 February 1984.

77. Don Melvin, "Aldermen Debate Utility Street Fee," *Burlington Free Press*, 13 March 1984.

78. Don Melvin, "Aldermen Pass Street Excavation Fee," *Burlington Free Press*, 20 March 1984.

79. Ted Tedford, "2 Utilities in Court Over Fees," *Burlington Free Press*, 12 April 1984; Scott McKay, "Vermont Gas Wants Customers to Pay Fee," *Burlington Free Press*, 28 April 1984.

80. Don Melvin, "Utilities to Pay City Fee While Judge Ponders," *Burlington Free Press*, 26 May 1984; Ted Tedford, "What Court Will Hear Fee Case?," *Burlington Free Press*, 8 June 1984; Ted Tedford, "Utility Lawyers Want Excavation Fee Heard in State Court," *Burlington Free Press*, 12 June 1984; Ted Tedford, "Fee Case Back in Superior Court," *Burlington Free Press*, 27 July 1984; Ted Tedford, "Excavation Fee Put on Hold while Court Weighs Dispute," *Burlington Free Press*, 3 August 1984.

81. Tedford, "Excavation Fee Put on Hold"; Don Melvin, "City Excavation Fee Back at Ground Level," *Burlington Free Press*, 10 October 1984.

82. Ibid.

83. Don Melvin, "Excavation Fee OK'd; Question: How Much?," *Burlington Free Press*, 23 January 1985.

84. Mark Johnson, "$1.76 Million Payment OK'd for Excavations," *Burlington Free Press*, 16 December 1985.

85. Ibid.

86. Ibid.

87. Mark Johnson, "City Departments Feel Sting of Fees," *Burlington Free Press*, 16 June 1986.

88. Sanders interviews, 12 December 1985 and 27 January 1986.

CHAPTER 8

1. The following material, unless otherwise indicated, is drawn from an interview with Doreen Kraft, 5 December 1985.

2. City of Burlington, Vermont, *117th Annual Report for the Year Ending June 30, 1982*, p. 51.

3. City of Burlington, Vermont, *118th Annual Report for the Year Ending June 30, 1983*, p. 55; Susan Green, "Burlington Gets a City-Sized WPA," *Burlington Free Press*, 6 October 1983.

4. Burlington, *1984 Annual Report*, pp. 87–90.

5. Burlington, *1985 Annual Report*, pp. 95–99; Don Melvin, "Burns Suggests . . . ," *Burlington Free Press*, 4 February 1985.

6. Burlington, *1986 Annual Report*, pp. 113–16.

7. Burlington, *1987 Annual Report*, pp. 98–101.

8. Burlington, *1988 Annual Report*, pp. 101–4.

9. Draft report from the Mayor's Council on the Arts for the year ending June 30, 1989.

10. The following material, unless otherwise noted, is drawn from an interview with Jane Driscoll, 7 November 1985.

11. Burlington, *1983 Annual Report*, p. 56.

12. Burlington, *1982 Annual Report*, p. 52; Burlington, *1983 Annual Report*, p. 57.

13. Burlington, *1983 Annual Report*, p. 57.

14. Ibid.

15. Burlington, *1984 Annual Report*, p. 95.

16. Burlington, *1983 Annual Report*, p. 57; "Beautification Program Gets Boost," *Burlington Free Press*, 11 April 1987; Burlington, *1985 Annual Report*, p. 66; Sanders interview, 12 December 1985.

17. Burlington, *1984 Annual Report*, pp. 94–95.

18. Burlington, *1985 Annual Report*, pp. 103–7.

19. Ibid.

20. Ibid.; "Youthful Arts," *Burlington Free Press*, 9 August 1985.

21. Burlington, *1986 Annual Report*, pp. 120–23.

22. Burlington, *1987 Annual Report*, pp. 105–8.

23. Burlington, *1988 Annual Report*, pp. 108–11.

24. Draft report from the Mayor's Youth Office for the year ending June 30, 1989.

25. Scott McKay, "Driscoll's Special Status of Concern to Some Aldermen," *Burlington Free Press*, 27 June 1983. Jane Driscoll became Jane O'Meara Sanders when she married Bernard Sanders in 1988.

26. Burlington, *1982 Annual Report*, p. 52; the following material, except where indicated, is drawn from an interview with Peggy Luhrs, 12 December 1985.

27. Sarah Baley, "Women's Council Plans 'Health Day,'" *Burlington Free Press*, 12 August 1981; Burlington, *1982 Annual Report*, p. 52; "Mayor's Council to Hold Series of Events on Working Women," *Burlington Free Press*, 14 January 1982; Burlington, *1982 Annual Report*, p. 52.

28. Burlington, *1983 Annual Report*, pp.55–56.

29. Burlington, *1984 Annual Report*, pp. 90–92.

30. Burlington, *1984 Annual Report*, pp. 90–91; Burlington, *1985 Annual Report*, p. 100–1; Burlington, *1984 Annual Report*, p. 92.

31. Burlington, *1985 Annual Report*, pp. 99–100.

32. Ibid.

33. Ibid., p. 101; Tina Adler, "Conference Discusses Violence against Women," *Burlington Free Press*, 24 November 1985.

34. Susan Youngwood, "City Seeks Ways to Provide More Jobs for Women," *Burlington Free Press*, 30 November 1985; Deborah Schoch, "Plans Afoot to Increase Number of Women in Construction Jobs," *Burlington Free Press*, 20 February 1986; Mark Johnson, "Rental Ordinance Gets Aldermanic Approval," *Burlington Free Press*, 11 March 1986; Mary Ann Lickteig, "Program Trains Females for Jobs They Didn't Think Could Be Theirs," *Burlington Free Press*, 21 December 1986; phone interview with Bruce Seifer, 10 June 1988.

35. "Women's Council Sponsors Job Forum," *Burlington Free Press*, 18 February 1986; Danica Kirka, "Contractors Struggling to Hire Required Number of Women," *Burlington Free Press*, 27 April 1987.

36. Leslie Brown, "Council Seeks Funds to Fight Sexual Assault," *Burlington Free Press*, 7 February 1987; "Women's Council Receives Funding, *Burlington Free Press*, 12 February 1987; Burlington, *1987 Annual Report*, pp. 102–4.

37. Burlington, *1988 Annual Report*, pp. 105–7.

38. Burlington, *1989 Annual Report*, pp. 111–13.

39. Scott McKay, "Candidates Support Rights for Women, Homosexuals," *Burlington Free Press*, 24 February 1983; Scott McKay, "Board Endorses Idea of Equal Pay for Women," *Burlington Free Press*, 8 March 1983.

40. Enrique Corredera, "Union, City Agree on Equal Worth," *Burlington Free Press*, 17 August 1988.

41. Burlington, *1982 Annual Report*, p. 35; Burlington, *Annual Reports*, 1983–1987.

42. Burlington, *1988 Annual Report*, p. 44.

43. Sanders interview, 27 January 1986.

44. Ibid.

45. "Panel Reports on Needs of Elderly," *Burlington Free Press*, 1 August 1981.

46. Burlington, *1982 Annual Report*, p. 51.

47. Sanders interview, 7 April 1986.

48. Ibid.

49. Burlington, *1988 Annual Report*, p. 113.

50. Ibid.

51. McKay, "Candidates Support Rights."

52. Scott McKay, "Burlington Aldermen to Back Downtown Gay Pride Rally and March," *Burlington Free Press*, 15 June 1983.

53. Don Melvin, "Aldermen Sidestep Proclamation for Gay Day," *Burlington Free Press*, 22 May 1984.

54. Don Melvin, "Aldermen Express Support for Rights of Homosexuals," *Burlington Free Press*, 18 June 1985.

55. "Gays March, Say No Turning Back," *Times-Argus*, 14 June 1986; "The Bernie Sanders Record of Support for Social Justice, Civil Liberties, and for Gay and Lesbian Rights," Sanders for Congress campaign literature, 1988.

56. Monica Allen, "Being Gay in Vermont—Their Issues," *Times-Argus/Rutland Herald* Vermont Sunday Magazine, 15 December 1985.

57. Scott McKay, "Sanders Optimistic About Getting Team," *Burlington Free Press*, 18 August 1983; "Aldermen Approve Baseball Contract," *Burlington Free Press*, 13 September 1983.

58. Kevin Iole, "Reds Aim for Fourth Flag," *Burlington Free Press* Vermont Vacation Magazine, 22 May 1987.

59. Kevin Iole, "Reds May Get New Affiliate," *Burlington Free Press*, 19 May 1987; Sports Section, *Burlington Free Press*, 18 March 1988; Seifer phone interview, 19 December 1989.

60. Kevin Iole, "City Loses Bid for Baseball," *Burlington Free Press*, 17 December 1988; Kevin Iole, "Baseball Strikes Out in Vermont," *Burlington Free Press*, 17 December 1988.

CHAPTER 9

1. "Sanders Writes President Criticizing Gramm-Rudman," *Burlington Free Press*, 24 December 1985; "Sanders Urges Congress to Re-Establish Priorities," *Burlington Free Press*, 27 November 1986; Ezra Palmer, "Sanders Calls for Disarmament," *Burlington Free Press*, 23 April 1982; "War Concerns Sanders," *Burlington Free Press*, 1 February 1983; Scott McKay, "Sanders Will Speak on Hunger," *Burlington Free Press*, 22 November 1983; Steve Farnsworth, "Ban on Russians Scalds Sanders," *Burlington Free Press*, 25 November 1983; Leslie Brown, "Sanders Urges Cadets to Meet with Soviets," *Burlington Free Press*, 25 January 1986; Debbie Bookchin, "Sanders Lands Soviet Sister," *Times-Argus*, 11 June 1988; Enrique Corredera, "Soviet City Agrees to Ties with Burlington," *Burlington Free Press*, 19 July 1988; Enrique Corredera, "Soviets Accept Invitation to Visit Burlington," *Burlington Free Press*, 23 August 1988; Enrique Corredera, "City Welcomes Mayor's Group from Yaroslavl," *Burlington Free Press*, 11 October 1988; Enrique Corredera, "Mayors Hope Sister City Will Strengthen U.S.–Soviet Ties," *Burlington Free Press*, 15 October 1988; Deborah Schoch, "Council Votes 5–5 on Grenada," *Burlington Free Press*, 1 November 1983; Michael Powell, "Aldermen Unanimously Approve Divestiture," *Burlington Free Press*, 1 May 1985; "Sanders Urges Reagan to Take Hard Stance on South Africa," *Burlington Free Press*, 18 August 1985; William H. Braun, "Sanders Defends Time Spent on World Politics," *Burlington Free Press*, 21 September 1984.

2. Debbie Bookchin, "GE Arms Production Protested," *Rutland-Herald*, 10 August 1982.

3. Greg Guma, "Foreign Policy in City Hall: A Progress Report." *Burlington Peace Coalition Newsletter* (January 1987), p. 1.

4. Scott McKay, "GE, Union, Sanders Join Forces to Protest Blockade," *Burlington Free Press*, 10 June 1983.

5. Ibid.

6. Ibid.

7. Sanders interview, 12 December 1985.

8. Hilary Stout, "General Electric Protesters Agree to Limited Sit-in," *Burlington Free Press*, 19 June 1983; Mike Donoghue, "Despite 88 Arrests, Protest at GE Plant Is Calm, Amicable," *Burlington Free Press*, 21 June 1983.

9. Sanders interview, 12 December 1985.

10. Deborah Schoch, "50 Protesters Sitting In at Stafford Office," *Burlington Free Press*, 24 March 1984.

11. Sanders interview, 27 January 1986.

12. Ibid.

13. Don Melvin, "Sanders Registers Protest with Police Commission," *Burlington Free Press*, 9 May 1985; Don Melvin, "Mayor and Burke Settle Differences," *Burlington Free Press*, 29 August 1985; Mark Johnson, "Commission Curbs Use of Undercover Policemen," *Burlington Free Press*, 13 November 1985.

14. Johnson, "Commission Curbs Use."

15. Ibid.

16. Sanders interview, 27 January 1986.

17. "Sanders Encourages Sandinistas," *Burlington Free Press*, 11 July 1984; John Gittlesohn, "250 Join in March and Rally for Nicaragua Revolution," *Burlington Free Press*, 29 July 1984.

18. Ted Tedford, "Burlington May Get Sister City in Nicaragua," *Burlington Free Press*, 28 July 1984.

19. Interview with Pat Peterson, 14 April 1986.

20. Tedford, "Burlington May Get Sister City"; Don Melvin, "Burlington Approves Sister City," *Burlington Free Press*, 18 September 1984; Enrique Corredera, "City Focuses on Nicaragua," *Burlington Free Press*, 5 April 1987.

21. Peggy Grodinsky, "Burlington Soon to Aim Spotlight on Sister City," *Burlington Free Press*, 12 May 1985; "Incomplete Vote," *Burlington Free Press*, 17 May 1985; Don Melvin, "Sister City Needs Material Goods," *Burlington Free Press*, 11 July 1985; "Organizers Seek Donations for Burlington's Sister City," *Burlington Free Press*, 1 August 1985.

22. Peterson interview, 14 April 1986.

23. Ibid.

24. Ibid.

25. "Supply Boat to Sail for Sister City," *Burlington Free Press*, 16 December 1985; Robert Campbell, "Puerto Cabezas to Get Supplies from Burlington," *Burlington Free Press*, 17 February 1986; Robert Campbell, "Sister City Gets Cargo Shipment," *Burlington Free Press*, 7 March 1986.

26. "Sister City Program Seeks Collections," *Burlington Free Press*, 27 November 1986; Elaine Guarnieri, "Two Delegations Travel to Nicaragua," *Burlington Free Press*, 20 January 1987.

27. Peterson interview, 14 April 1986.

28. Deborah Schoch, "City's Aldermen Tiptoe around Sanctuary Issue," *Burlington Free Press*, 16 April 1985.

29. Peterson interview, 14 April 1986.

30. Don Melvin, "Aldermen OK Encouraging Nicaragua Trade Despite Embargo," *Burlington Free Press*, 22 May 1985.

31. Michael Powell, "Mayor Sanders Planning to Go to Nicaragua," *Burlington Free Press*, 8 July 1985; Don Melvin, "Sanders Begins Nicaraguan Visit," *Burlington Free Press*, 16 July 1985; Don Melvin, "Mayor Sanders Visits Burlington's Sister City," *Burlington Free Press*, 17 July 1985; Don Melvin, "Sanders Pays Bedside Visit to Fasting Foreign Minister," *Burlington Free Press*, 18 July 1985; Don Melvin, "Sanders Hopes to Meet Ortega," *Burlington Free Press*, 19 July 1985; Don Melvin, "Mayor Rails Against U.S. Antagonism," *Burlington Free Press*, 20 July 1985.

32. Don Melvin, "Mayor Sanders Helps Sandinistas Celebrate Anniversary of Victory," *Burlington Free Press*, 20 July 1985; Don Melvin, "Mayor, Ortega Confer," *Burlington Free Press*, 21 July 1985; Don Melvin, "Sanders Says Nicaragua Is Not a Military Threat to Any Nation," *Burlington Free Press*, 22 July 1985; Michael Powell, "Sanders: 'U.S. Must Talk with Nicaragua,'" *Burlington Free Press*, 25 July 1985.

33. Michael Powell, "Political Response to Sanders Trip Mixed," *Burlington Free Press*, 26 July 1985; Don Melvin, "Politicians Debate Nicaragua Trip's Impact on Sanders," *Burlington Free Press*, 28 July 1985.

34. Diane Kearns, "Sanders Praises Nicaragua's Style of Government," *Burlington Free Press*, 2 August 1983; Don Melvin, "Sanders to Participate in Forum

with Ortega," *Burlington Free Press,* 23 October 1985; Danica Kirka, "Nicaraguan Governor Visits Burlington," *Burlington Free Press,* 15 May 1985.

35. Sanders interview, 12 December 1985.

36. *Idem,* 17 October 1985.

37. Mark Johnson, "Report Criticizes Speculation Tax, Splits Aldermen," *Burlington Free Press,* 19 February 1986.

38. Danica Kirka, "Sanders Slams Contra Aid Vote, Urges Protests," *Burlington Free Press,* 27 June 1986; Kathleen H. Cooley, "GE Officials Demand Apology for Protests," *Burlington Free Press,* 9 July 1986; Danica Kirka, "Mayor: GE Trying to Manipulate Burlington Politics," *Burlington Free Press,* 11 July 1986; "Sanders Owed Apology by GE, Union Leaders," *Burlington Free Press* editorial, 10 July 1986; Cooley, "GE Officials Demand."

39. Mark Johnson, "Board Hears Contra Frustrations," *Burlington Free Press,* 1 July 1986; Guma, "Foreign Policy in City Hall."

CHAPTER 10

1. I am indebted to my mentor and friend Dr. David Gil of Brandeis University for his insights on this issue.

2. Alan Abbey, "Community Leaders Lukewarm to Sanders," *Burlington Free Press,* 5 March 1981.

3. Deborah Sline, "Burlington's 'Tax Revolt' Could Spread Quickly," *Burlington Free Press,* 28 January 1982.

4. Sanders interview, 17 October 1985.

5. Ibid.

6. *Idem,* 12 December 1985.

7. *Idem,* 17 October 1985.

8. I am indebted to Bill Conroy's dissertation, "The Limits of a Radical Regime City: The Case of Burlington, Vermont" (Ph.D dissertation, Fordham University, 1987) and his subsequent book, *Challenging the Boundaries of Reform: Socialism in Burlington* (Philadelphia: Temple University Press, 1990), for his insightful analysis of the constraints of the federalist system on municipal politics and the possibilities of radical change. Conroy and I met at the 1987 Socialist Scholars Conference in New York. I am aware of one other book on the Sanders administration by Greg Guma entitled *The People's Republic: Vermont and the Sanders Revolution* (Shelburne, Vt.: New England Press, 1989).

9. André Gorz, *Strategy for Labor,* pp. 6–8.

10. Susanne Gowan et al., *Moving Toward a New Society,* pp. 270–81.

11. Clavel, *The Progressive City,* pp. 79–95.

CHAPTER 11

1. Nancy Wright, "Sanders Makes History," *Times-Argus,* 7 November 1990, pp. 1, 8; "Socialist Vows to Be Capitol Outsider," *New York Times,* 12 November 1990; "The Sanders Scoop," *Sanders for Congress* newsletter, 22 October 1990;

Timothy Noah, "Sanders, a Red Star in the Green Mountains, Is Making a Strong Bid for Congressional Seat," *Wall Street Journal*, 24 September 1990, p. A16; "Vermont Elects First Socialist Congressman in 40 Years," *Seattle Times*, 7 November 1990; Gerald Meyer, "Vito Marcantonio," in *Encyclopedia of the American Left*, eds. Mari Jo Buhle, Paul Buhle, & Dan Georgakas (New York: Garland Publishing, 1990), pp. 447–48.

2. "Text of Announcement Remarks by Former Burlington Mayor Bernard Sanders," *Bernie Sanders for Congress* campaign literature, 19 March 1990.

3. Lisa Scagliotti, "Sanders, Smith Are Deadlocked," *Burlington Free Press*, 8 July 1990, p. 1A.

4. Peggy Dillon, "A Grass-Roots Effort: Local Sanders Volunteers Organize," *Valley News* (Vt.), 13 July 1990; Paul Teetor, "Sanders' Election Bid under Study," *Burlington Free Press*, 18 August 1990.

5. *Sanders for Congress* letter, 25 September 1990; Adam Pertman, "Bernie Sanders: Unorthodoxy in Full Flower," *Boston Sunday Globe*, 22 July 1990, pp. 32, 34; John Cole, "Gunning for Smith," *In These Times* letter, 12–18 December 1990, p. 15.

6. Noah, "Sanders, a Red Star in the Green Mountains"; author's personal conversations with Vermonters; "Bernie Sanders: Independent for U.S. Congress," *Bernie Sanders for U.S. Congress* campaign brochure.

7. Kevin J. Kelley, "Congressional Campaign No Longer Just 'Symbolic,'" *In These Times*, 10–16 October 1990, pp. 13, 22.

8. Ibid; "The Sanders Scoop," *Sanders for Congress* newsletter, 26 October 1990; "The Sanders Scoop," *Sanders for Congress* newsletter, 31 October 1990; Scagliotti, "Sanders, Smith Are Deadlocked."

9. "Red-Letter Days in the Race for the House," *Burlington Free Press*, 4 November 1990, p. 10A; *Sanders for Congress* letter, 7 November 1990.

10. Kevin J. Kelley, "Another Reason to Cheer: Sanders Makes the House," *In These Times*, 14–20 November 1990, pp. 7, 22.

11. Lisa Scagliotti, "Sanders' Message Peaks in Nation's Hard Times," *Burlington Free Press*, 4 November 1990, p. 1A, 11A.

12. Paul Teetor, "It's Sanders," *Burlington Free Press*, 7 November 1990, pp. 1A, 4A.

13. Wright, "Sanders Makes History."

14. Teetor, "It's Sanders"; Kelley, "Another Reason to Cheer."

15. Scagliotti, "Sanders' Message Peaks"; "Socialist Vows to Be Capitol Outsider"; Teetor, "It's Sanders."

16. Kevin Phillips, *The Politics of Rich and Poor: Wealth and the American Electorate in the Reagan Aftermath* (New York: Random House, 1990); Adam Platt, "Wellstone's Senate Win Bodes Well for the Left," *In These Times*, 14–20 November 1990, p. 7.

17. Teetor, "It's Sanders"; Kelley, "Another Reason to Cheer"; CSPAN postelection interview with Bernie Sanders, 5 December 1990; phone conversation with Sander's Congressional office, 4 February 1991.

18. John B. Judis, "Take Two on the War: The Best Way Out," *In These Times*, 6–12 February 1991, pp. 12–13; "House Votes 399–6 in Praise of Troops," *The Seattle Times*, 19 January 1991, p. A6; Kevin J. Kelley, "Socialism, Nationalism Clash in Vermont," *In These Times*, 27 February–19 March 1991, p. 2.

Selected Bibliography

Burlington Free Press Library Archives.

Carnoy, Martin, and Shearer, Derek. *Economic Democracy: The Challenge of the 1980s.* Armonk, N.Y.: M.E. Sharpe, 1980.

City of Burlington. *Annual Report,* 1981–1988.

——. *Election Records,* 1953–1983.

Clavel, Pierre. *The Progressive City: Planning and Participation, 1969–1984.* New Brunswick, N.J.: Rutgers University Press, 1986.

Community and Economic Development Office. *Burlington Community and Economic Development Policies.* Burlington, Vt.: Community and Economic Development Office, 1984.

——. *Community and Economic Development Policies.* Burlington, Vt.: Community and Economic Development Office, n.d.

Conroy, William. *Challenging the Boundaries of Reform.* Philadelphia: Temple University Press, 1990.

——. "The Limits of a Radical City Regime: The Case of Burlington, Vermont." Ph.D. dissertation, Fordham University, 1987.

Gorz, André. *Strategy for Labor.* Boston: Beacon Press, 1967.

Gowan, Susanne; Lakey, George; Moyer, William; and Taylor, Richard. *Moving Toward a New Society.* Philadelphia: New Society Press, 1976.

Guma, Greg. "James Burke and the Progressive Era," May 1984. (Typewritten.)

——. *The People's Republic: Vermont and the Sanders Revolution.* Shelburne, Vt.: New England Press, 1989.

Hill, Melvin, Jr. *State Laws Governing Local Government Structure and Administration.* Athens: University of Georgia, Institute of Government, 1978.

Honigsberg, Peter Jan; Kamoroff, Bernard; and Beatty, Jim. *We Own It: Starting & Managing Coops, Collectives, & Employee-Owned Ventures.* Laytonville, Calif.: Bell Springs Publishing, 1982.

Industrial Cooperative Association. *Jobs and People: A Strategic Analysis of the Greater Burlington Economy*. Burlington, Vt.: Community and Economic Development Office, December 1984.

Kann, Mark E. "Radicals in Power: Lessons From Santa Monica." *Socialist Review* 3 (May-June 1983), pp. 81–101.

Meyer, Gerald. "Vito Marcantonio." In *Encyclopedia of the American Left*, pp. 447–48. Edited by Mari Jo Buhle, Paul Buhle, & Dan Georgakas. New York: Garland Publishing, 1990.

Phillips, Kevin. *The Politics of Rich and Poor: Wealth and the American Electorate in the Reagan Aftermath*. New York: Random House, 1990.

Rice, Tom. "Who Votes for a Socialist Mayor?: The Case of Burlington, Vermont." *Polity* 4 (Summer 1985), pp. 795–806.

———. "Why Vote for a Socialist Mayor: The Case of Burlington, Vermont," 1986. (Typewritten.)

Rosenstone, Steven J.; Behr, Roy L.; and Lazarus, Edward H. *Third Parties in America: Citizen Response to Major Party Failure*. Princeton, N.J.: Princeton University Press, 1984.

Soifer, Steven. "Electoral Politics and Social Change: The Case of Burlington, Vermont." Ph.D. dissertation, Brandeis University, 1988. (Available from University Microfilms No. 88–19, 289.)

Stave, Bruce, ed. *Socialism and the Cities*. Port Washington, N.Y.: Kennikat Press, 1975.

Stephens, John. *The Transition from Capitalism to Socialism*. London: Macmillan Press, 1979.

Sweezy, Paul M. *The Theory of Capitalist Development: Principles of Marxian Political Economy*. New York: Monthly Review Press, 1970.

Szymanski, Albert. *The Capitalist State and the Politics of Class*. Cambridge, Mass.: Winthrop Publishers, 1978.

Weinstein, James S. *The Decline of Socialism in America: 1912–1925*. New Brunswick, N.J.: Rutgers University Press, 1984.

Wright, Erik Olin. *Class, Crisis and the State*. London: Verso Press, 1970.

Index